Culture and Customs of the Sioux Indians

Short Bull, Spiritual Leader and Ghost Dance teacher, Winter Count Historian, and Pictograph Artist. (Photo courtesy of Thomas Shortbull)

Norman Shortbull, Lakota Artist. (Photo courtesy of Thomas Shortbull)

Thomas Shortbull, Former South Dakota State Senator and current president of Oglala Lakota College. (Photo courtesy of Thomas Shortbull)

Vanessa Shortbull, Miss South Dakota 2002 and Cancer Study Coordinator. (Photo courtesy of Thomas Shortbull)

Culture and Customs
of the Sioux Indians

GREGORY O. GAGNON

Culture and Customs of Native Peoples in America

Tom Holm, Series Editor

 GREENWOOD

AN IMPRINT OF ABC-CLIO, LLC
Santa Barbara, California • Denver, Colorado • Oxford, England

Library of Congress Cataloging-in-Publication Data

Gagnon, Gregory O. (Gregory Omer), 1942–
    Culture and customs of the Sioux indians / Gregory O. Gagnon.
        p. cm. — (Culture and customs of native peoples in America)
    Includes bibliographical references and index.
    ISBN 978–0–313–38454–7 (hard copy : alk. paper) — ISBN 978–0–313–38455–4 (ebook)
1. Dakota Indians—History. 2. Dakota Indians—Social life and customs. I. Title.
E99.D1G34   2011
978.004′975243—dc22   2011007279

ISBN: 978–0–313–38454–7
EISBN: 978–0–313–38455–4

15 14 13 12 11   1 2 3 4 5

This book is also available on the World Wide Web as an eBook.
Visit www.abc-clio.com for details.

Greenwood
An Imprint of ABC-CLIO, LLC

ABC-CLIO, LLC
130 Cremona Drive, P.O. Box 1911
Santa Barbara, California 93116-1911

This book is printed on acid-free paper (∞)

Manufactured in the United States of America

Contents

Series Foreword

Since the 1960s, Native and non-Native scholars have diligently sought to disassemble and understand the false and, frankly, harmful stereotypes and images of Native American peoples. Many Americans have recognized that stereotypes of indigenous people are not only often wrong, but have actually fostered adverse political and legal decisions and even sporadic and arbitrary attempts to have whole Native American communities eradicated. The steep and steady decline of the indigenous population, the dissolution of Native governments, and the loss of culture and lands stem from an almost perverse lack of knowledge about Native American peoples.

Despite the dispossession of lands and many, many cultural features, Native American peoples have been astonishingly resilient. White Earth Anishinaabe author Gerald Vizenor, a wordcraftsman of no mean abilities and talents, coined the term "survivance" from the words "survival" and "resistance" to capture the two-fold nature of why indigenous customs and cultures are still alive. The Greenwood Press series *Culture and Customs of Native Peoples in America* attempts not to cast aspersions on the motives, desires, and policies of the Europeans and Euro-Americans who colonized North America, but to highlight, especially to young people and a general audience, the beauty, knowledge, pride, and resiliency of the indigenous peoples of this land. "Survivance" is very real. Native Americans, as our authors show, are not extinct, nor have they become a single, relatively small U.S. ethnic group.

Rather, Native Americans are here today as members of many indigenous nation-states that have utterly unique relationships with the United States. Today, the federal government recognizes 562 and American Indian and Native Alaskan tribes and communities that are self-governing and hold certain sovereign rights and powers. Over 1 million people are citizens or members of these nation-states. Nearly 4.5 million people in the United States claim some degree of American Indian or Alaska Native racial heritage.

Most Americans do not quite understand that Native American sovereignty relates specifically to the survival of tribal cultures. When the Europeans came to North American shores, there were hundreds of indigenous peoples, each group with its own territorial boundaries, distinct language, religious customs and ceremonial cycles attuned to the place in which they lived, and a unique and sacred history. All had developed governing bodies that maintained order within and could raise military forces to protect and defend their territories. Each was, therefore, sovereign, but each had different forms of governance, whether by council, kingship, or priesthood. Nearly all of the native nation-states based their social organization on kinship.

The European colonists came for land and human and natural resources. At first, they attempted to displace the indigenous nation-states or enter into largely unequal and oftentimes destructive trade relationships. Very many Native Americans perished as a result of new, pandemic diseases that were endemic to European populations. Native nations were also caught up in a series of colonial wars that led to further depopulation.

In an effort to end violence and bring about stability, Native nations entered into a series of treaties with foreign powers. When the United States emerged from the stew of colonialism, it continued the treaty-making policies in order to expand its eminent domain from coast to coast. Of course, numerous terrible wars resulted from this policy, but for the most part Native nations and the United States maintained the relationships they created in the treaty-making process. Native nations lost territory and many were displaced from their homelands, but 562 of them have maintained what has been called "limited sovereignty." What this means is that although Native nation-states have certainly lost some of their powers as sovereigns, they have maintained the rights of taxation, territorial integrity, determination of citizenship, and cultural sovereignty. Despite the fact that the U.S. government has violated nearly every one of their treaties with the Native nations, the treaties nevertheless established today's general guarantee that Native peoples can continue as autonomous cultural entities with the ability to change or adapt on their own terms. This is only one of the reasons that Native peoples assert their sovereignty rather than simply become assimilated into the general U.S. society.

Another indigenous people, the Native Hawaiians, were treated similarly. The descendents of Native Hawaiians number over 4 million people. Their own nation-state, established over all the islands by King Kamehameha the Great in 1810, was undermined and finally usurped in 1893. Queen Lili'uo-kalani was actually imprisoned and replaced by a ruling cabal of businessmen and plantation owners. For a time, these men ruled the islands as "the Republic of Hawaii." In 1898, the United States annexed the islands and the territory eventually became a state of the union in 1959. Since then, Native Hawaiians have adapted their customs and culture to insure their survival. Cultural have multiplied and the Native language has been preserved in place names, ceremonies, and in a number of households.

The *Culture and Customs of Native Peoples in America* series hopes to serve as an exploration of the vibrant cultures and intriguing customs of several North American indigenous groups, from religious practice and folklore to traditional costumes and cuisine. It is an enjoyable and stimulating journey.

Tom Holm
Tucson, Arizona

Preface

Writing a book about Sioux history and culture poses a number of issues. Perhaps the most difficult task is distilling the hundreds of studies of the Sioux and decades of personal research into a single treatment of a people. One goal was to emphasize not only the development of Sioux cultures and societies but also to explain the meaning of the course of Sioux history. Another goal was to explain how developments throughout the rest of the world influenced Sioux societies because the Sioux did not exist in a vacuum.

Each scholar develops a perspective about his or subject derived from his or her own background, not just the sources. In my case, this perspective emanates from an experiential base that includes being Indian (Chippewa), a PhD in British Empire Studies, a scholarly interest in the Oglala Lakota in particular, and nearly 17 years as an administrator-instructor at Oglala Lakota College on Pine Ridge Reservation. Since 1997, I have taught American Indian Studies at the University of North Dakota. This experience has allowed me to incorporate historic and cultural studies for other societies into a maturing view of Sioux history and culture.

Explanation of some vocabulary I have used is obligatory because many readers are confused by the complexity of the Sioux. "Sioux" is a problematic word as it is imprecise and yet is used to encompass a people, society, and a history of societies that have formed and changed over more than 700 years. But we are stuck with it. Suffice it to say that "Sioux" is used to indicate the

Siouan language family branch that includes Dakota and Lakota dialects of a language that became distinct by 1300. These societies are variously known also as Santee-Dakota (the parent Sioux traditionally within Minnesota), Yankton-Dakota (the river culture that settled in areas near where Iowa-Minnesota-South Dakota-Nebraska come together), Yanktonai-Dakota, and Teton-Lakota (the plains Sioux) from the Missouri River westward to the Big Horn Mountains. Nakota speakers are not included because linguistic scholars have concluded that the Yankton and Yanktonai spoke Dakota with Nakota being the dialect of another Siouan speaking tribe, the Assiniboine. Where appropriate, I have used terms that designate subdivisions of these societies, for instance, Oglala Lakota or Wahpekute Dakota.

I have chosen to use Sioux words where English does not convey meaning accurately. For instance, the Sioux were led by *Itancan,* which means "leader"; Itancan were not chiefs. The word "chief" assigns powers and roles that itancan did not have. *Tiyospaye* can be translated as community and can apply to the fluid plains communities as well as to the semi-permanent Yankton and Dakota towns, although it is most applicable to the plains Sioux. I try to keep all of these words from being too confusing to the reader. The terms "Indian," "American Indian," and "Native American" are used interchangeably to indicate the indigenous first peoples of the Americas.

Another challenge I encountered is conveying a sense of the constancy of cultural change and diversity that characterizes the Sioux over the 700 years of their existence. Some Sioux have lived in the Woodlands and prairies of Minnesota while others lived along the rivers and yet others lived on the Northern plains. Each group had distinct economies, homes, organization, and dialect. Each also had different historical experiences. There was no single Sioux experience anymore than there was a single English experience.

Sioux life was intensely spiritual, a daunting challenge to readers who live in a twenty-first century American society. To the Sioux, all things were interconnected through a symbiotic interaction among humans, animals, and supernatural Beings. The world was one that had been given to the Sioux in the same way that their culture was given to them, by the supernatural Beings. It was the place of humans, the Sioux, to show respect for this revealed world through ceremonies and personal prayer.

Pragmatic adaptability was also a continuing characteristic of Sioux societies. The integration of the horse by the Lakota is a clear example of taking a new element and making it pivotal for Teton-Lakota culture. The horse is usually part of the picture evoked by the word Sioux. It was embedded in Sioux religion, economy, war, marriage, manhood, status, and substance. Change in Sioux religion during the reservation period is an example of pragmatic adaptation to colonialism. The creation of tribal colleges to usher Sioux into the twenty-first century while retaining and enhancing traditional values is another example of adaptability to new conditions while maintaining important elements of the Sioux culture and values in these adaptations.

I have also tried to picture the reality that all Sioux are not and were not the same. Unfortunately, histories and cultural studies too often paint a picture of one Sioux viewpoint and a society frozen in time. There is no single Sioux belief and no single viewpoint. Sioux reactions to an expanding America ranged from efforts to conciliate and accept American dominance to turning to war against the invading Americans. In matters of religion some Sioux have accepted Christianity as a substitute for traditional religion, while others have rejected it. Sioux Christian fundamentalists coexist alongside traditional religion fundamentalists. Sioux leaders have always tried to lead in the best way, but there has been much debate about what is the best way at any time in Sioux history.

Sioux culture and history has a rich past and a continuing future. I hope that readers enjoy the narrative journey.

Writing a survey history requires building and interpreting the work of many scholars and makers of Sioux history. They are too many to name, but the short bibliography indicates those scholars whose work I have drawn on the most. The makers of Sioux history that I have been fortunate enough to work with over the years helped create this book and have informed all of my teaching and learning. I thank them all. It may be an obligatory statement, but Ellen Gagnon is the most important supporter and, in her unique way, contributor to my work.

Chronology

10,000 years ago	The Misty Past. The ancestors of the Sioux begin the cultural differentiation that will lead to the development of Sioux society and culture. These ancestral Sioux live in the Appalachians perhaps in or near Kentucky and Ohio. Ancestral Sioux are descended from the Paleo-Indians who entered North America millennia ago.
500 BC	The Proto-Siouan language family divides into western, central, and eastern branches as its members begin a migration westward and northward. The Proto-Sioux are part of the central branch.
By 1300 AD	The ancestors of the Sioux migrate to the headwaters of the Mississippi, presently northern Minnesota. They create The Blackduck-Kathio-Clam River Continuum, which, influenced by Mississippian and Oneota cultures, becomes the Proto-Sioux/Psinomani culture. Fortified villages, agriculture, some pottery making, and wild rice gathering complement hunting and gathering. As they pass through the territory of the Mississippian culture, and because many of the current Siouan speaking tribes are direct descendents of Mississippian chiefdoms, the Proto-Sioux are most likely influenced by this widespread culture. At most, the Proto-Sioux were Mississippians. It is also possible than some Proto-Sioux were remnants of Oneota culture. As with all ancient history, there is much debate about what really

	happened. Archaeology cannot be conclusive; it is possible only to infer what did happen.
By 1500 AD	The Proto-Sioux have become Sioux and the divisions into the Seven Council Fires have occurred. The Santee (Dakota), Yankton and Yanktonai (Dakota); and Teton (Lakota) have begun their movement from the homeland at the headwaters of the Mississippi toward the west and south. The Assiniboine (Nakota) branch northward from the Sioux and cease to be considered part of the Sioux. Some of the Sioux expand eastward toward Michigan and northwestern Wisconsin.
1630s–1660s	Dakotas feel the effects of the shattering of the eastern tribes by Iroquois invasions. Refugees are pushed westward where they encounter Dakota, Ottawa, Ho-Chunk (Winnebago), Potawatomi, Menominee, Wyandot, and others. Intertribal wars continued as tribes contended for territory.
1641–	The first mention of the *Nadouessis* is made. Jesuit missionaries Charles Raymbaut and Isaac Jogues are told by Ojibwe that the *Nadouessis (Sioux)* lived 14 days from Sault St. Marie. Direct French-Sioux contact takes place probably about 1640.
1690s–1700	Dakota-Chippewa economic alliances are formed. Dakota leaders allow Chippewa settlement as far into their land as Wisconsin in return for the Chippewa acting as middlemen to bring French goods to Dakota country. Alliance includes some military assistance and intermarriage between the tribes.
1730s	Teton bands obtain horses from Shoshone traders and begin a transformation of their culture from woodlands to plains. Teton bands become a nomadic, buffalo hunting, and territorially expanding society.
1737	A smallpox epidemic kills nearly 15,000 plains Indians including more than 4,000 Yankton.
1740	The Dakota-Chippewa War begins. Chippewa expansionists use the killing of French traders by Dakota as an opportunity to launch an invasion from Madeline Island in Lake Superior into northern Minnesota. The war continues intermittently well into the 1860s. Dakota bands gradually shift from their homelands to southern Minnesota and westward.
1744	The Battle of Sandy Lake takes place. The Dakota lose to the Chippewa and begin a gradual withdrawal from their ancestral lands in northern Minnesota.

The Battle of Kathio-Mille Lacs takes place. A large Dakota force is defeated by Chippewa.

1755   The Battle of St. Croix River takes place. The Dakota lose their lands in northeastern Minnesota and the adjacent area, now present-day Wisconsin.

1760   The Battle of Leech Lake takes place. A Chippewa band of pillagers secures the lake in spite of a Dakota counteroffensive.

1770   The Battle of Red Lake takes place. A Chippewa victory reinforces the Dakota focus on southern Minnesota and marks the last effort of the Dakota to regain territory from the Chippewa.

1776   A Winter Count chronicles that an Oglala Lakota band reached the Black Hills.

1786   A smallpox epidemic kills thousands of plains Indians.

1787   The United States passes the Northwest Ordinance, which begins a formal Indian policy for the new nation that "the utmost good faith shall always be observed towards the Indians; their lands and property shall never be taken from them without their consent; and in their property rights and liberty, they shall never be invaded or disturbed." The Constitution is adopted, and Article 1, section 8, states that Congress has the power to "regulate commerce with foreign nations, and among the several states, and with the Indian tribes."

1804–1806   Lewis and Clark explore much of Sioux country, as does Zebulon Pike.

1819   The United States creates a Civilization Fund to pay missionary societies to establish schools. Proselytizing is seen as a given and deemed desirable.

1823   The Treaty of Prairie du Chien is signed, a treaty of land cession between the United States and the Dakota.

1824   The Bureau of Indian Affairs is created as part of the War Department. It will be transferred to the newly created Department of the Interior in 1849.

1830   The Indian Removal Act and the Indian Country Act initiate the policy of moving Indians to a specially created territory out of the way of American expansion.

1832   The American Fur Company, having bought out some competitors, establishes a trading center at Fort Laramie (Wyoming) and

Fort Pierre (South Dakota). The Kiowa, Cheyenne, Crow, Pawnee, Blackfeet, Shoshone, and Ponca tribes are displaced by the Sioux. Fort Laramie becomes a relatively permanent home for many Lakota, particularly Oglala and Brule after the Oglala leaders Bull Bear and Smoke move their entire bands to this southern border of their country.

American fur company traders from the St. Louis area move to Lakota country, and many marry Teton women. Men whose last names are Richard, Bordeaux, Janis, and Pourier, and many other "Frenchmen" are integrated into the Lakota bands and their children as well. By the 1860s, Red Cloud will note that he has about 100 mixed-blood relatives.

1837	A smallpox pandemic nearly eradicates the Mandan, and other tribes suffer immensely. The Teton and Yanktons are not as severely affected because the United States provided inoculations and because these tribes' nomadic bands are scattered. Any obstacle that the river tribes pose to Sioux expansion disappears.
ca. 1840	Crazy Horse is born.
1840	Bull Bear, the dominant itancan of the Oglala, is killed by members of Smoke's tiyospaye. Red Cloud, from Smoke's band, begins his ascent to dominance among the southern Lakota.
1840s	American immigrants use the Platte River as a route to Utah, Oregon (via the Oregon Trail), and to California (the Gold Rush). Thousands of Americans wreak ecological havoc by driving away buffalo, consuming grass and wood, strewing garbage, and spreading disease through Lakota country.

A precipitate decline in demand for beaver causes the Dakota economy to collapse, and leaders must scramble for a substitute source of income for their bands. Without the fur trade, land is the only commodity that Americans want so leaders will sell in treaties.

1849	The United States buys Fort Laramie and Fort Pierre in order to protect immigrants along the Oregon Trail and east of the Missouri in the Dakotas.
1850s	The United States begins a reservation policy. The goal is to confine Indians to specific plots of land taken from their homelands. Treaties of purchase are the main means to effect the creation of reservations. The United States begins the creation of army posts to control Indian populations.

American miners establish the Bozeman Trail just north of the Black Hills as a route from Fort Laramie to Montana's mines.

Lakota itancan point out that this is a violation of the 1851 treaty and demand that Americans adhere to the terms of the treaty.

1851 The Treaty of Traverse des Sioux and the Treaty of Mendota are signed. Treaties of land cession are amended by Congress to leave the Dakota without any land at all, contrary to the terms that were originally negotiated. The four Santee tribes, threatened by the presence of 100, 000 soldiers, cede most of southern Minnesota and parts of South Dakota and Iowa to the United States for $3.075 million in cash and annuities.

The First Fort Laramie Treaty (Horse Creek Treaty) is signed. Thousands of Indians from several tribes, even the Crow, gather in Sioux country at the behest of the United States. They agree to let wagon trains pass unmolested in return for payment. The U.S. commissioners and Indian leaders describe where the boundaries of the various tribes are. Americans now know with whom to negotiate when issues arise in particular areas. Some Teton Sioux and some representatives of other plains tribes agree to a description of their tribal boundaries and to allow passage on the Oregon Trail, are provided compensation for the depredation of natural resources caused by Americans, and recognize the Brule itancan Brave Bear (Conquering Bear) as "head chief," a position that did not exist in Teton society, something that band leaders point out. At least one Sioux leader indicates to the Americans that the Sioux had driven the Crows, Cheyenne, Pawnee and others out of the area and the same thing could happen to the Americans. This was the first major contact between the U.S. government and at least some of the Tetons.

1851–52 Seven thousand Santee move to land along the Minnesota River where they become subject to removal at the pleasure of the President. It was an area roughly 10 miles by 6 miles. The Santee are dependent on Americans paying the annuities because there is no game and they are surrounded by American and recent immigrant communities such as New Ulm.

1854 The Mormon's Cow Incident at Fort Laramie leads to the killing of Conquering Bear and some Brule. Brule retaliation wipes out the attacking Americans and inspires a series of Brule retaliatory attacks along the Oregon Trail.

An American force led by General Harney invades Sioux country, attacks a Brule tiyospaye at Ash Hollow, captures a large number of hostages, and demands the surrender of the Brule who had attacked Americans along the Platte River. Spotted Tail, an emerging Brule itancan, gives himself up and is imprisoned for a year in Kansas. Harney moves to Fort Pierre and negotiates a treaty with the northern Sioux, but the President and Congress ignore it. Aside from minor incidents, a temporary peace reigns.

1856	Smallpox decimates the Yankton.
1858	The Dakota cede additional land, the North Bank of the Minnesota River, bowing to U.S. pressure.
1862 (August)	Dakota annuities are late, but agent Thomas Galbraith refuses to distribute food. One trader, Andrew Myrick, remarks, "Let them eat grass." Dakota kill some settlers near Litchfield and after much debate, Little Crow, a Mdewakanton Santee itancan agrees to lead a war. Many Santee leaders choose not to be engaged in the war, but others attack the Redwood Agency where trader Myrick is later found dead with grass stuffed in his mouth.

Minnesota Governor Ramsey appoints Henry Sibley, a fur trade magnate formerly married to a Dakota, to head the Minnesota militia. Some Dakota join the militia too.

New Ulm is attacked, and where 34 settles die, with 60 wounded. Fort Ridgely is also attacked.

In September, the Battle of Birch Coulee is a victory for the Dakota.

Major General John Pope, loser of the Battle of Bull Run, is given command of the American Army with orders to stop the uprising.

American troops win the Battle of Wood Lake. Some Dakota, not part of the war, take control of 269 American captives from the Dakota who are at war. The captives are released.

Colonel Sibley enters the peaceful Dakota camp and places all 1,200 under arrest.

After 37 days of fighting, about 500 Americans and about 60 Dakota have been killed.

Sibley initiates summary military trials for the Dakota outlaws who have committed "outrages." Before all the trials end (42 on the last day), 393 have led to hanging sentences for 323 Dakota.

President Lincoln, urged by Reverend Riggs, Bishop Whipple, and others reviews the sentences and reduces the number to 38.

1862 (December 26)	Thirty-eight Dakota sing their death songs and are hanged in Mankato to drumbeats and the cheers of the crowd. This is the largest single execution in American history. The Dakota were at war and were not citizens of the United States, but they were tried as if they were criminals.
1863	Congress expels all Dakota from Minnesota and abrogated all treaties with the Dakota. Dakota territory is opened for homesteading after passage of the Homestead Act.
1863–67	Dakota refugees flee to Canada and to Dakota territory; some join Yankton, and even Teton, bands to escape. Little Crow is killed by a farmer who receives a bounty for his scalp. Canada creates four reserves for refugee Dakota. American forces chase Santee refugees into the Dakotas and attack a Yankton tiyospaye at Whitestone Hill and Lakota at Killdeer Mountain. About 1,700 Dakota prisoners are sent to Crow Creek, a reservation along the Missouri River in the Dakotas.
1866	Red Cloud's War begins because the United States built forts along the Bozeman Trail rather than closing it. Americans did try to purchase the area, but Red Cloud and other leaders refused, especially after the troops arrived while negotiations were taking place. Lakota shut down the Bozeman Trail and are joined by many tiyospaye itancan in laying siege to the forts.
	Fetterman Battle and Wagon Box Battle take place. Lakota led by Red Cloud, with Crazy Horse leading a decoy party, defeat and kill an entire force led by Lieutenant Fetterman. A Lakota attack on a wood-chopping expedition turns into a major battle because additional troops were concealed in the wagons. The siege continues.
1867	The Dakota sign a treaty surrendering any claim to Minnesota and Red River Valley in return for reservations in Santee (Nebraska), Lake Traverse (South Dakota), and Devil's Lake-Fort Totten (North Dakota).
1868	American commissioners sue for peace and agree to abandon the Bozeman Trail. Lakota and their allies burn the forts.
	The Fort Laramie Treaty ends the Red Cloud War by guaranteeing an abandonment of the fort, establishing a Red Cloud agency, and recognizing the Great Sioux Reservation—roughly from the Missouri River to the Big Horns. The Lakota agree to remain north of the Platte River, but the United States acknowledges their right

to hunt as long as the buffalo exist in the Big Horns and up to the Little Big Horn area. The Sioux receive a payment schedule for lands ceded east of the Missouri. The United States agrees to keep all Americans out of the Great Sioux Reservation and stipulates that any additional land cessions would have to be approved by three-quarters of all adult Sioux males.

1869	Grand River, Cheyenne River, and Whitestone agencies are established by the United States. These are forerunners to the Standing Rock, Cheyenne River, and Rosebud agencies created a decade later.
1871	Congress formally ends treaty-making because the House of Representatives objected to the Senate's having agreed on funding for which the House had to supply appropriations. The United States pledges to honor all treaties and later "agreements" that operate similar to treaties, except that both houses of Congress will need to approve.
1874	George Custer leads an expedition into the Black Hills, and a gold rush follows, despite desultory efforts by the army to expel squatters. The Sioux respond with some harassment and some skirmishes with the squatters.
	A U.S. commission tries to buy the Black Hills, but assembled itancan refuse.
1875	The United States orders all Lakota to go to the agencies designated or be declared hostiles even if they were in the unceded territory where they had a treaty right to be. After a bitter winter, the army launches a three-pronged attack into the unceded territory to punish the Lakota and their Cheyenne and Arapaho allies.
1876	General Crook's column is defeated June 1 by Lakota led principally by Crazy Horse, and he retreats to Fort Laramie. Sitting Bull and other leaders conduct a large Sun Dance where Sitting Bull dreams that soldiers will fall into the Lakota's camp. June 26, Lieutenant Colonel George Armstrong Custer attacks the multiband camp at Little Big Horn River. Custer and 267 men are killed. The Sioux and their allies disperse to continue their usual summer activities, but Crook pursues them with troops. The Battle of Slim Buttes forces most of the Lakota to return to their agencies, and Sitting Bull goes to Canada with part of his tiyospaye.
1877	Crazy Horse surrenders with about 1,000 of his multi-tiyospaye band at Fort Robinson where the Red Cloud Agency has been

relocated. Crazy Horse is bayoneted later as he is being taken into custody by the military; the plan was to ship him to Florida to prevent his leading a "breakout."

Congress votes to take the Black Hills despite not being able to get three-quarters of Sioux males to agree. A Catholic boarding school is opened on Standing Rock Reservation.

1879 Carlisle Indian School, the first off-reservation boarding school, is opened with the goal of "destroying the Indian to save the man," as will be the goal of Bureau of Indian Affairs schools until the 1960s. The first Sioux students are from Rosebud, Pine Ridge, and Standing Rock reservations.

President Grant turns reservations over to religious denominations and allows them to nominate Indian agents. For instance, the Episcopal Church is "given" Pine Ridge Reservation and has the exclusive right to proselytize. Indian land to support missionaries and schools is given to churches. Red Cloud wanted Catholic priests, but they were excluded from the reservation. Eventually, other denominations were allowed on all of the reservations.

1883 In an ex parte decision regarding Crow Dog, the Supreme Court ruled that Indian against Indian crimes were the jurisdiction of the tribes. This decision allowed for the release of Crow Dog who had been tried for killing the Brule itancan Spotted Tail.

The Indian Offenses Act makes the practice of traditional religion a punishable crime. Courts of Indian Offenses appointed by Indian agents are charged with carrying out the terms of the act. Indians are judges, and some are hired as BIA police, but all are employees of the agency.

1885 The Major Crimes Act is passed in response to Crow Dog's case. Congress essentially requires that all felonies (major crimes) committed on a reservation have to be tried in federal courts. This eliminates tribal justice systems and assures that Indians are to be tried and judged by non-Indians and that trials are to be held away from reservations.

1886 The Commissioner of Indian Affairs orders that only English be used in Indian schools stating: "It is believed that teaching an Indian youth in his own barbarous dialect is a positive detriment to him."

1887 The Dawes Severalty Act (the Allotment Act) begins the process of forcing Indians to become private property owners. After surveying, Indian heads of household are to be allotted 160 acres from tribal land, with women and single adult men receiving lesser amounts. Any land unallotted is to be declared surplus and sold to pay expenses for Indians to receive farm equipment, seeds, and so on. After 25 years, allotees are to be given fee patents, and the land will become state land and, therefore, taxable. No provisions are made for Indians who become adults after the reservation is allotted or sold to non-Indians. Indians were not consulted.

1889	North and South Dakota become states.

After an intense campaign and creative vote-counting, the United States declares that three-quarters of Teton males have agreed to reduce the Great Sioux Reservation by selling nine million acres, leaving six smaller reservations. Cheyenne River, Standing Rock, Rosebud, Pine Ridge, Crow Creek, and Fort Thompson are the reservations carved from the Great Sioux Reservation.

The Ghost Dance, imported to the Plains by Lakota who learned it and its prophecies from Wovoka, a Paiute, sets off panic among American settlers and consternation among American agents. Many Lakota begin dancing, and troops from Kansas are sent toward the reservations.

1890	Sitting Bull is killed in a melee caused when BIA Indian police try to arrest him. Many Sioux expect the U.S. military to massacre them. Several itancan, including Big Foot from Cheyenne River Reservation, decamp for the perceived safety of Pine Ridge Reservation where Red Cloud is still the dominant leader.

The Massacre of Wounded Knee takes place. On December 28, Big Foot's band is intercepted by the Seventh Cavalry. After spending a night encamped at Wounded Knee Creek on Pine Ridge Reservation, cavalrymen try to disarm the Lakota. One shot fired leads to all of the surrounding soldiers firing into the camp. After charging the camp, cavalrymen chase and kill men, women, and children for as far as two miles. Almost 300 Lakota die and are buried in a mass grave. Some survivors are rescued by Pine Ridge Sioux. Several soldiers are killed, according to a military inquiry. Later, many were killed by friendly fire. Some consider this the last battle of the Indian wars, and the Lakota still commemorate the massacre.

1890–1934	Allotment proceeds on each of the Sioux Reservations, and surplus is sold to non-Sioux. This process has the checkerboard

effect envisioned by American policy makers and leaves a jurisdictional nightmare for future tribal and state governments. Land loss continues as the United States shortens the time between allotment and allottees receiving deeds to their allotments. County tax sales alienate lands, and non-Indian neighbors also buy land from Sioux owners. Reservations such as Lake Traverse (Sisseton-Wahpeton) are nearly all taken by white owners; only the less desirable land, as on Pine Ridge and Standing Rock, is not purchased, even when declared surplus.

1900–34 Many agents, urged on by tribal leaders, allow tribal councils, and several, like Rosebud, write constitutions and have reservation-wide elections.

1914–19 Many Sioux volunteer to fight in World War I. Congress extends citizenship to veterans.

1915 Teton reservations cede more land so homesteaders add to the non-Indian owners within reservation boundaries.

1923 The Black Hills Treaty Council, started in the 1890s, files suit to regain the Black Hills.

1924 All Indians born within the boundaries of the United States are made citizens.

1929–45 The Great Depression and World War II distract American attention, and reservations see a loss in resources. Many men and women join the military and/or leave the reservation to work in war industries. Their experiences contribute to an increased knowledge of the United States and add to the skills pool on reservations. During the war, Indian lands are appropriated for use as bombing ranges and even Japanese internment camps.

1932–44 John Collier, Commissioner of Indian Affairs not only pushes through the IRA but also uses executive orders to affirm and enable Indians to practice traditional culture. The prohibitions on Indian religion are lifted, and Indian ceremonies no longer have to be practiced secretly. Tetons hold public Sun Dances as early as in 1936.

1933–36 Several New Deal programs such as the Civilian Conservation Corps and Works Progress Administration are extended to reservations; this boosts Sioux economies.

1934 The Indian Reorganization Act allows reservation members to vote on whether or not they want to have a tribal government recognized by the United States and not existing only at the whim of agents. Each reservation holds a referendum, and those reservations passing the referendum then hold a constitutional convention followed by another reservation-wide vote. Standing Rock Reservation in North Dakota declines, but each of the other reservations approve the IRA and promulgate constitutions in the 1930s. The BIA retains control of appropriations and programs, so new tribal councils have little power.

1936	Sun Dances are held publicly on Pine Ridge and Standing Rock Reservations. Traditional Sioux religion is openly practiced again.
1946	Congress creates the Indian Claims Commission, which allows Indians and tribal governments to sue the United States for redress of grievances such as the taking of land and violations of treaties. Sioux claims include a transfer of the Black Hills claim, denied by federal courts in 1940, to the Commission.
1948	The Army Corps of Engineers starts construction of the Oahe Dam and takes 170,000 acres of prime farmland for its reservoir. Crow Creek, Fort Thompson, and Yankton reservations suffer as well. No due process is provided.
1952	The Indian Relocation Program is started as part of the new policy of Termination. Congress indicates its intention to eliminate all reservations. Many Sioux are lured into moving to urban areas where many become disadvantaged minorities living in Indian ghettos. Many also return home. The result is that every major city has a Sioux population.
1968	Congress passes the Indian Civil Rights Act. It extends most of the Bill of Rights to Indian reservations in order to provide the kind of civil rights other Americans have. Tribal governments are not consulted as the United States extends its sovereignty more deeply into tribal government jurisdiction.
	The American Indian Movement (AIM) is founded. Modeled on the Black Panthers and SNCC, AIM began as an urban movement to protect Indian civil rights and deter police brutality. AIM evolved into a movement to return to traditional culture, and the organization affected reservation politics as well. AIM did not seek equality but, instead, wanted tribal sovereignty. Many Sioux joined the movement.
1970	President Richard Nixon announces a new Indian policy, Self-Determination in a Government-to-Government Relationship. He also promises that there will be no more termination of reservations and their citizens. Self-Determination is the current policy of the United States, and it recognizes that tribal

governments are sovereign and that the United States has a Trust Responsibility to support sovereignty and protect Indian rights as the third form of sovereign government within the United States (the other two are the federal and state governments).

1973   The occupation of Wounded Knee takes place. Traditional leaders aligned with American Indian Movement (AIM) members occupy the town and demand that the United States listen to grievances about treaty rights and the corruption of the Pine Ridge tribal government. Seventy-one days of spectacular siege focuses the American public on Indian claims of injustices and corruption in the management of Indian affairs as well as racism. 1973 is also the year of Wounded Knee II. After participating in several national demonstrations including the Trail of Broken Treaties, Sioux on Pine Ridge Reservation occupied the community of Wounded Knee, a symbol of American brutality. AIM members, traditional leaders, non-Indian national supporters, tribal members from around the United States, and leaders like Russell Means used the 170-day standoff/siege as a springboard to highlight American Indian issues. The occupation was a nationally televised event and featured a great deal of gunfire, violence, and threats. It remains a symbol of American Indian pride in their traditional cultures and a symbol of renewed tribal sovereignty.

1974   The Indian Claims Commission awards $17.5 million plus interest to the Great Sioux Nation for the illegal taking of the Black Hills in 1877. The U.S. Court of Claims reverses the decision one year later.

1975   Congress passes PL 93-638, the Indian Self-Determination and Education Assistance Act. It reverses 200 years of American policy by allowing tribal governments to take over BIA programs and schools and administer them. The process, called "contracting," still requires BIA approval of tribal plans, and the contracts require that BIA/legislative requirements be fulfilled, but tribes now have the resources and flexibility to run programs locally. A new policy—Indian Self-Determination in a Government-to-Government Relationship—allows tribes a modicum of sovereignty.

1976   Congress enacts the American Indian Religious Freedoms Act. This act pledges to protect the rights of Indian freedom of religion and to instruct federal officials to facilitate Indian ceremonial use of parks lands. It also recognizes and reinforces the removal of restrictions on Indian religion that dates back to 1934.

The Indian Child Welfare Act is enacted. Reservation courts are recognized as having the right to control the adoption and placement of tribal children no matter where they live. The intent was to stop welfare agencies from removing Indian children from their cultures.

1978	The Indian Child Welfare Act passes. Indians lobbied for this act because so many Indian children were being taken from their tribe and adopted into or placed in non-Indian homes. It establishes jurisdiction over Indian children in their "home" tribe, regardless of where they are residing. Tribal courts must be offered jurisdiction by state social agencies when Indian children are involved.
1979	The Court of Claims, directed to review its previous denial, awards the Great Sioux Nation $17.5 million plus interest for American taking of the Black Hills.
1980	The Supreme Court affirms the Court of Claims ruling but increases the award to $106 million plus interest. The Court concludes that illegal seizure of the Black Hills. "A more ripe and rank case of dishonorable dealings will never, in all probability, be found in our history." Sioux tribes refuse to take the money, as they want the Black Hills returned. Interest continues to build, but the courts are only authorized to provide monetary compensation. Only Congress can make a political settlement that might include returning land.
1980–present	Sioux people and governments have shared many of the same milestones as other American Indian tribes. The U.S. government remains the builder of all Indian legal parameters whether by executive action, Congressional acts, or court decisions. However, individual Sioux reservations have experienced their special local histories. Indicating events for each reservation is not possible in a spacelimited chronology, and indicating all Indian events is restricted by the same limitation. The events listed below hint at the major events since 1980.
1981	Tim Giago establishes *The Lakota Times* on Pine Ridge Reservation. It is among the first Indian-owned, independent newspapers in the United States. Most Indian newspapers before 1981 were tribally controlled organs. *The Lakota Times* is now owned by the Oneida tribe, but it remains an important source of news throughout Indian Country.
1990	The Native American Graves Protection and Repatriation Act is passed. It continues the trend of supporting the rights of tribal

governments by requiring all museums to repatriate identifiable cultural legacy and sacred objects as well as human remains to the tribal governments of the identified tribes. Because the Sioux have been so featured in American museums, numerous human remains and Sioux artifacts have been returned to their homelands.

1991   Little Big Horn Battlefield replaces Custer Battlefield Monument as the name of the place where Sioux and Cheyenne defeated the Custer military expedition. This symbolic act recognizes that the Indians were bravely defending their homelands.

1992   The Shakopee band of Dakota opens Mystic Lake Casino near the Minneapolis-St Paul urban concentration. It becomes one of the most profitable Indian casinos. The Dakota established a foundation that now provides loans and grants for other American Indian communities that do not have highly profitable communities. Funds have gone to many Sioux communities like Spirit Lake Nation Reservation (Dakota) and to other reservations like Red Lake Reservation (Chippewa).

2004   The National Museum of the American Indian is established on the National Mall in Washington, DC. American Indians contributed to the design of the museum, and it reflects this input. Several tribes made large donations, including the Shakopee.

In *U.S. v Lara,* the Supreme Court reaffirms that tribal governments are inherently sovereign and were not created by the United States. The incident leading to the decision occurred on Spirit Lake Nation Reservation.

Cecelia Fire Thunder is elected Chairperson of the Oglala Sioux Tribe (Pine Ridge Reservation). She is later impeached by the tribal council. As a single incident, it indicates that Sioux governments are including women and that sovereign tribal governments are not always run smoothly—there are ideological divisions within reservations. Myra Pearson has served as chairperson on Spirit Lake Reservation for years.

2008   In the Cobbell decision, federal courts decide that the Bureau of Indian Affairs has mismanaged Indian trust funds and owes individual Indian land owners at least 455 million dollars. In 2009, the 13-year lawsuit is settled by an agreement with the United States accepting a penalty of $3.4 billion. Congress still needs to appropriate the funds. The decision does reinforce the Trust Responsibility and indicates that tribes or individual Indians can require the federal government to continue the Trust Responsibility.

2009   Tribal Law and Order Act is passed. Apparently, this act will address many of the problems of jurisdiction by encouraging cross-deputization of tribal and federal police as well as state and local police. Tribes should be able to enforce laws for all residents within reservations, not only Indians. The bill provides measures to address reservation suicide rates, drugs, and courts. Details were not worked out for funding and other measures as late as 2010, but the goal of the Act is to reinforce tribal exercise of sovereignty.

The Indian Health Care Improvement Act is passed. Congress makes another attempt to provide adequate health care by expanding the Indian Health Service and the ability of tribal governments to administer health programs according to tribal priorities. This is a reinforcement of tribal sovereignty within the policy of Self-Determination in a Government-to-Government Relationship.

1

Introduction to Sioux History and Culture

Nearly everyone in Canada and the United States has an internalized portrait of the Sioux buried in his or her subconscious. This portrait—a tall, handsome, painted warrior on horseback sporting an eagle feather war bonnet—springs to mind whenever the word *Indian* is mentioned. If one adds a tipi or two with a river running by it and an Indian "maiden" standing nearby, the common stereotype is complete. There is even a narrative to accompany the picture. The Sioux were a fierce, cruel, proud people who pluckily resisted the Manifest Destiny policies of the United States and Canada. They had valiant leaders like Sitting Bull, Crazy Horse, and Red Cloud; however, they lost and disappeared from history altogether. The plains Sioux are enshrined in stereotype as the epitome of all Indians.

Unfortunately, the stereotype is not accurate for American Indians, not even for the Sioux. In fact, the Sioux were really three distinct subdivisions with a tribal origin in the misty past. They are known as one tribe because European, and later American, explorers and government officials institutionalized the name to designate one group identified as Algonquian Indians and then extended the name to include additional groups who spoke dialects of the Algonquian language.

It is true that the Sioux were once a single culture, but that was between 1300 and 1500 AD. By the time French, English, and Americans came into contact with these Siouan speakers, they had divided into three distinct societies. These "Sioux" were as distinct from one another as the English, Australians, and Americans are today, perhaps more so, because each had a different economy. A "Sioux" living on the Minnesota River was distinctly different from a "Sioux" living on the western high plains.

TRIBE

The term "tribe" poses a difficulty too. Europeans indicated that Indian societies were tribes because they concluded that Indian societies were like the European "tribal" ancestors. Similarly, Europeans used their own ancestral history to apply terms like chief, pagan, barbarian, and savage to Indians. The study of societies, especially the non-European tribes of the Americas, Africa, and the Pacific islands, grew into anthropology. Unfortunately, they adopted the familiar term, tribe, for American Indian societies whether these societies met the newly minted definition or not.

Arbitrarily, tribes are "generally egalitarian, functionally generalized multi-community societies linked together through kinship and friendship ties, a common derivation and customs, and a common language."[1] Although each of the communities is self-sufficient and politically independent, there are pan-community unifying avenues such as warrior's societies, intermarriage, frequent ceremonies of unity that bring communities together, and extensive interaction. The Sioux, in about 1800, probably had as many as 300 independent yet interconnected societies.

In other words, a tribe is a conglomeration of independent societies sharing a culture. This is easy enough, but one needs to realize that tribes were named by outsiders like Americans, French, and English before they were aware of the complexity of Indian societies and according to preconceptions that they brought with them from Europe. The United States decided that the Sioux were a tribe, no matter what differences existed among them, and treated them as such. The Sioux themselves recognized that they had a common ancestral culture and accepted that they were one people but, in practice, went their separate ways. So, scholars and the American public have kept the term Sioux, and the Sioux accept it most of the time.

SOURCES OF KNOWLEDGE

Another impediment to studying the history and culture of the Sioux needs emphasis. Sources for reconstructing Sioux history and culture are quite limited the farther back we go in time. Even today, there are no means to construct a history as complete as that we could have for the United States, nationally. For the Misty Past, scholars have archaeology, linguistics, DNA,

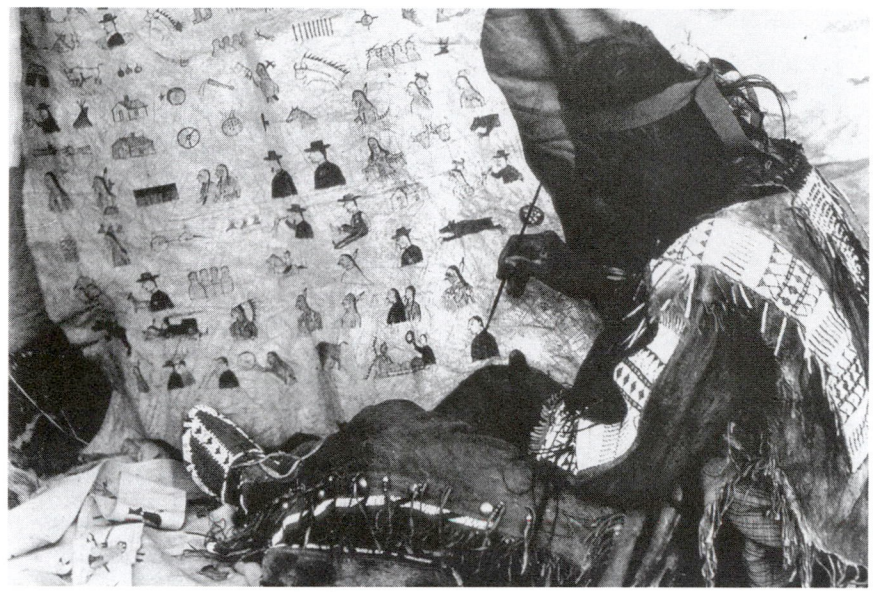

A Teton/Lakota man painting a winter count. Winter counts included a pictograph for each year that was significant for each band. Several Winter counts have survived as sources of Sioux history. (Nativestock.com/Marilyn Angel Wynn)

and oral histories. Each of these provides only snippets of information. European contact with the Sioux did not begin until the seventeenth century, and the various traders and government officials only added sporadic commentary—sometimes it is difficult to know if a particular journal is even describing the Sioux or some other culture/tribe. Additionally, written commentary was shaped by the preoccupations and prejudices of the observers.

For the Tetons, we also have a scattering of Winter Counts. It was the custom for each band to track years by identifying a particular event that was prominent for that year. Each winter, a picture of the previous year was painted on the hide that held pictures of previous years, as a mnemonic device allowing the keeper of the Winter Count to narrate a chronological history. Since some Winter Counts identify events noted in other histories, it is possible to construct knowledge of which events some bands felt were important to them. As with other histories, the closer we get to today, the better the records.

Oral traditions and oral histories provide another source of information about the Sioux past. These need to be used as carefully as the scattered written sources. Sioux historians did not see the world in the linear fashion used by today's historians, and histories were often related without time references.

Teton/Lakota Sioux posing in classic plains regalia on Pine Ridge Reservation, 1910. (Library of Congress)

However, using all of the sources available in a comparative way can allow a reasonable picture of the past.

Many anthropologists have worked with tribal members to describe traditional culture, but even the most detailed ethnographic reports are based on the memories and records of only a few people or a particular group. For instance, in the nineteenth century, several ethnologists and commentators focused on the Oglala Teton Lakota of the Pine Ridge Reservation, but we have nearly nothing about several of the other seven bands and their reservations.

Sioux Genesis

The Sioux 2011 tribal population within the United States is approximately 120,000, with another 6,000 within Canada. More than half of the Sioux do not live on American reservations or Canadian reserves. They are scattered as minority groups in cities and towns throughout Canada and the United States. However, the remaining 50 percent continue the historic pattern of living within separate political jurisdictions—currently, reservations and reserves are subject to the ultimate control of the two countries, but they are uniquely sovereign too. Eight reserves in Canada and sixteen reservations in the United States constitute the current "Sioux Country."

Historic population figures for the Sioux are problematic as are demographic data for most societies. For the most part, the Europeans estimated populations from indirect evidence and extrapolations from observations. Historians have compiled various sources and applied current demographic techniques. Probably, the Sioux population was about 28,000 in 1660, 24,000 in 1700, and 22,000 in 1760. Depopulation was a result of increased warfare but, most importantly, of disease. The smallpox pandemic of 1780–82 was noted by all of the Sioux Winter Counts. The pre-reservation nadir was about 17,000. After 1785, the Sioux population began to rebound because resistance to the introduced diseases grew and the United States launched a smallpox vaccination campaign for the Tetons in the 1830s. They were mostly spared the devastating 1837 epidemic that almost eliminated the Arikara, Mandan, and Hidatsa, for instance. Total Sioux population reached more than 40,000 by around 1855. In 1881, Sioux reservation populations stood at closer to 30,000.

Historically, the Sioux developed as a distinct culture around the year 1300 near the headwaters of the Mississippi river and once included northwest Wisconsin and northern Minnesota as their territory. Sioux cultural and political similarities gradually differentiated in this ancestral homeland as portions of the Sioux moved westward and southward and developed increasingly different life styles. By 1500, the Sioux "tribe" had come to include three distinct identities that became more differentiated as the centuries passed. Scholars have characterized the Sioux historical identities based on dialect, homelands in the eighteenth and nineteenth centuries, and economies. There are cultural differences as well.

All of the Sioux recognize that they are part of a single mythic nation, the Oceti Sakowin (Seven Council Fires). The Seven Council Fires that existed in around 1800 are grouped according to dialect and other characteristics. They are the:

- Dakota/Santee. The speakers of this dialect resided in southern Minnesota by the time the Americans arrived around 1800. They had four "fires": the Mdewakanton, Wahpeton, Wahpekute, and Sisseton. Sometimes, anthropologists call these fires either bands or tribes. The Dakota/Santee were a relatively coherent culture, living in the Woodlands style of hunting, gathering, some farming, fishing, and fur trading. They lived in rather large towns usually on rivers. Their dialect of the original Dakota is characterized by the use of "D" in many key words. The word "Dakota" itself, meaning ally or relative or friend depending on context, is an example.

- Dakota/Yankton and Yanktonai. These two council fires diverged from the Dakota about 1500 and moved to the area where the Sioux and Missouri rivers meet in southeastern South Dakota, northwestern Iowa, and southwestern Minnesota. They changed location for access to fur traders and buffalo as food and hides for commerce. The Yankton quickly adopted the earth lodge-agriculture style of the other river cultures like the Arikara; they also used hide tipis, made familiar by the Teton, when they went buffalo hunting. Some scholars have indicated that they spoke an "N" dialect but, if they ever did, it was before French contact in the eighteenth century. Scholarly disputes about the N dialect illustrate the problems in being precise about much of early Sioux history and cultures.
- Lakota/Teton. Although this was the largest council fire by the 1800s, it is only a single fire in the oral history of the Sioux. When French and Americans interacted with them, beginning in the eighteenth century, the Lakota/Teton had seven separately identified multiband subdivisions: the Oglala, Sicangu/Brule, Minneconju, Two Kettles, Sans Arc, Blackfoot, and Hunkpapa. Sometimes these subdivisions are called tribes rather than bands. Each of these tribes was divided into bands. The Lakota are the stereotypical plains Indians, and "Lakota Country" was more or less bounded by the Big Horn Mountains in the West, the Canadian border in the North, the Platte River in the South, and the Missouri River in the East. This book will use Santee/Dakota, Yankton, Yanktonai, and Lakota/Teton interchangeably, so Sioux can refer to any of them as well as collectively. Other names of subdivisions of the four basic political terms will be added for clarity, so for instance, Teton Oglala or Teton Hunkpapa.

Readers should simply remember that Dakota refers to those Sioux who lived in the woodlands and prairies of Minnesota until the 1860s when most became refugees or were relocated to the eastern Dakotas and Nebraska. Yankton Sioux indicates that these Sioux were centered along rivers like the James, Missouri, and Big Sioux where Iowa, Minnesota, and South Dakota meet. The Teton are the largest of the Sioux subdivisions, and their country is the northern high plains from Montana to Nebraska and east to the Missouri River. The Yanktonai are a separate society also of plains culture Sioux.

CONSTANT CHANGE

What existed clearly around 1800 was not always the way it was. One of the truly difficult considerations in any tribal history is to accept that change was constant. The Sioux peoples constantly adapted their customs and culture to meet their needs, and even their belief systems were always in flux. The Sioux are not, and never have been, static captives of their culture.

"Culture" is another word that muddies the waters of understanding. Anthropologists use the term to refer "to a group of people who share common customs, speak a common language, and occupy a particular territory. Cultures have an ideological, symbolic dimension that must be understood in order to comprehend the activities of its members."[2] We, however, bow to conventional usage and use the term "Sioux" to describe the Seven Council Fires with all of their cultural, political, economic, and homeland differences.

THE TRADITIONAL SIOUX

"Traditional" is the descriptive term selected to describe the Sioux of the eighteenth through much of the nineteenth century. This is the period when Sioux culture reached is florescence. It is when Sioux cultural development was most distinct and when the Sioux were politically sovereign. The Sioux of common imagination lived in this period with a distinctly Sioux world view, religion, and way of life. Traditional Sioux society and history is a major focus of this book.

Describing over 600 years of a constantly changing society is a difficult task. Not only is Sioux society today quite different from 1300 or 1500 or 1750, but the Sioux have also undergone major changes periodically. The transition of some Sioux from hunter-gatherers existing on the edges and rivers of the northern plains to a warrior horse culture sovereign over hundreds of square miles is one example. Changes resulting from the fur trade within all of the Sioux subdivisions drastically affected Sioux life. The best that an historian can do is to remind readers that change occurs regularly and try to convey some sense of change while courting the danger of leaving readers with a sense that the traditional society was immutable and that the Sioux of today are Indian only to the extent that they act like their pre-reservation ancestors.

Notes

1. Gibson, p. 20.
2. Gibson, p. 21.

2

Early Sioux History

INTRODUCTION

SIOUX HISTORY exists in two domains of knowledge. First is the history that describes what happened as determined by the tools of empirical scholarship. Historians, archaeologists, and other scholars have created an historical narrative using written documents, DNA research, oral histories, geological records, dendrochronology, and a host of other sources. These sources trace the emergence of Sioux cultures, migrations, interactions with other tribes, economies, warfare, relations with colonial powers, and U.S.-Sioux political developments.

The alternate domain is cultural history that integrates sacred knowledge. This history begins with the origin traditions of the Sioux bands. Sacred knowledge reflects how they became the Oyate (the people) of the Oceti Sakowin (the Seven Council Fires), a distinct society with a revealed culture. Sacred narratives reveal the creation of humans and of the society eventually called the Sioux by Europeans and Americans.

According to Lakota sacred knowledge, the Oyate emerged from the earth in the Black Hills and became Lakota when they were taught the way of the pipe by White Buffalo Calf Woman. In some sources of Dakota traditional knowledge, the Oyate came from the North and were guided to the place where they learned the ways of the people. In another origin history, the Dakota came from the east guided by the Underwater Panther *Umketehi* along the Red Road, Chanke Duta. Regardless, it is from these beginnings that the Sioux learned to be a distinct culture through supernatural assistance.

The history domain provides another form of explanation for the beginnings of Sioux history and is the focus of this chapter. Sioux history can be divided, approximately, into five chronological periods:

1. Tribal Developmental Period (from the Misty Past to about 1650). Sioux ancestors arrived in the Americas, moved to the East Coast/Appalachians and migrated in bands to the headwaters of the Mississippi. The Sioux emerged as a distinct tribal culture, the Santee/Dakota, around 1300 and established themselves throughout the upper Midwest from the shores of Lake Michigan to the Red River of the North. Expansion continued southward and westward due to the pressures of other tribal expansions in and in response to the search for more resources. Some bands separated from the Dakota/Santee by around 1500. One group of bands became identified as the Yankton and Yanktonai and took portions of eastern South Dakota and North Dakota as their homelands. Another group became the Teton-Lakota and by the eighteenth century had encompassed a new homeland, roughly from the Missouri River to the Black Hills. Each of the three groups adopted the living styles of other tribes around them and was a distinct subculture of the original Dakota by approximately 1500 AD or thereabout.

2. Sioux Expansion Period (ca. 1650s–1800). The various Sioux subdivisions solidified their boundaries and continued developing distinctive cultures. Chippewa and European merchants introduced manufactured goods and stimulated the beginnings of Sioux fur trade in the 1680s. Horses became the underpinning of the transformation of the Tetons and Yanktons into plains horse cultures. Guns altered balances of power for all of the Sioux. Introduced diseases altered Sioux life as well. By the end of the period, most of the Sioux were still not directly involved with European expansion or wars as were eastern Indians.

3. Incorporation into the United States (1800–81). The U.S. expansion following the expulsion of the French and British required responses from each of the Sioux subdivisions. The fur trade became a dominant facet of Sioux economies. The Dakota and Yankton focused on beaver and luxury furs, and the Teton-Lakota brought piles of buffalo hides to the fur trade posts in the plains. As the century progressed, American determination to control and to expand its occupation of the continent lead to treaties of cession, war, and the creation of reservations for all of the Sioux by 1881. Sioux institutions and culture were targeted for eradication by American officials pursuing a policy of assimilation on the reservations.

4. Reservations as colonies (ca. 1890–1960s). The U.S. political control of even the details of the daily lives of the Sioux was created by congressional and executive actions. The Bureau of Indian Affairs (BIA) assumed control of the reservations directly. Assimilation programs and instruments of control were institutionalized. Sioux actions and changing American societal goals resulted

in movement toward allowing a revitalization of Sioux culture and a return to limited self-government. By the 1960s, Americans were moving toward policies to release the Sioux and other Indians from a paternalistic colonialism.

5. Self-Determination (1960s–present). Reservation governments reclaimed sovereignty within American law and began a process of ameliorating the negative effects of the colonial period, a process that occurred within an American society that had changed its attitudes toward minorities and multiculturalism. Indian, including many Sioux, leaders supported by reformist Americans proclaimed a government-to-government relationship and tried to provide ways to deal with the legacies of the past. Legislation and federal court decisions provided a framework for this new American approach to the Sioux and their governments.

TRIBAL DEVELOPMENT PERIOD: FROM THE MISTY PAST TO THE 1950S

After ancestral Indians arrived in America via the Bering Strait, whether by boat or by foot, and whether 12,000 years ago or 30,000 years ago, they gradually spread throughout the continents while developing increasingly more distinct communities over the millennia. Population drift and migrations, language development, increasing technological variation, and greater differentiation of worldviews led to distinct societies. One such society, consisting of many bands, developed the Siouan language family. In many ways, language is the best marker available to describe cultures because nearly all of the other attributes of culture and its accompanying technology are transferable from one group to another. Anyone can use a pot from a different culture, and we know that commerce was prevalent from the beginning of human time.

Early Siouan speakers originally lived in the area of the Appalachians in today's Kentucky and the Carolinas. As the original population expanded and subdivided, these Sioux created 19 distinct languages. Seven groups became woodland tribes, including the Dakota. After 1300, the Teton dialect of Dakota, Lakota,[1] evolved on the plains along with eleven other Siouan languages such as Hidatsa.

This linguistic progression narrative is derived from linguistic recreations augmented by archaeological evidence and buttressed by at least part of the Dakota origin narrative. As Siouan speakers migrated westward, most likely along river routes, they scattered among various environments and locations while forming and re-forming societies. A major split probably occurred about 500 BC. One group eventually became the western Siouan speakers (Mandan, Hidatsa, Crow). The largest group evolved into the central Siouan speakers (Dakota, Stoney, Assiniboine, Quapaw, Kansa, Osage, Omaha, Iowa, Otoe, Missouri, and Winnebago). Eastern Siouan speakers (Ofo, Biloxi, and Tutelo) remained along the southeastern coast of North America. Another split occurred around 700 AD when the proto-Dakota and Winnebago left the other groups. Each of the tribes involved has oral histories that explain the causes of most of the separations. Access to resources, internal disputes, and supernatural guidance provided the impetus for tribal genesis.

By 1300 AD, the Proto-Dakota (Sioux) were located in numerous communities in northern Minnesota. Archaeological attempts to identify specific ethnic communities found in northern Minnesota are hampered by the limitations imposed by only being able to use pottery, worked stone, and skeletons as evidence. Generally, archaeologists operate on the premise that when pottery styles change, new cultures have arisen. Given the pottery and skeletal evidence, it is probable that the Proto-Dakota Sioux were what archaeologists have defined as the Clam River-Kathio-Blackduck continuum. The proto-Dakota further differentiated into a culture called Psinomani.

The Psinomani were apparently influenced by, interacted with, or actually were part of larger cultures throughout the 1300s. Evidence is somewhat vague, but widespread cultures such as the Mississippian and Oneota played a role in the continued evolution of the ancestral Dakota Sioux. Over at least two centuries, the proto-Dakota developed a distinct Dakota culture. Dakota-expanding societies spun off to new locations over time and developed cultural variations. The birth of new communities probably occurred because of some combination of a need for greater resources, local resource depletion, internal disputes, war with other expanding tribes, or supernatural intervention.

Somewhere around 1500, community fracturing reached the point that former Dakota had relocated sufficiently distant from the core homeland to identify themselves as distinct. Yankton, Yanktonai, and Lakota were now seen as separate council fires. Within the Dakota, strong affinities continued, but four groups were sufficiently separate to form the four council fires of the Dakota. By 1500 or so, the Seven Council Fires that make up the Sioux existed. Following internal disputes, speakers of the Assiniboine Nakota dialect moved so far away that they affiliated with Cree and Chippewa, Algonquian speakers, and actually became enemies of the Sioux and were excluded from the Oyate. Expansion westward by the Teton continued until the mid-nineteenth century as it did for the Yanktonai.

Sioux expansion was not the movement of the tribes into uncontested, unoccupied land. It was not uniform and constant either. Santee bands moved as far east as the Wisconsin-Michigan border while others were moving west and south. Areas like those around Hayward, Wisconsin, and Lac Courte Oreilles were at times Dakota and at other times Chippewa. Winnebago bands clashed with Dakota bands as each sought better resources and safety. The oral histories of most of the upper midwestern tribes describe warfare and the ebb and flow of military success. Dakota bands and tribes both fought against and allied with the other tribes throughout the period. The Iowa moved to the state that bears their name because they lost to expanding Yankton Sioux. Other tribes were developing along the same lines as the Sioux and were determined to secure specific areas for themselves.

The tribes that fought the Sioux during these centuries were the Winnebago, Cree, Chippewa, Menominee, Iowa, Arikara, Assiniboine, Pawnee, Ponca, Ottawa, Illinois, Miami, and several others. This was a period of conflict but also one of securing alliances with other tribes. Just as in Europe, enemies could become friends as circumstances changed, and Indian leaders sought to secure their people. However, it is probable that a warrior/male supremacist ideology emerged during this period and operated to encourage conflict. Sioux society became a warrior-dominated society where success in war was required for all males and was demanded by the society.

During this period, Santee/Dakota territory was secured and their culture solidified. They were valued as allies and feared as enemies according to other tribal oral histories. Some pictured them as predators who reveled in warfare. During the seventeenth century, the Santee were aware that threats to other tribes were causing disruptions, but the Santee had to be confident that they would remain secure in their woodlands. Farther West and near the southwestern Minnesota border, the Teton, Yankton, and Yanktonai council fires had moved to the edges of the vast northern plains and established secure boundaries also.

THE SIOUX EXPANSION PERIOD: 1650s–1800

Although the Sioux had long been entwined with events beyond their country, the 1650s ushered in a period of massive change precipitated by the arrival of Europeans in the Americas. French establishment of the colonies of Quebec, Montreal, and Acadia (later Nova Scotia) and Dutch creation of trade posts along the Hudson River, soon acquired by the English, set forces in motion that would alter Sioux society and help shape Santee history for decades. Chippewa initial control of access to French goods and the Beaver Wars of conquest and devastation launched by the Iroquois—both in the seventeenth century—were the indirect result of European colonialism. Much of America was a maelstrom of constant motion as tribes and Europeans sought access to and control of resources.

Chippewa traders arrived in Dakota/Santee country in the 1660s and 1670s with French goods, which they exchanged for furs. The Chippewa obtained French products because they were accessible to French traders through the Saint Lawrence region and, by the end of the century, at Sault Ste. Marie, their homeland, where Lakes Superior, Michigan, and Huron met to form a thriving entrepôt for Indian and French goods. French traders joined Chippewa communities and built trading post forts like Michilimackinaw. A Chippewa-Dakota alliance, formalized at Fond du Lac, allowed some Chippewa to relocate from their homeland to Madeleine Island near northern Lake Superior and permitted their use of Santee territory in Wisconsin and northwestern Minnesota. The Dakota gained the Chippewa as allies and suppliers of European goods. Ironically, the Chippewa were invited to occupy Dakota territory just as later the Dakota would invite French and British merchants. This mutually beneficial Chippewa-Santee alliance endured for nearly a century and was sealed by intermarriage, joint warfare, and commerce.

Dutch and English challenges to French commerce and perceived control of Indian nations led to their alliance with the Iroquois Confederacy that controlled access to Albany markets as a counterweight to the French. Iroquois leaders, particularly the Mohawk, did not allow the English to trade directly with other tribes, and they exercised a monopoly that rapidly depleted the supply of beaver in their domain. The only answer to the need of the Iroquois for ever more furs was to take resources from other tribes, and in the 1650s, Iroquois expeditions decimated multiple tribes like the Huron, Tobacco, and Erie. The Iroquois assaulted the Chippewa, Ottawa, Potawatomi, Menominee, Illinois, and other Great Lakes tribes as well. This created a domino effect of tribes fleeing westward to escape the fury of the Iroquois. Refugees, in turn, displaced other tribes, resulting in the roiling of the entire upper Midwest into Canada. Chippewa leaders managed to put together an alliance by the 1680s that defeated the Big Snakes (the Iroquois) and forced them to retreat to their homelands in northern New York. French-Chippewa expeditions into Iroquoia completed the defeat of the Confederacy. French colonial officials, along with leaders of the tribes involved, crafted the Great Peace in 1701 that established a measure of stability.

Santee bands felt the effects of these wars even as far away as their homeland in Minnesota. One result was that their enemies became more aggressive and some Santee bands began moving westward, seeking alternatives to Chippewa traders for European goods. The buffalo-populated plains beckoned, and French traders moving up the Mississippi were also a temptation. The Yankton responded first, moving westward until they eventually stayed in the area where Iowa, Minnesota, and South Dakota merge. Spanish and French traders established trading posts in Yankton country. Dakota-Santee leaders sought to entice French merchants to Minnesota.

Pierre Radisson and Medart Chouart de Groseliers were the first to explore market possibilities, in 1660. Then, Sieur du Luth and Father Hennepin trekked to Dakota towns in Minnesota in 1679. Nicholas Perrot established a trading post on Lake Pepin and grandiosely claimed the area for the King of

France. Perrot added to other reports of the military ability of the Santee with descriptions of their battles with the Chippewa, Ottawa, and Hurons. Written commentary by Europeans allowed historians to begin identifying Sioux leaders, although the descriptions are often perfunctory and the spelling so haphazard that deciphering the names can be a challenge. As contact increased in frequency and duration, leaders' personalities and intentions became clearer, but nonetheless little can be gleaned about the Dakotas' daily lives.

French merchants and officials contented themselves with sporadic trading expeditions to about 1750 as they were preoccupied with their struggle with the British for the Ohio Valley and were blocked from Santee country by both the Chippewa—their trading partners—and the Fox, who fought the French and Chippewa for control of trade routes. Santee hopes for increased trade were not realized by the spasmodic interludes of French trade and they continued their movement out of the Mille Lacs-Sandy Lake homeland in northern Minnesota to secure safer, more lucrative sites.

In 1736, a Santee-Chippewa band attacked wintering French traders and killed them. The French blamed the Dakota for the killings and offered the Chippewa a choice of joining them against the Dakota or remaining allies of the Dakota. Chippewa leaders chose the French alliance because choosing the Dakota would have damaged the Chippewa economy and courted military disaster. This incident precipitated about a century of Dakota-Chippewa war that would eventually realign the boundaries of each tribe.

In 1750, the four-day Battle of Kathio resulted in the Chippewa hastening the departure of the Santee toward the south. As with many events in oral histories, Kathio is much shrouded in legend, but, clearly, there was a battle followed by many more that continued the Dakota-Chippewa War. As the war progressed, the Santee abandoned their towns of Cass Lake, Sandy Lake, Winnibigoshish, Leech Lake, and Red Lake to the Chippewa. The last effort of the Santee to regain their homeland through a major retaliatory expedition in 1768 failed. From 1768 until well into the nineteenth century, Santee attacks on Chippewa were either reprisals or merely attacks on an enemy for booty and glory rather than for land. The Chippewa answered in kind.

Access to buffalo and the fur traders heading up the river from St. Louis, a disease that spread among the deer herds, and other factors magnified the effects of the war and made relocation rewarding for the Sioux. Southern Minnesota below St. Anthony's Falls (St. Paul, Minnesota) was solidified as the home of the Dakota. Their towns dotted the Mississippi and Minnesota rivers and their tributaries. Many towns, such as Wabasha, Red Wing, Mankato, and Shakopee, were identified by the names of their *itancan* (leaders).

While the Santee were pursuing their interest in trade and moving in a southwesterly direction from their homeland, the other council fires were becoming plains Indians. As with much of the history of the Santee, the narratives about Yankton, Yanktonai, and Teton expansion are gleaned from oral histories that did not necessarily have the same concerns for chronological flow that would become a fixation of modern historians. However, enough survives that can be corroborated not only in Sioux sources but also in a mixture of European records and the oral histories of other tribes. Early history has had to remain less detailed than current history, but its broad outlines are discernible.

Yankton bands moved to meet French traders probing northward up the Mississippi and Missouri rivers from St. Genevieve and other French communities. The Yankton expelled such other tribes as the Omaha and Iowa. They were firmly established in several earth lodge towns by the 1760s. Ethnically French and politically Spanish, traders secured Yankton permission and built a trading post near modern Yankton, South Dakota. Other small posts were situated up the river systems of the St. James and Missouri as markets ebbed and flowed.

Yankton communities borrowed life styles as well as architecture from the Arikara and other plains neighbors. However, they did not stop considering themselves one of the council fires of the Sioux and retained a trading-visiting-cultural relationship with the other Sioux council fires. Horses arrived from the West in the 1700s to assist their physical transition to plains people who farmed and hunted buffalo. The Yankton often joined their western Teton relatives in war, trade, and social interaction. Like their Santee relatives, the Yankton did not ally with either the French or the English in the French and Indian War. They were too far removed from the theaters of conflict.

Teton/Lakota bands headed west from many points along the Missouri River. Rapid expansion and conquest were made possible by the acquisition of horses from the Shoshoni trade network. Horses allowed the transformation of these Sioux into a nomadic, buffalo hunting, warrior, culture that was the most formidable military power on the northern plains.

The Teton-Lakota bands grew large enough to be considered tribes by the nomenclature-confused Europeans and Americans. Until well into the twentieth century, Americans called these bands either Sioux or Dakota. Teton subdivisions included the Brule and Oglala, which had the largest populations and moved westward along the Platte, Niobrara, and White rivers toward the Black Hills and from the Missouri where it meets the Bad River. Other major bands (tribes) were the Hunkpapapa, Sans Arc, Sisapa, Minniconju, and Two Kettles. In turn, each of the bands was divided into many *tiyospaye* (families and affiliated living communities). From the Lakota perspective, they pushed aside Arikara, Pawnee, Ponca, and others as they moved westward. By 1776, some Ogala had reached the Black Hills and begun the

Teton/Lakota, the quintessential plains tribe, was a common motif in Karl Bodmer's paintings that branded the Sioux in the American and European mind. Horse racing was a favorite sport. (Library of Congress)

process of making them the heart of the Teton nation. The Cheyenne, Crow, and Kiowa vacated the Black Hills under pressure from the Tetons.

The northern bands displaced the Mandan, Hidatsa, Blackfeet, Gros Ventres, and others. The Mandan and Hidatsa were useful suppliers of corn, beans, squash, guns, and other European products for the nomadic Tetons. These urban dwellers suffered greatly from small pox in the latter eighteenth century and ceased to be even a small deterrent to Teton expansion. However, Mandan and Hidatsa cities did remain important centers of commerce where European and Indian goods were traded to the benefit of the Sioux and others until the 1837 smallpox pandemic forced the two tribes to huddle in a single town. After a few years, the two tribes were joined by the Arikara.

In the process of moving westward, Sioux organization changed to reflect the nearly constant warfare and dependence on buffalo and gathering for food. Men's lives came to depend on their prowess at horse stealing from other tribes, their bravery and success in open warfare, and the prestige of belonging to the several warrior societies. Horses provided the means and the arena for displaying the glory of warfare and the mobility of the Tetons that allowed them to dominate the entire northern plains from the Platte River northward into southern Canada. By around 1750, the Tetons were recognized by both Europeans and Americans as Lords of the Plains. Some historians have likened their expansion to the imperialism of the United States westward expansion. Parenthetically, the Tetons made a large number of enemies.

As westward expansion continued, the Santee/Dakota had shifted their home bases to the Minnesota and Mississippi rivers where they continued their woodlands culture with ever-increasing forays westward to hunt buffalo. Southern Minnesota, which consisted of rolling hills and prairies, lent itself to ever-larger Dakota towns than had been possible in northern Minnesota.

British trade out of Canada with the Santee did not develop on a large scale. At first, some Santee made the trek to Hudson's Bay Company posts and some British traders entered southern Minnesota, but the large entrepots of the British were quite distant from Santee country. Nevertheless, many French-surnamed British traders did filter into Santee country and become influential relatives through intermarriage. British goods remained desirable and were the only ones available to the Santee. Although the Santee remained customers of middlemen from other tribes including Yankton relatives from the west and south, the Santee considered the British as their friends.

British involvement was enough for a few Santee to join British forces during the American Revolution. Wabasha, a Mdewakanton itancan, journeyed to Fort Macinac in 1779 and later led men in the campaigns along the upper Mississippi. He was present at Prairie du Chien in 1783 when the victory of the Americans over the British was announced. He indicated that he was "content."

For the most part, Santee lives were changed very little by French and British merchants. Changes occurred because other tribes were displaced westward during the wars for resources, particularly by the expansion of their Chippewa allies who became enemies after 1836. Life continued to follow familiar cycles determined by the seasonal availability of resources, and towns were established by itancans such as Wabasha, Red Wing, and Little Crow.

INCORPORATION INTO THE UNITED STATES: 1800–81

The height of Sioux wealth, power, and well-being occurred in the first half of the nineteenth century. Santee bands were secure in the large towns, were successful in war against most of their enemies, and had access to more material goods than ever before. The Yankton had embraced the earth lodge-buffalo hunting lifestyle of the plains communities and were successful against other tribes. The fur trading posts, horses, and material goods in their country surpassed their earlier experience. Teton bands were the lords of the plains, feared by their enemies and free to pursue their continuing territorial expansion. Fur traders brought goods to them and built trading posts to supply their needs. Fort Laramie and Fort Pierre were American Fur Company posts and acted like capitals for the Teton/Lakota. Americans came to the Lakota for peace and sought them as allies. Buffalo were abundant and the source of commercial wealth. It was good to be Sioux. Parenthetically the plains Sioux made a lot of enemies.

The Americans won their war of independence from the British and acquired title to the land east of the Mississippi, excluding Canada. Then, the United States purchased French title over the Louisiana Territory in 1803. This title gave the United States the exclusive right to interact with the Indian tribes within their new borders. Indian titles would have to be acquired through direct negotiations with the tribes. President Jefferson sent Lieutenant Zebulon Pike and others to explore the land added to the United States through the Louisiana Purchase. Pike's mission was to establish that the United States was sovereign and tribes were subjects of the United States. Of course, the Sioux did not picture their world this way.

The Sioux opened diplomatic relations with the Americans in 1805 when Lieutenant Pike met with several Dakota leaders. The initial treaty between the two nations involved the purchase by the United States of a tract of land where Minneapolis-St. Paul is located today. In American eyes, signing of the treaty began the process of incorporating all of the Sioux within the legal-political system of the United States. Even when allowed to maintain tribal governments, the Dakota and other Indians were expected to be subject to American laws. The United States was sovereign, and only the Americans had the power to make decisions about land usage.

Sioux society viewed sovereignty and land ownership similarly to most American Indian societies, and their view did not resemble that of the Americans. Land belonged to particular tribes and was subdivided into band areas. Usage was determined by tradition, but no single individual had ownership of pieces of land. Other tribes recognized or challenged the boundaries as situations changed. Everyone recognized that a tribe could cede land to other tribes or grant permission of occupancy or attack invaders according to a complex series of protocols. For instance, the Chippewa were allowed to live on the western shores of Lake Superior by the Sioux after the two negotiated with each other. French and English merchants were allowed to live in Sioux Country following negotiations. After 1736, Chippewa power was such that they took land and added it to the Chippewa domain. Eventually, both tribes recognized new boundaries, although the Sioux were never content with their loss.

Within Sioux country, each band or community had its particular land area. The Red Wing community, for instance, exercised political and proprietary control over an area accepted by members of the tribe. Red Wing community/ village leaders could grant usage to others or even surrender land to others. Hunting, gathering, and farming rights were controlled by the Red Wing, although access to other Sioux was a given. This usage approach to ownership was difficult for Americans to understand because there was no private property for exclusive use by individuals and there were no rigid national boundaries. Sovereignty in the hands of a central government that controlled all of its citizens and other inhabitants within national boundaries was not part of Sioux political theory.

When Lieutenant Zebulon Pike arrived in Sioux Country representing the United States, American political theory had borrowed the idea of The Doctrine of Discovery from international law. This theory held that Sioux Country was already part of the United States because the United States had acquired sovereignty from the English and French—the "discoverers" of North America. Indians were entitled to use of the land but the United States had the right to acquire the right to use it through payment (purchase) or through just wars. Indians, including the Sioux, merely had aboriginal title. In the 1820s and 1830s, Chief Justice John Marshall would make the Doctrine of Discovery the legal justification for extinguishing Indian title and making them subject to American law.

In this trope, the United States wrested sovereignty from England through the American Revolution and bought sovereignty from France. Later, it would conquer Mexico and assume its sovereignty over much of the rest of the lands that became the United States. In the 1780s, the United States began negotiating treaties with Indian nations to purchase Indian lands for American use—the United States already had sovereignty according to American law. Americans chose to follow British precedent and utilize treaties to describe American relationships with Indian nations. In effect, the use of treaties recognized that Indian nations, like the Sioux, were sovereign nations. International law recognized that treaties were agreements between sovereign governments.

Another facet of American Indian policy was based on the American idea that American culture was superior to the cultures of primitive Indians. American civilization was based on private property and Christianity as well as representative democracy. It was expected that Indians would recognize the self-evident superiority of American culture, choose to replace their culture with American and thereby become "civilized." At any rate, Americans insisted that Indians, including the Sioux, would have to give way to the needs of Americans. Indians would have to conform to American laws and accept American sovereignty. American policies toward Indians would follow these assumptions well into the 1960s.

Neither Indians nor Americans understood the other's views of sovereignty and land ownership when Zebulon Pike sought out Santee leaders in 1805. He met with seven Mdewakanton itancan and negotiated a treaty of purchase. Nine square miles were sold for $2,000 so the United States could build a fort (Fort Snelling). Only two leaders, Little Crow and Way Ago Enagee, signed the treaty. America decided that their signatures constituted an obligation for the entire Sioux tribe. Although we cannot know for certain, these Mdewakanton leaders probably thought they were granting the right of occupation and concluded that the United States provided gifts as expected in any diplomatic protocol. The United States never paid the $2,000 and did not build the fort until after the War of 1812.

Renewed war between British trade partners and the United States led some Dakota to join the British. A British trader, Robert Dickson, gathered several Santee leaders including Wabasha and Little Crow with 300 other Dakota to gain support even before the war started. Santee leaders indicated that British traders were important to them. Dickson brought a force of 130 Sioux, Menominee, and Winnebago to Mackinac where they helped capture the American fort located there. In 1813, as Indian Superintendent, Dickson brought another 600 men to augment British forces at Mackinac. A few Santee leaders chose to support the British, but most remained neutral, and some even went over to the Americans. Santee leaders did what they considered best for their people.

After the war, the United States invited Sioux leaders to Portage des Sioux. Santee, Yankton and Teton leaders ended the war with the United States by treaty. Americans moved to secure the peace by building Fort St. Anthony in 1819 (renamed Fort Snelling in 1820) and appointed Lawrence Taliaferro as Indian agent. His job was to secure peace between the Sioux and the Chippewa, distribute gifts to visiting Indians, and reduce the influence of British traders.

Several American Fur Company traders had plied their goods even before the war. Taliaferro attempted to control these traders by designating 17 sites for trade and fulminating against the use of alcohol as a trade item. Two of the merchants, Joseph Rolette, a relative of Wahbasha, and Joseph Renville, also married into a prominent Sioux family, were particularly difficult for Taliaferro to control. Commerce remained an important activity and fur trader-kinsmen had influence among Santee leaders throughout the century. Their influence was so pervasive that Indian agents, settlers, military leaders, and other government officials saw them as necessary to any effective communication with the Santee.

The Sioux word for mixed bloods is *iyeska*. It literally means "talks white." From the first exchange between Europeans and Sioux, both realized the importance of kinship in business, political, and cultural relations. Intermarriage was desirable for Sioux and Europeans alike. By the time the Americans arrived to interact with the Sioux, each of the Seven Council Fires included descendents of intermarriage as part of the tribe. These mixed bloods often formed a separate part of each band because they were engaged in trade, were not completely integrated, and were treated differently by Santee and outsiders alike. Most of the mixed bloods were of French descent, and their descendents remain prominent in the Sioux population. Kinsmen and Sioux with surnames such as Renville, Rolette, LaFramboise, Richard, Bordeaux, Boudreaux, Janis, Cadotte, St.Clair, and Picotte are prominent throughout Sioux history.

The influence of the *iyeska* is much debated because they were both widespread and necessary as interpreters and merchants for Sioux-American relations. Most Americans were suspicious of their influence because they felt that these "half breeds" led the "real" Sioux leaders to oppose American leadership and goals. They were accused of being a pernicious, selfish group who were not even real Indians. As time went on, Sioux leaders often complained that the mixed bloods misled them or selfishly took treaty money at the expense of others. There were mixed bloods who were selfish and who manipulated their kin to their own advantage. Many others provided leadership in defense of Sioux sovereignty throughout the centuries.

THE DAKOTA IN THE NINETEENTH CENTURY

The first major American effort to assert control over the Sioux occurred at Prairie du Chien in 1823. Santee, Chippewa, Sacs and Fox, Menominee, Iowa, Winnebago, Potawatomie, and Ottawa bands were invited to participate in a treaty conference. Amidst the feasting, games, gift-giving, and military displays, Americans led by Superintendent William Clark hoped to convince tribes to draw borders, establish neutral zones separating Chippewa from Dakota and other Sioux enemies from them, and agree to general terms for peace. The Treaty of Prairie du Chien seemed to accomplish American goals and Sioux recognition of American sovereignty. It is likely that the assembled tribes did agree that peace was a good idea and that they had already established neutral zones in Minnesota.

Unfortunately, a number of Dakota and Chippewa leaders died on the way home for Prairie du Chien and this led to a continuing legend that Americans deliberately had killed them. The Santee did not trust Americans because they sensed that the Americans often seemed to favor other tribes. Stories about American killing of Dakota by poisoning did not contribute to establishing trust.

Leaders of the Dakota, Chippewa, and other tribes signed a treaty with the United States that recognized the tribal boundaries and committed all of the nations to peace. It marked the beginning of a continuous official presence of the United States in Dakota country. (Library of Congress)

Acceptance of American sovereignty was another matter. It is quite likely that the Dakota and other tribes envisioned sovereignty as establishing a kind of supportive relationship with the Americans and promising American largesse as the Dakota needed it. Certainly, no itancan would surrender his band's independence to Americans. Shortly after the treaty, war as usual continued among the tribes. In 1832, Dakota from Wabasha's band gleefully attacked Sac and Fox fleeing from the American army during the Black Hawk War. They killed approximately 70 men, women, and children. As with the Chippewa, war continued for several decades.

American influence did grow as military activity increased at Fort Snelling and a regular agent tried to direct Dakota behavior. Lawrence Taliaferro began a 19-year career as Indian agent in 1820. His task was to oversee the civilization of the Sioux and other tribes. American Indian policy drew on the assumption that Indians had to become Christian farmers and relinquish their pagan cultures and their land to the Americans. The United States planned that all of Sioux country would soon be divided into states and Indians would be a minority guided toward civilization by American agents, missionaries, and their civilized American neighbors. The Dakota indicated repeatedly that they did saw no improvement to their lives and culture by becoming Americans; they already knew how to live the right way.

Taliaferro encouraged missionaries to combine preaching with school classes and instruction in farming. He established the Eatonville experiment in Dakota farming with two families that became 45 families by 1833. Gideon and Samuel Pond, volunteer missionaries, were given land near Lake Calhoun and hired to teach farming with Sioux treaty money. They were joined by Thomas Williamson and Alexander Huggins along with their families. These ministers were soon involved in conflicts with each other, and Taliaferro dispersed them to other Sioux communities. Despite the flood of missionaries, most Dakota ignored their conversion efforts. The Dakota did not convert in significant numbers until the 1850s and 1860s.

One missionary accomplishment was the result of Stephen Riggs's systematizing of the Dakota language in his 1852 *Grammar and Dictionary of the Dakota Language*. Joseph Renville, a mixed-blood Dakota and trader, provided linguistic knowledge to Riggs so he could create a written representation of the language. Riggs's book was preceded by the use of Dakota in church services, partial translation of the Bible into Dakota, and publication of numerous tracts in Dakota. Riggs and other missionaries used Dakota as the language of instruction in their schools too. The book and the extended use of the language left later Dakota with a written language that helped maintain their distinctive culture. By the 1860s, enough Dakota had become Christian to have established their own towns, separate from other Dakota communities.

Ironically, one of Taliaferro's major problems was controlling the soldiers, traders, and American squatters who had flocked to the area. Alcohol trade was a key part of their activities, and Dakota leaders complained bitterly about Americans who sold liquor and abused women. They expected Taliaferro and the military commanders to keep Americans from allowing their pigs and cattle destroy Dakota resources and from driving off game. Neither Taliaferro nor the post officers were able to control the Americans despite efforts to do so. Many Indian agents and missionaries lamented the negative effects of Americans on Sioux morals and behavior over the next several decades. Few recognized the irony of Americans as bad influences when they were supposed to assist in the assimilation of Indians into the "superior" American civilization.

Taliaferro, urged by missionaries and settlers, soon decided that the best option for the Dakota was to sell more of their land. He concluded that the sale of land would distance the Dakota from bad American influences, provide them with financing for their transition to farming, and satisfy demands for land of the growing American population. Only the fur traders opposed land cession because they felt it would reduce their income. Taliaferro worked out a draft to allow treaty payments to include payment of debts to traders.

By the late 1830s, fewer of the traders were kinsmen in the old way—traders were mostly Americans of recent arrival who operated businesses, not profit-making kinship networks. Yet the traders remained a vital part of the Santee economy and their voices had to be heard by Dakota and American officials alike.

In 1837, Agent Taliaferro convinced 26 Sioux leaders to go to Washington to negotiate a peace treaty with the Sac and Fox. But when they arrived, they found that the Bureau of Indian Affairs had other plans. The treaty presented to the itancan surrendered western Wisconsin and most of east central Minnesota. The United States would provide an investment of $300,000 with annuities paid through annual interest of not less than 5 percent, and one-third of the amount was would be used at the discretion of the president. The rest of the interest would be provide money and goods for each Dakota who had at least one-quarter Indian blood. A sum of $90,000 was to be used to pay merchants for Dakota debts. Other payments were to be doled out in varying quantities and used to purchase farm implements, buy seeds, and pay for farm instructors and blacksmiths, and these payments would continue for 20 years. After they signed the treaty, the itancan were allowed to go home. These Dakota signers were all Mdewakanton Dakota so represented only one of the four Dakota council fires.

The Dakota suffered as they awaited Senate ratification of the treaty and delivery of the goods. Instances of lashing out at missionary schools and forays against the wandering cattle of Americans kept the area in turmoil. The main problem was an intensification of war with the Chippewa. The Dakota killed more than a hundred Chippewa who had traveled to Fort Snelling and were on their way home. Chippewa raids intensified in response. In the interim, crops failed, and delayed annuities from an earlier treaty left the Dakota facing starvation.

Taliaferro resigned because Washington annuities arrived late once the treaty was confirmed and continued warfare confirmed that he could not control the Indians he was meant to direct toward civilization. Successive agents faced the same problems: Dakota hostility toward missionaries for the most part, agricultural failure by the few who tried, increased influence of alcohol, Washington's failure to deliver on promises and annuities, the greediness of traders who extended credit for overpriced goods and then demanded the debts be paid, warfare amongst the tribes, and disease. During the 1840s, Governor Doty of the Wisconsin Territory negotiated a treaty designed to create a northern Indian territory for all of the tribes. He wanted the Dakotas to share a reservation with other tribes. Congress rejected this treaty, but the turmoil created by its negotiations kept the Dakota uneasy, and they were bitter about the promises made but ignored.

In 1849, Minnesota became a territory and its ambitious governor Alexander Ramsey was also ex officio Indian agent. The two positions created a conflict of interest, but not in the mind of Ramsey and other Minnesotans such as the former fur trader, Henry Sibley. Eager expansionist devised means to take Dakota land and open Minnesota to the non-Indian settlers and economic interests that would help make it a state. Federal officials such as A. H. H. Stuart, Secretary of the newly created Department of the Interior, and Commissioner of Indian Affairs Luke Lea urged the purchase of all of Minnesota from the Dakota and other tribes.

Two treaties in 1851, Traverse des Sioux and Mendota, accomplished most of what the Americans wanted. They were negotiated as a package. Luke Lea and Governor Ramsey first met with the Sisseton and Wahpeton bands and presented them with the terms of the treaties. Within a few days, the Wahpekute and Mdewakanaton heard the terms as well. The proceedings of the treaty discussions are evidence of the level of distrust Dakota leaders had for American claims of benevolence and fairness. At Mendota, in particular, Wabasha, Little Crow, and other itancan pressed the Americans about their violations of the 1837 treaty and misuse of treaty funds. Eventually, Lea threatened that the Great Father, if he chose, "could come with 100,000 men and drive you off to the Rocky Mountains."[2]

After being exposed to threats and cajolery, the Dakota leaders signed the treaties. Taken together, the four Dakota Council Fires sold over 21 million acres to the United States in return for about $3,000,000 with annuities for 50 years drawn from the interest. They were allowed to keep enough land for a 60-square-mile reservation along the Minnesota River. As the Dakota finished signing the Treaty of Traverse des Sioux, they were ushered to another table to sign an agreement to use their money to pay debts to the traders.

As it often happened, the Senate changed the terms of the treaty and did not ratify it until 1852. However, as soon as the treaty was signed by the Santee, white settlers moved onto the land to be ceded and even began expelling Dakota. Indian agent Nathaniel McLean did protest to the squatters but was told by Ramsey, in words that were echoed by Fort Snelling's commander, that nothing could be done. The Dakota were left with no land because of the Senate's amendments and received only ten cents per acre as compensation, yet they had to agree to these amendments or receive nothing; Americans were already occupying the land.

In order to make the amendments striking out provisions for a reservation more palatable, Governor Ramsey promised the Dakota that they could remain on the land "until the whites wanted it." After national elections in 1853 replaced the Whig party's appointed officials, Democrats made Willis

Gorman governor and appointed a new Indian agent, Robert Murphy. They created a Dakota reservation but its title and status was ambiguous until clarified in 1860. The Dakota had a reservation, but its title was clouded until 1860.

Gorman managed to convince the Dakota to move to a reservation carved out north of Fort Ridgeley, but they soon left to hunt. Annuities were late, and Santee had to find food off the reservation because their tiny reservation did not have enough game. Even when annuities did arrive, Dakota leaders such as Little Crow were sure that they were being cheated and that the government was keeping their money. Little Crow even went to Washington in 1855 and was assured, as Little Crow heard it, that the rest of the money would be delivered. Congress had reduced appropriations to the point that they were not meeting the treaty obligations. BIA Commissioner Manypenny investigated and found that over $30,000 was owed the Santee. Then, Minnesota was transferred to the Northern Indian Superintendency, and Agent Murphy was replaced by Charles Flandrau for about 13 months in 1857.

Dakota leaders strove to keep their bands fed and protected as itancan always had done, but the constant stress caused by late annuities, the hostility of American settlers, and the shortage of game kept the Dakota bands in a state of penury compounded by hunger. Americans in Red Wing even burned Dakota homes, so the Dakota just moved to another area to plant their corn. The Dakota world was one of being dominated by, in their view, capricious Americans. Dakota roved throughout their old lands, begged for food from the settlers, and sometimes threatened whites.

Dakota society was stressed, and bitter feuds divided bands. The murder of a Wahpekute itancan, Tasagi, led to the exile of the murderer, Black Eagle, and his followers. This new band turned to Inkpaduta as their leader, and they wandered about, begging, in their old homeland. The severity of the winter of 1856–57 increased tensions as the band foraged for food. After an incident in which a settler's dog was killed, Inkpaduta's band was disarmed by an American posse. In retaliation, Inkpaduta's band killed 34 settlers and took three women hostage. They attacked two more communities, killing some settlers, and then fled. Americans called this attack the Spirit Lake Massacre, and panic spread throughout the state.

Americans fled to forts for safety, and rumors of an Indian war multiplied. Inkpaduta may have had a total of 14 men in his band. Panic-stricken, vengeful militia attacked Dakota bands simply because they were Indians. The Minnesota legislature appropriated $10,000 to rescue the women captives. Two Wahpetons returned one of the captives and a month later found the other surviving captive. An expedition killed Inkpaduta's son and captured his wife, but the Dakota forced Agent Flandrau to free her. Little Crow agreed to lead an expedition to punish Inkpaduta if the military would protect the Dakota force from Americans. After a month-long effort, Little Crow returned and reported that Inkpaduta had escaped.

Inkpaduta never was found, and the Dakota discovered and Dakota leaders drew the conclusion that Americans blustered instead of retaliating against Dakota opponents. Dakota itancan felt that a more aggressive approach to American failures to meet treaty obligation would be effective. Another result of the Inkpaduta incident was that American settlers were in constant fear of an Indian uprising. They renewed demands for the military to drive them out of Minnesota. The tension filled situation was ripe for explosion.

Meanwhile, other Dakota continued efforts to acculturate. In 1856, a number of Dakota encouraged by missionary Riggs formed the "Hazelwood Republic" to begin the process of private landholding and farming that was America's stated goal for Indians. Another new agent, Joseph Renshaw Brown, pushed for an assimilation policy and rewarded Christian Dakotas who farmed. He also called for reservation land to be given to individual Dakotas and any Indian land unclaimed for individuals should be sold to American settlers. Revenue from land sales would help pay toward civilizing the Dakota. Brown was ahead of his time. Americans would adopt this policy for all reservations in the late 1880s through the Dawes Allotment Act.

Most historians evaluate Brown's efforts as sincere and as effective as any could have been given the problems he faced. American citizens wanted to take the land and to be rid of the danger of Indians. Washington officials pushed Brown to cajole the Dakota into assimilation but provided late annuities, changed treaties, and ignored Dakota needs. The Dakota wanted their payments, to be protected against white encroachment, to be allowed to hunt, fish, and gather on their former lands, and to be left alone on their reservation. Dakotas were increasingly prepared to challenge American authority with the threat of retaliation. Brown did manage to keep the peace most of the time, and his efforts to civilize the Dakota had some positive results, but the bulk of the tasks set for him were not achievable.

The Washington Treaty of 1858 put the civilizing policy into effect. Each Dakota was to receive an allotment from the southern half of the reservation with some land retained for future generations. The northern half was to be purchased for a price to be determined by the Senate (in 1860, the tribe was confirmed in its title, and 30 cents per acre was the compensation offered). Congress appropriated the compensation ($266,880), but most of it was taken to pay claims by merchants. Dakota leaders and the Dakota people were bitter about what they considered lies and a travesty of justice.

Dakota restiveness increased as they perceived American perfidiousness and recognized that they could get away with more and more opposition.

The agency warehouse was raided several times, provoking no retaliation from American officials. White settlers sent numerous complaints of Indian thievery to the agency. Even within the Dakota, tensions between those trying to acculturate and those adamantly opposed to any assimilation led to clashes, threats, burning of farms and killing of animals. Many Dakota were determined to defend their independence. Yankton and Yanktonai relatives encouraged the Dakota resistance and offered sanctuary for any who fell afoul of the Americans.

The situation in Dakota country and Minnesota was volatile in 1860 when national elections occurred. Republicans replaced Democrats. Loyal Republicans were rewarded with government appointments, as was the common practice. Clark Thompson became Northern Superintendent, and Thomas Galbraith became Sioux agent. Neither Republican had experience with Indians. Dakota itancan were Little Crow, Big Eagle, Wabasha, Wacouta, Traveling Hail, Standing Buffalo, Shakopee, and Mankato, among other veterans of dealing with Americans.

The spark for the Dakota Conflict was created by yet another year of late arrival of the payments to the Dakota. In 1862, although food had arrived at the Upper Agency, Agent Galbraith refused to distribute it. Little Crow demanded that the agent distribute the food while the Dakota waited for the money. Galbraith asked the traders what he should do, and Andrew Myrick, the spokesperson for the traders, said, "So far as I am concerned, if they are hungry, let them eat grass."[3] A few days later, four Mdewakanton killed Robinson Jones, his wife, his daughter, and two other white men. They hurried home to ask Little Crow to preempt American reprisals with war. The Dakota grievances were many and were augmented by their sense that this was the time to pay Americans back for all that had been done to them. The Santee peoples were hungry, and their way of life was challenged from all sides.

After much discussion, as was the Dakota political process, Little Crow agreed to lead the war. On August 18, 1862, Dakota attacked the lower agency and killed all of the Americans they could, including Myrick, who was found with his mouth stuffed with grass. During the first week, the Dakota forces, mainly Mdewakanton and Wapekute, swept the area of Americans and killed many. At Redwood Ferry, Dakota forces killed about 20 members of a relief force.

Two strategic sites blocked the Dakota from attacking the heavily populated Minnesota Valley, Fort Ridgeley, and New Ulm. The city of New Ulm was attacked twice but was successfully defended, despite most of the city having been burned. Americans lost 34 dead, and 60 more were wounded, but they kept the Dakota from spreading the war to the Minnesota Valley.

Little Crow, a Dakota itancan, was the primary leader of the war against Minnesota and the United States. The 1862 Dakota Conflict led to the Dakota being expelled from Minnesota and the loss of many Dakota and American lives. Little Crow was shot by a farmer who collected the bounty on his scalp. (Library of Congress)

Fort Ridgeley was assaulted several times over three days, but its cannon and the arrival of reinforcements spared it too. As the main battles raged, smaller Dakota forces burned towns and farms, killed men as they could, captured women and children, and looted. White responses included hysteria and wild accusations of babies slaughtered, women violated, and bodies hacked into pieces. Later, investigations and the testimony of witnesses revealed few atrocities and frequent Dakota protection of women and children. The facts did not matter, as Americans called for extermination of the savages.

The Minnesotan-American response began with the appointment of Henry Sibley, former territorial governor and Indian trade merchant, as commander of the relief force. After an inconclusive battle at Birch Coulee, Sibley sent messages to Little Crow urging him to surrender. Several Dakota leaders, such as Wabasha, Taopi, and Paul Mazakutemane, began distancing themselves from the war and discussing surrender with Sibley. The Battle of Wood Lake (16 Dakota and 8 Minnesotans killed) turned the tide completely. Three days later, Sibley entered the camp, named Camp Release, of the non-combatant Dakota who surrendered to him 269 captives that they had been protecting. Sibley imprisoned the 1,200 Dakota in the camp. Little Crow and most of those involved in the war dispersed westward, although there would be continued raiding over the next two years.

Public rage against the Dakota led to Sibley establishing military tribunals to punish Santee outlaws. Each of the men taken into custody was presumed to have been part of the "uprising" but was offered a chance to prove his innocence in trials. Isaac Heard, one of the commissioners examining the Dakota framed the dominant view: "The fact that they were Indians . . . would raise the moral certainty that, as soon as the first murders were committed, all the young men were impelled by the sight of blood and plunder . . . to become participants in the same class of acts."[4] Nearly 400 Indians were tried, sometimes 40 in one day, and 303 were sentenced to death. They were marched to Mankato through New Ulm where they were attacked by a mob and 15 were seriously injured. The innocent prisoners, including women and children, were attacked on the way to Fort Snelling; one infant was killed.

By the end of the tribunals, General John Pope had arrived with federal troops and was in command of the war. Reverend Steven Riggs and Bishop Henry Whipple, among many Minnesotans, protested the injustices of the tribunals and insisted that many Dakota had not fought against the Americans but had helped and protected them. President Lincoln was aghast when he was told about the tribunals and ordered Pope to send all of the records for review. Lincoln was warned that some retribution had to occur or the Minnesotans would kill them all. After his review, Lincoln reduced the number of condemned to 39.

On December 26, 1862, 38 Dakota sang their death songs as they mounted a scaffold designed to hang them simultaneously. The hangman's family had been killed in the war. After burial in a shallow grave, the bodies were exhumed for medical students.

The rest of the Dakota prisoners, about 1,900, were held at Mankato and Fort Snelling. Conditions at the camps were primitive, and 130 died during the winter. Missionaries tried to ameliorate the conditions, and hundreds of Dakota were baptized by Protestants Thomas Williamson, the Dakota Robert Hopkins, Gideon Pond, and Samuel Hinman. Father Augustin Ravoux baptized 184 at Mankato. Those who worked with the Dakota were condemned for it by the press and public; Hinman was beaten by a mob.

Although the hangings ended the war in Minnesota for the most part, two military expeditions totaling 4,200 soldiers pursued refugee Dakota into North Dakota in 1863. Most of the Sissetons and Wahpetons had fled to the Dakotas, near Devil's Lake, as the war began, and Brigadier Sibley went after these "hostiles." Few had participated in the war. Three North Dakota skirmishes in July 1863, at Big Mound, Dead Buffalo Lake, and Stony Lake were won by Sibley's forces. General Alfred Sully led another expedition from

Dakota who surrendered to end the war with the United States were summarily tried as criminals by the United States. More than 300 were condemned to death. President Lincoln commuted most of the sentences. Thirty-eight Dakota were hanged in the largest public execution in American history. It is an event well remembered throughout Sioux Country and commemorated annually. (Library of Congress)

Fort Randall. They found a large number of Yankton at Whitestone Hill in North Dakota, attacked them, and burned their winter food, tipis, and household goods. A similar attack on mostly Lakota occurred at Killdeer Mountain.

As the large scale expeditions headed west, Dakotas continued to attack Minnesotans in small skirmishes and ambushes. These attacks led the Minnesota legislature to authorize a $25 bounty per Sioux scalp for members of the militia and $75 per scalp to civilians. Later the reward was raised to $200. On July 3, 1863, Little Crow was killed, scalped, and the reward was collected. The scalp was given to the Minnesota historical society. Some Dakotas fled to Canada, and others joined their Lakota relatives on the plains or moved to their buffalo hunting grounds in North Dakota.

In 1863, Congress abrogated all treaties with the Dakota and expelled them from Minnesota. Compensation was voted for victims of the war. The president was authorized to find another place for the Dakotas. Another bill removed the Winnebago, a tribe with no involvement in the war, from Minnesota. The first reservation selected for the Dakota was Crow Creek on the Missouri River in South Dakota. About 1,300 Dakota were shipped to Crow Creek in freight cars and by boat; within a year, 300 had died. The Dakota were not allowed to hunt, drought and grasshoppers destroyed the few crops planted, and government rations were supplied from food condemned for military use. Despite the addition of several hundred Dakota who had been captured or who had surrendered over the next three years, the population in 1865 was 1,043. In 1866, Santee Reservation in Nebraska became the new home of the Crow Creek Dakota.

Sissetons and Wahpetons who had fled to the Dakotas remained in a kind of administrative limbo until 1867. After the intense demands for revenge abated, most Americans, including Sibley and Brown who had commanded forces during the war, acknowledged that these Dakota had not been part of the war. Some rations and supplies were sent to them, but for the most part, they were left alone. In 1866, most gathered in communities near Lake Traverse in northern South Dakota and others remained near Devil's Lake in North Dakota. In 1867, 21 Dakota were brought to Washington to renew a treaty relationship.

Lake Traverse Reservation and Devil's Lake Reservation were created in the 1867 Treaty. Dakota chiefs, a position recognized by the United States, who signed the treaty were Gabriel Renville, head chief, and Scarlet Plume. Most of the itancan were hunting buffalo. In return for surrendering all claims in Minnesota, the Sissetons and Wahpetons would receive government funding. There were no treaty payments to individuals, and the reservations were to be divided into 160-acre allotments for the men to farm. In effect, the Dakota received homesteads on their own land.

The incorporation of the Dakota was complete. All Dakota were assigned to reservations and were governed by American agents according to American laws and regulations. Dakota culture and sense of identity would survive on reservations, but the Dakota had to adapt to a world they only partially controlled.

THE YANKTON AND YANKTONAI IN THE NINETEENTH CENTURY

By the mid-1700s, the seven Yankton bands had settled into their new lands extending from the James and Big Sioux rivers in South Dakota to the Missouri River's Big Bend. Although they adapted to living in earth lodges and farming like their neighbors, the Arikara, Ponca, Omaha, and Iowa, they maintained close contacts with their Santee relatives. They also used tipis like the western plains tribes after acquiring horses. The Yanktonai followed a similar pattern but lived northward along the Red River of the North Valley as far as Devil's Lake.

European contact began with the creation of Pierre Dorion's trade out of Spanish Louisiana and the establishment of fur trading posts in the area of

Vermillion and Yankton, South Dakota. The first contact the Yankton had with Americans involved a treaty of friendship and "acceptance" of both American sovereignty and the end of hostilities in 1815. Few, if any, Yankton had been in the War of 1812, but the United States wanted to make sure that their presence and jurisdiction were acknowledged. Britain had maintained trade relations with both the Yankton and Yanktonai before 1812. White Bear, Mosquito, Iron, and Partisan were among the leaders who signed the treaty.

As the Americans solidified their control of the Missouri River after the Louisiana Purchase and the American Fur Company replaced independent traders and merged with Choteau and Company. In 1825, Yankton and Yanktonai leaders concluded another treaty with the United States. It required the Sioux to recover lost American goods, capture and turn foreigners over to American authorities, and to not ally with any enemies, tribal or Canadian, of the United States. Americans agreed to indemnify Sioux for thefts by Americans, if they could be proven, and to license traders. Twenty-eight Yankton and Yanktonai signed the treaty. Mosquito, Mad Face, Black Bear, and Running Bear were among them.

These treaties had little effect on the lives of the Yankton and Yanktonai. Life continued as before. They fought their enemies, hunted and farmed, governed by consensus, and sold beaver and buffalo hides to ethnic Frenchmen and mixed bloods even if they were legally Americans now. Many of the Yanktonai moved westward and, essentially, became bands of the Lakota.

In 1851, Smutty Bear, along with itancan from the Tetons, signed the Fort Laramie Treaty. When the first agent arrived at Fort Pierre in 1851, he found that the Yankton needed food, so he purchased some food for them. In 1853, Smutty Bear, Struck By The Ree, and Standing Medicine Crow signed an amendment to the treaty and received their first treaty goods at the mouth of the Vermillion River. American settlers continued to demand that the Yankton be forced to surrender more land. In 1857 and 1858, Yanktons drove American squatters away and burned their buildings. American response to the growing tensions caused by encroaching Americans was to transport Yankton to Washington for yet another treaty of land cession.

The Treaty of Washington relinquished all of Yankton land, except a reservation of 400,000 acres near Fort Randall on the Missouri River, to the United States. The Yankton received $1,600,000 spread out in payments over 50 years, a school, and the promise of assistance in becoming farmers. Many Yankton complained that Charles Picotte, the interpreter, and Struck By The Ree, a Washington-recognized chief, had given away their land.

Nearly 2,000 Yankton met Agent A. H. Redfield at Greenwood, South Dakota. After distributing annuities, Redfield supervised the selection of

Yanktons to police their reservation and prevent the importation of alcohol. A sawmill was built, acreage plowed, and farming begun. Yankton who had opposed the reservation appeared at the end of harvest and took all of the crops except the rutabagas. Most Yankton then went buffalo hunting. By 1861, Walter Burleigh, the new agent, had built houses and assisted the band leaders in selecting their sites. He bought 100 cows to share with each band. All the band leaders received a one and one-half story house in an attempt to convince them to stay on the reservation. Illness and drought made keeping the Yankton on their new reservation nearly impossible; they left to search for food. Missionaries joined the effort to lure Yankton into assimilation and had some success but most avoided school and conversion to Christianity. Gradually, agents control grew less tenuous and most Yankton accepted their incorporation into the reservation system.

Yanktonai were not included in the 1851 Fort Laramie Treaty, but they received rations, anyway. General Harney recognized two Yankton head chiefs and 18 subordinate chiefs in a conference at Fort Pierre in 1856. Black Cat and Two Bears selected their subchiefs. Yanktonai bands bore the brunt of the punitive expeditions of 1863 that were intended to punish Dakota rebels. At Whitestone Hill and Killdeer Mountain, General Sully's forces attacked mainly Yanktonai tiyospaye. About 150, along with their itancan, Big Head, were sent to Crow Creek Agency.

Sully established Fort Union at the mouth of the Yellowstone River to intimidate all of the Sioux. It was later moved and renamed Fort Buford. Fort Wadsworth near Lake Traverse in North Dakota performed a similar role in Yanktonai territory. In 1865, the Yankton signed a treaty giving them their first annuities. In return, they had to accept roads and military posts throughout their land. As with most treaties, the Yanktonai objected strenuously to the terms but had little choice. Yankton were assigned to Crow Creek Reservation in 1866 when the Dakota were moved to Santee Reservation. Other bands located at Devil's Lake after 1871, at Standing Rock Reservation in 1871, and at Fort Peck Reservation in Montana in 1874. Many others joined the Tetons in their war against the Americans and fought in the Teton-American wars from 1866–77. Like the Yankton, the Yanktonai were used to reservation life and, however tenuously, had been incorporated into the American world of agents, missionaries, schools, and BIA laws and regulations.

TETON LAKOTA IN THE NINETEENTH CENTURY

By the 1800s, the Tetons had completed their expansion across Missouri into the northern plains and their transformation from a woodlands tribe similar to the Dakota into a nomadic plains tribe. As early as the 1820s, the Teton/Lakota bands divided into northern and southern groupings. The northern, fewer in number, branch was called the Saones. They moved north of the Cheyenne River and extended their domain to the Big Horn Mountains. By 1800, the Saones had evolved into five multibands, the Minneconjou, Hunkpapa, Two Kettles, Sans Arc, and Blackfeet. The southern branch evolved into the Oglala and the Brule and expanded westward along the Platte and toward the Black Hills. Each of these subdivisions included many tiyospaye led by their own itancan. Although each tipospaye had its own general territory, boundaries were flexible. Frequent intermarriage and movement among the various bands maintained a cultural unity and identity for all of the Tetons.

Many of the bands gathered each summer to Sun Dance, hold various other ceremonies, and have their itancan discuss common policies. Warrior societies included members from many bands, and their meetings served to reinforce tribal unity. During the large encampments, specific leaders were chosen to provide direction, settle disputes, and reinforce the concept that the Oyate, the people, were one. During the nineteenth century, interband gatherings also facilitated the recruitment of large numbers of men for specific expeditions against the Crow, Mandan, Hidatsa, Arikara, Pawnee, and Ponca, and, in the 1860s, against the Americans. War was a constant in the Teton world, and the Teton were successful at expanding Sioux Country and enriching themselves with the horses and other goods taken from the other tribes. Lakota men such as Red Cloud, Crazy Horse, Young Man Afraid Of His Horses, Sitting Bull, Gall, and Red Shirt earned their honors against Indian enemies long before they fought the United States.

Until the 1820s, Lakota generally utilized the tribal trade networks to acquire European and American goods in addition to the usual intertribal trade. In return, they sold buffalo robes, horses, and pemmican. Independent and company traders moved up the Missouri from the St. Louis area and along the Platte to reach the southern Lakota. Some Lakota even allied with the United States in the 1823 campaign to force the Arikara to open the Missouri river route for American trade. Although they were disgusted with the way the Americans conducted their ineffectual war, the Sioux demonstrated their commitment to expanding their commerce.

By 1832, the American Fur Company of John Jacob Astor and Pierre Chouteau had developed the infrastructure to maintain trading centers in the plains. Fort Pierre and Fort Laramie were built to reach Lakota customers, and both sites quickly became nearly permanent population centers for Lakota bands. Lakota harvested thousands of buffalo hides annually and purchased the goods they wanted commodities like guns, ammunition, needles, pots, blankets, cotton cloth, paint, beads, and other metal tools. For the most part, the presence of the Lakota prevented other tribes from using these centers. The centers were guarded by Lakota bands.

The history of any society, including Indian tribes, is often redirected through external events. For the Lakota, the Mexican War ending in 1846 is one such event. Defeat of Mexico by the United States opened former Mexican territory to American trade and population expansion all the way to the Pacific Ocean. Earlier, Mormons fleeing American jurisdiction moved through Oglala and Brule territory along the Platte River. Fort Laramie was an important midway destination for immigrants because the river forked to the North and South here, and supplies could be acquired too. The Oregon Trail, traversed by thousands each year, went through Sioux country. In 1849, the Gold Rush brought more thousands through the Fort Laramie gateway, and the United States bought the trading post from the American Fur Company. American troops were now in Sioux country to protect Americans and begin the process of bringing the plains tribes under U.S. control.

Hordes of immigrants trekked through Sioux Country and laid waste to a swath of land for several hundred miles on both sides of the Platte River. They killed or drove away game, their cattle consumed the grass, their fires eliminated the woods, their garbage littered the trail, and their diseases killed Sioux. They also had a fear of Indian attacks so they often fired on Indian groups seeking trade or just satisfying their curiosity. Teton/Lakota retaliated by stealing horses, killing cattle, charging tolls paid in goods from the wagon trains, and menacing immigrants. Although Teton reactions were not part of a systematic response but immigrants demanded that their government protect them.

The government responded as it had for nearly a century. It offered to pay the Indians to move away, accept American jurisdiction, and define their tribal boundaries. The government also wanted the tribes to agree to allow free passage by the immigrants and to stop waging wars with one another. American officials invited all of the northern plains tribes to a treaty conference at Fort Laramie in 1851.

Over 10,000 Tetons, Yankton, Arapaho, Cheyenne, Shoshone, Crow, Assiniboine, Arikara, Mandan, and Hidatsa gathered to meet with the U.S. commissioners. In the end, the tribes described their boundaries, although reserving the right to change them, agreed to have the United States provide $50,000 over 50 years for passage and damages already done, and allowed the United States to build military roads and military posts. The American commissioner asked the Tetons to select a single chief, but they refused because no one itancan was the leader of all of the Sioux, The commissioners just appointed the Brule itancan, Brave Bear, as the head chief of the Sioux.

He acquiesced in the title while assuring the Americans that he had no such authority. The treaty was signed by only six itancan; significantly, none of them were Oglala, and none of them were northern Sioux. The Oglala were the acknowledged dominant band of the southern Lakota and the northerners were a little less than half of the Teton/Lakota. After the signing, 27 wagon-loads of presents were distributed. The tribes dispersed and returned to living as they had for generations.

Conflicts between the continuing streams of immigrants and the Lakota multiplied along the entire length of the Platte. In 1854, a Lakota killed a Mormon's wandering cow near Ft. Laramie. The Mormon refused the compensation offered by Brave Bear because he wanted the miscreant punished. Lieutenant Grattan and the Fort Laramie commander decided to make the incident an opportunity to teach the Lakota a lesson. He took 29 men, a drunken interpreter, and two howitzers to the Brule camp. Again, Brave Bear offered restitution, but Grattan insisted that the cow killer be surrendered, and Brave Bear could not do that. Grattan ordered a volley, Brave Bear was killed, and the Brule and nearby Oglala killed all of the soldiers. Some of Brave Bear's relatives avenged his death a few months later by attacking a mail coach and killing three Americans.

According to Lakota justice, the issue was settled. Americans dubbed the incident "The Grattan Massacre" and insisted that the Indians be punished. American leaders and the public were sure that the Sioux had committed atrocities and did not accept that the Lakota were defending themselves. General William Harney was sent from Fort Leavenworth with 600 men. He found Little Thunder's Brule tiyospaye at Ash Hollow (Nebraska) and attacked the camp. About 86 Lakota were killed, half of whom were women, and another 70 women and children were captured. Prisoners were brought to Fort Laramie where Harney held them hostage until the killers of the men on the mail coach surrendered themselves for punishment. Spotted Tail and three others surrendered to gain the release of their women and children. The Brule men were then incarcerated at Fort Leavenworth, Kansas. They were released after a year.

Harney continued to Fort Pierre, which he secured as an army post. He met with leaders from most of the Sioux bands. The Oglala did not attend. Harney dictated a treaty with the threat of his 600 men plus scouts from other tribes to intimidate the Sioux leaders. This treaty required each tribe to select a head chief who would then appoint subchiefs. The head chief would be responsible for the behavior of his people. Harney was convinced that his expedition had cowed the Lakota, but, in actuality, it had the opposite effect. Those Lakota who had harbored doubts were now ready to fight. Those who were in favor of war were convinced they were right.

In 1856, a pipe was sent to summon Lakota to a meeting at Bear Butte. This solemn clarion call indicated the importance of the meeting for all Teton/Lakota. About 5,000 attended. The consensus reached was that the Lakota would stop all whites from entering Sioux country north of the Platte or west of the Missouri, with the exception of approved traders. No roads would be allowed, and Lakota would press their expansion into Crow Country to secure the buffalo herds there. All Lakota would refuse the annuities that bound them to the Americans. The Lakota strategy worked for a few years. Trading posts were attacked, intruding Americans were driven off, and even some Lakota who accepted treaty payments were killed or harassed.

At the same time, many Lakota itancan decided that the best choice for the good of their bands was to make accommodations with the Americans. Game was growing scarce in the southern part of Sioux country, and American annuities offered an alternative—the treaty rations that the Lakota had first received after the Fort Laramie Treaty of 1851 and that they knew about from their Yankton and Dakota relatives. Spotted Tail, now an itancan of the Brule, was the leading advocate for cooperation and other itancan agreed with him. The Lakota leaders were conflicted, but their form of government allowed each tiyospaye to act as an independent government. Government by consensus permitted irreconcilable tiyospaye to go their own way.

In 1863, General Sully brought the Dakota War to the northern plains as he pursued refugee Dakota. He found and attacked Yankton at Whitestone Hill and a mixed Yankton-Lakota-Dakota community at Killdeer Mountain. In the same year, Colonel Chivington of the Colorado militia massacred Cheyenne at Sand Creek. The Lakota and Cheyenne responded. Even Spotted Tail, an advocate of accommodation, joined the retaliatory expeditions that closed routes to Denver.

Several tribes, including the Sioux, attacked stage depots, outlying ranches, and towns, such as Julesburg, Colorado. The conflicts increased when miners headed for Montana's silver mines branched off from the Oregon Trail to travel on the west side of the Black Hills, the heart of buffalo country for the tribes. The new route was called the Bozeman Trail. Lakota and Cheyenne forces attacked the miners, and the government decided it had to react more forcefully.

In 1866, U.S. officials tried to end the war through a treaty of purchase and compensation. However, Lakota and other tribal leaders were incensed when soldiers arrived at Fort Laramie during the negotiations with orders to build forts. Red Cloud and the other itancan left the meeting, and soldiers starting building forts along the Bozeman Trail to protect the miners. Lakota, Yankton, Cheyenne, and Arapaho laid siege to the forts and kept the Bozeman Trail closed. Lakota warfare did not include assaults on fortified positions, but

Spotted Tail became one of the main itancan of the Brule subdivision of the Teton/ Lakota in the 1850s after he had fought in the 1854–56 campaigns along the Oregon Trail. He was considered friendly by the United States because he advocated accommodation with the reservation order. His efforts, combined with those of Red Cloud, an Oglala itancan, were instrumental in establishing the Rosebud Reservation. He was killed by a political rival in 1881. The Rosebud Reservation tribal college bears his name. (Mercaldo Archives)

they were willing to wait for soldiers to venture outside the safety of their forts. Woodcutting required large protective forces, and still the Lakota hit and ran.

Americans decided that this was Red Cloud's War and that he was the architect of the entire "resistance." The reality was that the war was led by several blotahunka, or war leaders, including Red Cloud. Other leaders included Iron Shell, American Horse, Swift Bear, White Bull, White Crane, Big Dog, Red Thunder, Blue Horse, Red Plume, Thunder Bull, and Plenty Crow. However, there were many others among the several thousand who took part in the sieges up and down the Bozeman Trail.

One sortie by the Americans was led by Colonel William Fetterman. He was enticed to pursue an apparently panicked small band led by Crazy Horse. After the ambush, planned by Red Cloud, Fetterman and his 80 men were dead. The

Lakota called this battle "They Killed One Hundred Whites." [5] The Americans called it the Fetterman Massacre. General William Tecumseh Sherman, commander of the Division of the Missouri, called for punishment, "with vindictive earnestness against the Sioux, even to their extermination, men, women, and children." [6] In 1867, another notable battle, the Wagon Box Fight was a victory for the army defending Fort Kearney; five or six Sioux were killed, but the army claimed 60 died and 120 were severely wounded.

American geopolitical concerns and a wave of sympathy for Indians caused the United States to seek peace and, despite the generals, to try dealing with Indians as promised in treaties. American forces were stretched thinly because the army occupied the South and the railroad needed to be defended more than the Bozeman Trail. Organizations like the Friends of the Indians carried the day as they argued that Christian humanitarianism would bring peace, save the Indians from extermination, and allow Americans to guide them toward Christian civilization. The immediate result of the redefined needs of the United States was the creation of a Peace Commission. Should Indians refuse to negotiate, then there would be time to exercise the military option.

After successful negotiations in the southern plains led to the Treaty of Medicine Creek, the commissioners moved to Fort Laramie. Red Cloud refused even to talk until the Bozeman Trail forts were abandoned. In 1868, the forts were evacuated, the Lakota burned them, and Red Cloud added his mark to those of the many other leaders who had signed the treaty. This victory over the United States confirmed Lakotas' sense of superiority and represents the high-water mark of their power.

The Fort Laramie Treaty of 1868 represents the apex of Lakota power, even as it laid out the clear intentions of the United States—assimilation and American incorporation of the Lakota into the American reservation system. The treaty guaranteed "The Great Sioux Nation" from the Missouri to the Big Horn Mountains and pledged American forces would keep Americans out of Sioux country, including out of the Black Hills. The United States agreed to pay annuities for 30 years. Other provisions called for the establishment of agencies for the Lakota, schools, and farming equipment. The right of the Sioux to hunt in the unceded territory was attenuated by the proviso that it only be in effect while the buffalo were "in sufficient numbers." Sioux were supposed to cease interfering with the Union Pacific and Northern Pacific railroads, turn over accused criminals, including Lakota, to U.S. organs of justice, and agree to a census. An important article had the United States agreeing that any future land purchase had to be approved by three-quarters of all Lakota males.

Although Red Cloud and most of the other southern itancan ended their war with the United States, some Oglala and Brule headed north to join their

American Peace Commissioners met with victorious Sioux leaders and signed the Fort Laramie Treaty ending Red Cloud's War. The United States agreed to abandon all forts in Sioux country and to protect the Great Sioux Reservation from encroachment by Americans. The United States also agreed that land cessions could only occur if three quarters of all Sioux males agreed. In 1877, the United States confiscated the gold-laden Black Hills, "the heart of the nation." (National Archives)

Teton/Lakota relatives in continuing war with the United States. The northern Lakota were not included in the 1868 Fort Laramie Treaty, even if Americans insisted that they were. Sitting Bull, a renowned Hunkpapa itancan, was joined by many who opposed signing the 1868 treaty. Crazy Horse, Black Twin, Hump, and Big Road added their tiyospaye to the northern bands. Sitting Bull led an attack on Fort Buford at the head of the Yellowstone River in 1868. He then laid siege to Fort Rice and Fort Stevens. Even Fort Totten near the eastern border of the Dakotas was attacked.

In 1870, those determined to maintain independence had formed an alliance with Cheyenne and Arapaho bands and developed a common policy. They told the Americans they would withdraw to the area west of the Yellowstone (roughly the border between Montana and North Dakota). They would winter north and summer south of the Yellowstone River. The alliance

Most Americans considered Sitting Bull as the image of a Sioux chief. He was a renowned war leader, itancan, and holy person. He surrendered after the Battle of the Little Big Horn and a brief sojourn in Canada. He was the dominant leader of the northern Teton/Lakota and acted as leader of resistance to the BIA on Standing Rock Reservation. He was killed by BIA police in 1890. The death of Sitting Bull resulted in Big Foot leading his band to Wounded Knee where he was killed along with his people. Big Foot's death was also symbolic of the end of Lakota independence. (Library of Congress)

would respond to American incursions with force. This tactic provided a solid line of resistance from the northern Black Hills to the Yellowstone. The alliance even tried to create a centralized leadership at a ceremony attended by 4,000 Indians. Sitting Bull was named war leader of the Lakota with Gall as second in command. Crazy Horse was declared war leader of the Oglala, Cheyenne, and Arapaho. All agreed to obey Sitting Bull. The Lakota clearly felt the need for centralized power. The degree to which such power was effective cannot be measured.

In 1871, the military deployed 2,000 troops to protect the engineers and crews of the Northern Pacific. Lakota harassed the troops and engineers to the point that they retreated to the safety of the forts. In 1873, Lieutenant Colonel George Custer narrowly averted an ambush of his two companies of the Seventh Cavalry. Once again, the outside world intervened. The economic panic of 1873 halted the Northern Pacific, but the Lakota drew the logical conclusion as they watched the Americans leave: they had defeated the United States.

The economic panic and continuing war with the plains tribes combined to move President Ulysses Grant to abandon his Peace Policy. He had announced in 1869 that the military would no longer appoint Indian agents; instead, the churches would be asked to recommend honest, God-fearing men to supervise Indian agencies. Each reservation was to be given to a church as its exclusive area for missionary work. Among the Tetons, both Catholic and Episcopal agents and missionaries were appointed. The need for gold to restore the American economy led Grant to approve an exploratory expedition to the Black Hills. George Custer led an array of soldiers, geologists, and reporters along a route the Lakota later dubbed the Thieves' Road. Custer's group found gold, and the policy of keeping Americans out of Sioux country went by the wayside.

Grant dispatched a commission to buy the Black Hills, which would solve any moral dilemma, but those Lakota at the agencies refused to sell. In 1875, the Secretary of the Interior issued orders to the non-reservation Indians to "return" to their agencies by January 1, 1876 or be considered hostiles. Sitting Bull, Crazy Horse, Gall, and the Northern Cheyenne had never signed the treaty and had no intention of moving to the agencies.

Three military expeditions set out after the recalcitrant hostiles located in the Yellowstone-Black Hills corridor on the west side of the Black Hills in the spring of 1876. General Crook's column left Fort Laramie and met a combined Lakota-Cheyenne force at Rosebud River. After the battle, Crook retreated to Fort Laramie. Lieutenant Colonel George Custer led the Seventh Cavalry toward the Little Big Horn where his Arikara allies found the Lakota for him. Rather than await reinforcements, Custer attacked a multiband camp of about 6,000 Teton, Cheyenne, Arapaho, Yankton, and Dakota. He was killed along with some 300 Seventh Cavalrymen.

Custer's Last Stand, as it was immortalized in American opinion, roused the ire of the U.S. government, which determined to subdue the Lakota, Cheyenne, and Arapaho for good. Colonel McKenzie managed to capture a large Cheyenne band led by Dull Knife and destroy its supplies. General Crook stumbled upon several Lakota camps at Slim Buttes. After an indecisive battle, he did manage to destroy food, supplies, and tipis and capture some horses. General Miles, commander of the third column, fought a skirmish with Lakota led by Sitting Bull and then retreated. Lakota-Cheyenne continued raids on Americans. As the war continued, Lakota leaders such as Red Cloud and Spotted Tail worried that Americans would kill them even

Although romanticized for Americans in this painting, the Battle of the Rosebud drove General Crook into retreat and was followed eight days later with the Battle of the Little Big Horn. (Library of Congress)

if they were camped at their agencies. Crook heightened Lakota concern by disarming the reservation Lakota, taking their horses, and setting a guard on them. Lakota itancan at each of the four Sioux agencies (Red Cloud, Spotted Tail, Grand River, and Standing Rock) had opposed every effort of appointed agents to assert control over the Lakota. One agent had the temerity to announce to Red Cloud that he was no longer a chief, that Spotted Tail was now "head chief" of the Sioux. Even Spotted Tail ignored the agent; no one Lakota was a "head chief."

Both Crook and Miles continued to send Lakota and mixed-blood traders to make promises to the "hostiles," if they would just come to the agencies. In the face of declining game, continuing harassment by the military, and the loss of so much food in the campaigns, many Lakota and Cheyenne moved to agencies. They were promised to be given food, to be allowed to keep their guns and horses, and to be allowed to stay in their homelands. In 1877, Crazy Horse surrendered at the Fort Robinson-Red Cloud Agency. Crazy Horse was killed a few months later when the military tried to arrest him so they could send him to Florida. The Northern Cheyenne were sent to Indian Territory. Sitting Bull crossed the Canadian border and was able to exist there at the sufferance of the Cree and Canadians. He returned and surrendered at Fort Buford in 1881.

Sitting Bull's surrender marks the end of Indian independence as nations in North America. By 1881, every Indian in the United States had been assigned to a reservation. Every Indian was subject to the authority of Indian agents who could call in the military if he needed them. The Teton Council Fire, like the other council fires of the Sioux, was now incorporated into the United States.

Notes

1. Nakota is a dialect of the original Dakota that has been mistakenly identified with the Yankton and Yanktonai fires, according to Douglas Parks and Robert Rankin, "Siouan Languages," in *Handbook of North American Indians,* XIII, pp. 94–114. The confusion seems to arise from the fact that the Yankton, Yanktonai, and, at times, the Dakota Sisseton also use the "N" pronunciation for some words. All call themselves Dakota. To simplify, I have just used Yankton or Yanktonai for these fires and only use either Dakota or Lakota for the other Sioux.

2. Quoted in Roy W. Meyer, *History of the Santee Sioux United States Indian Policy on Trial.* Lincoln: U. of Nebraska Press, 1967, p. 83.

3. Quoted in Meyer, p. 114.

4. Quoted in Meyer, p. 126.

5. Quoted in Jeffrey Ostler, *The Plains Sioux and U.S. Colonialism From Lewis and Clark to Wounded Knee.* London: Cambridge University Press, 2004, pp. 45–46.

6. Quoted in Ostler, pp. 45–46.

3

Modern Sioux History

Reservations as Colonies, 1881–1960s

Colonies are created when a nation takes complete control of another. Colonized peoples are directly governed by the controlling country. They are incorporated under the policies, laws, and institutions of the colonial power. The process began with acquiring Indian lands and continued with applying American administration and laws to Indian nations within the boundaries of the United States. For the Sioux, the process began later than for the eastern tribes but was a steadily accelerating process throughout the nineteenth century. By the surrender of Sitting Bull in 1881, all Sioux were living on reservations surrounded by American communities and forts. They were governed by Bureau of Indian Affairs agents who used various instruments of control to carry out American policies. Reservations were colonies of the United States—islands of Indian societies subject to decisions and laws made elsewhere.

Being incorporated into the United States meant that the Sioux were subject to the policies of the United States. As the United States expanded from its 13-state base in 1781, it developed policies to guide its interactions with the Indian nations and continued the practice of signing treaties with Indian nations, thus accepting that Indian nations were independent, sovereign nations.

It is easier to understand American policies if one knows how the United States expanded its territory, how policies were determined, how the Supreme Court described the relationship of Indians and their governments to the

United States, and what the functions of the executive branch in Indian affairs are. As the Sioux increased their relations with the United States, American policies toward all Indians provided the context.

American Indian policy is determined within the context of American political culture. Americans, from the inception of the country in 1781, assumed that Indians would disappear or be brushed aside by the culturally superior Americans. Indian nations would not be allowed to stand in the way of American expansion, would be encouraged or forced to become Christians and private landowners so they could assimilate, and would surrender their lands for American use. Of course, Indian nations could not be allowed to remain as independent sovereign nations within the boundaries of the United States. There was disagreement within the United States about the best way to govern Indians in a way that was best for them once American interests were achieved. Americans never doubted that they had the right to govern Indians.

The foundation of American Indian law was established by 1832, even before the Sioux lost their independence. In three cases, Chief Justice John Marshall wrote the majority opinion establishing basic principles of Indian law. *Johnson v. McIntosh* (1823) explained the reasons why the United States had sovereignty and jurisdictional ownership of all Indian land within the boundaries of the United States. Marshall indicated that Indians had aboriginal title and that the United States needed to acquire that title if it wanted to use the land for Americans. Indian nations could sell land only to the United States and not to individuals or other countries. This decision explains why America wanted clear understanding of which tribes owned which lands and why treaties of cession became a feature of U.S.-tribal relations.

Cherokee Nation v Georgia (1831) recognized that Indian nations had inherent sovereignty that predated the United States, and that sovereignty was recognized by the United States as it entered into treaties with Indian nations. This decision supports the principle that today's Sioux reservation governments are sovereign. John Marshall also pointed out that the United States had a responsibility to protect Indian lands and to provide the Indians with support just as a trustee does for a minor or incompetent. The relationship of Indians to the United States was like that of a "guardian to a ward." This principle forms the basis for the U.S. control of Indians and their governments through the Bureau of Indian Affairs and other agencies. It explains why Congress appropriated funds for reservations and Indians toward education and other services. The legal principle is known as the Trust Responsibility.

Worcester v Georgia (1832) established that states did not have jurisdiction within the boundaries of tribal governments. The federal government was the only outside government that could make and enforce laws that it decided to apply to Indians within their own boundaries. This general principle explains why current reservations are governed by tribal/reservation governments that are subject only to federal and tribal law. Reservations are within the boundaries of states but are not subject to state law unless Congress decides to allow that relationship as it does, for instance, with Sioux reservations in Minnesota.

The right of the federal government to govern Indians was applied systematically after all of the Sioux were forced onto reservations. The 1880s coincided with American concerns about immigrants and the development of the Progressive Era in the United States as a whole. As translated to Indian policy, such concerns led to a policy of assimilation of Indians through a deliberate elimination of Indian cultures. The goal was to eliminate tribalism completely, including Sioux land ownership, Sioux religion, and Sioux government, in effect, the entirety of Sioux culture. Sioux independence no longer existed, so the colonized Sioux had to adapt to a new economy and governance according to rules devised by the United States.[1]

Sioux reservations were established from Montana to Minnesota by 1881. They varied in size from the miniscule plots reacquired by the Dakota in Minnesota to millions of acres in South Dakota. Each reservation society experienced American control in different ways because of the personalities of Indian leaders and BIA agents, their location, the particular denomination of Christianity that was proselytized, and the variations in character of American territorial and state leaders. However, all reservations were subject to the same policies determined by the United States and experienced roughly the same patterns of governance.

Elimination of traditional tribal government was achieved through BIA agents who determined the distribution of rations, developed their own police forces and courts, had the ability to call in troops to support their decisions, and controlled employment on the reservations. The BIA issued regulations to agents who were expected to enforce them with "their Indians." A significant marker of the elimination on tribal justice was the passage of the Major Crimes Act (1885) which required that all felons be tried in federal courts and not according to tribal practices.

In 1883, agents were allowed to establish police forces and courts to control the Sioux. Among the regulations were provisions to punish Indians for practicing their religion and marriage customs, for males wearing long hair, using tribal healers, dancing, and refusing to force their children to go to school. All aspects of Sioux life were subject to the rules established by the BIA.

Perhaps the most devastating federal action was the implementation of the Dawes Severalty Act (1887), also known as the Allotment Act. In order to force Indians to become private farming landowners, the act authorized the allotment of 160 acres of tribal reservation land to each male head of household and smaller acreage for women and single men. Indians were then expected to live and farm on this land. It would be held in trust and be tax exempt for 25 years. Then, the assimilated Indian would be given a deed (fee patent) to his land along with American citizenship and would be subject to taxation and could sell the land to anyone. Once all of the tribal members received their allotments, then the remaining land was considered surplus and could be sold by the federal government to anyone. Revenue would be used to buy farming supplies and to teach Indians to farm.

The proponents of the act included many Americans. In fact, there was a loose organization called the Friends of the Indians who created the groundswell of support for the Dawes Act and other assimilationist laws and directives. This group felt that Americans who bought surplus land within reservations would be role models for Indians and would help them learn about the "superior" American civilization.

The effects of allotment were pervasive. Theodore Roosevelt, justifiably, called the Dawes Act "a mighty pulverizing engine to break up the tribal mass."[2] Indian land use had been based on communal holdings and communal use according to tradition, but the introduction of private property removed this lynchpin of traditional Sioux culture. Scattering individuals around the reservation on separate parcels of land broke up the extended families and made itancan almost superfluous.

By the time allotments were stopped in 1934, Indians had lost two-thirds of their land to non-Indian owners, even the federal government. Roughly 30 million acres was what remained within the United States; it had once been all Indian land. Sioux reservations were reduced drastically. For example, the Sisseton-Wahpeton Reservation lost over 90 percent of its land to non-Indians and the large reservations like Standing Rock and Pine Ridge lost up to 50 percent. The land lost was often the most desirable for farming.

Non-Indians purchased surplus land, land taken through tax sales, and land for which individual Sioux allottees had received deeds when the waiting period expired. Muddled jurisdictions were a pernicious effect of non-Indian land ownership within reservations. Americans did not expect to be under the control of the Bureau of Indian Affairs or the vestiges of Indian governments. They demanded jurisdiction by states. Today this means that the ability of Sioux governments to govern their own reservations is severely hampered. The same is true for the efforts of states to govern their own citizens. Reservations were supposed to be exclusively reserved for Indians, but the reality after 1887 was that many non-Indians owned land and lived within the boundaries of reservations.

Education provided another means to undermine Indian cultures. Several of the treaties promised schools, and the United States took steps to provide them. At first, Christian denominations built a few schools on a few Sioux reservations and received federal subsidies. As early as the 1830s, Protestants combined proselytizing with reading, writing, and arithmetic for Dakota children. These schools were voluntary but often supported by federal agents, federal funds, and the BIA through cajolery. As the reservation system spread, mission schools appeared on reservations, and they were often given Indian land to support the churches. In 1878, Major Pratt started the first off-reservation boarding school at Carlisle Military Barracks, Pennsylvania. He recruited his first classes from the Rosebud and Pine Ridge agencies but also added Indians from other reservations.

Off-reservation boarding schools, federally funded and staffed, reached 30 by the 1920s. Many Sioux children were recruited and sometimes their parents were coerced. Sioux children attended these schools along with the children from other tribes. As Pratt indicated, their purpose was "to kill the Indian to save the man."[3] Boarding schools required use of the English language at all the times, attendance at Christian services, no vestige of tribal cultural behaviors, and rigid discipline. They also required students to work half-days to learn the patterns of "civilized" labor. Students also did most of the work to maintain the school. Perhaps the most important facet of the boarding schools was the extended separation from their cultural support and their extended families. Many never learned to be Sioux. Many were also abused, and every reservation community bears testimony to the abuses.

Education on reservations was a combination of BIA "day schools" and boarding schools. On Sioux reservations such as Pine Ridge and Standing Rock, Catholic boarding schools supplemented the BIA schools. The Catholic schools followed the same curriculum and rules as the off-reservation boarding schools. Until the 1960s, assimilation was the goal, which meant a concerted denigration of traditional values and culture.

It is tempting to picture the Sioux as helpless victims to whom things were done because the U.S. colonial rule was so pervasive and the goals so thoroughly anti-Sioux culture. The reality is that the subjected Sioux did not accept their fates without effective resistance. As with colonized peoples throughout the world, the Sioux developed means of resistance that allowed them to survive as Sioux until policies changed in the 1960s and 1970s.

The most immediate response to the devastating effects of colonization was a revitalization movement Wanagi Wacipi which was translated as Ghost Dance. In the late 1880s, word circulated throughout the West that a new prophet, Wovoka, had had a vision of a new religion that would bring back the traditional days. Lakota holy men went to Nevada where the Paiute,

Wovoka, was teaching a new ceremony that would restore the world. He revealed that if Indians would dance and sing as he taught, the ancestors and buffalo would return and an apocalypse would make the whites disappear. His message was a syncretic one that blended calls for individual work, monogamy, and prayer as well as a return to the Indian values of generosity and kinship.

Lakota holy men like Short Bull brought the message back to the plains Sioux. Rosebud, Standing Rock, Cheyenne River, and Pine Ridge converts soon began dancing around the clock, and Teton visions altered Wovoka's message to include shirts adorned with special symbols and their power would deflect bullets. Although sincere in their conversion, Sioux Ghost dancers were responding, in desperation, to the loss of their way of life. Some agents and settlers were fearful of a Sioux uprising against America. The military was summoned from as far away as Kansas.

James McLaughlin, agent at Standing Rock, ordered Sitting Bull arrested by the BIA police. Sitting Bull was killed in 1890 in the attempt at arrest, and panic spread throughout Sioux country. They feared that the soldiers were there to kill them all. One tiyospaye, led by the itancan Big Foot, fled the Cheyenne River Reservation in an attempt to reach the Pine Ridge Reservation and the protection of Red Cloud. When they had almost reached Pine Ridge, they were intercepted by the Seventh Cavalry and told to wait overnight at Wounded Knee Creek. The next morning, soldiers attempted to disarm the band. A shot was fired, and the surrounding soldiers opened fire with Hotchkiss rapid firing guns. As the Lakota men grabbed their guns to return fire, the women fled with their children. Soldiers pursued them, and before the killings were over, about 300 Lakota had been massacred. Some bodies of women and children were found as far as two miles from the camp. Later they were buried in a mass grave. Survivors were rescued by Oglala Lakota of Pine Ridge Reservation and simply absorbed into existing Oglala tiyospaye.

After some skirmishes and a brief siege at Holy Rosary Mission near Pine Ridge, the Lakota Ghost Dancers surrendered. Revival movements like the Ghost Dance are a common response of people in desperation, and prophets were very much a part of the religion of the Sioux and most other tribes. Many Lakota, like Black Elk, lamented that the Massacre at Wounded Knee had "broken the circle" that was the Sioux Nation.

Most Sioux religious leaders simply held ceremonies and taught traditional values away from the scrutiny of American agents. Most of the seven Lakota ceremonies were practiced throughout the colonial period despite prohibition under the law. Although some Sioux emphasized the old ways, the teachings of the Native American Church appealed to others. This

This dramatization of the Wounded Knee Massacre was widely circulated in the press. Big Foot's band had fled to Pine Ridge Reservation for safety after the killing of Sitting Bull. The Seventh Cavalry surrounded them and then started disarming them, but a shot rang out, and the troops opened fire. Estimates of Sioux men, women, and children killed vary up to about 300. Many Indians and non-Indians consider the Massacre as the last event of the Indian wars. Black Elk said "the Circle was broken at Wounded Knee." (Library of Congress)

religion reached the Yankton Reservation first and spread to the Lakota Reservations. Pine Ridge, Rosebud, and Yankton reservations were the main centers of the Native American Church. The religion was developed in the southwest and legally incorporated by the state of Oklahoma which gave the Native American Church legal standing.

The Native American Church blended traditional ceremonies with Christian practices and even absorbed Jesus Christ. Use of peyote buttons and tea to induce dreams and visions made the "peyote religion" controversial amongst traditional religious leaders as well as with the Christian Indian agents who promulgated laws against the church and succeeded in getting peyote on the list of prohibited hallucinogenic drugs. Persecution had little effect on members of the church.

All opposition was not religious. As long as they survived, traditional itancan received continued support from the Lakota, and they used this support as leverage to influence federal efforts. Agents realized that they had to have the help of Lakota if they were to govern effectively. On each reservation, leaders were able to influence the agents' decisions on hiring ration distribution, school attendance, and various other aspects of governing by the BIA. Many agents succumbed to demands that they recognize councils as quasi-governmental bodies. By the 1920s, several Sioux reservations, such as Rosebud, had written constitutions and reservation-wide elections. Elections returned a combination of traditional leaders and newly educated young men. All of them were well versed in what the treaties specified and how they, as leaders, could influence American decisions through national churches and other national organizations.

Campaigning for Indian Rights in the Early 1900s

The Society of American Indians, established in 1911, was the first pan-Indian association devoted to all Indian causes. Dr. Charles Eastman (Ohiyesa), a Dakota, and Gertrude Bonnin (Zitakala-za), a Yankton, were leaders of the organization and were joined by other college educated Indians from several tribes. These "Red Progressives" published the *American Indian Magazine* that advocated for Indian causes. By the 1920s, they were campaigning for treaty rights, the legitimacy of tribal cultures, and funding to alleviate suffering on reservations. They allied with various reform organizations such as the American Indian Defense Association. This association led the resistance to efforts to legalize occupation of pueblo land for white squatters in the 1920s; John Collier was one of its leaders. The association also defended the right of Indian citizens to freedom of religion and government.

Reservation-based Sioux organizations included the Treaty Rights Association. A group of Cheyenne River Reservation Sioux formed the Black Hills Treaty Council. It lobbied effectively to get Congress to allow Sioux to contest the taking of the Black Hills. In 1915, Congress allowed the Court of Claims to hear Indian-filed cases and in 1921, the Black Hills Treaty Council asked the courts for compensation for the illegal taking of the Black Hills. The case had a rocky history until the Supreme Court ruled that the taking was illegal—in 1980.

Many of the most vociferous and effective voices for Indians came from boarding school graduates. Other Indians had been recruited by religious schools and educated for assimilation, but they did not necessarily abandon all Indian culture and were often defenders of tribal rights. Sioux realized that they had to adjust to the realities of being governed by American law; they had to learn to be both Indian and American, and many did so effectively. Gertrude Bonnin is an example. This Yankton, born in a tipi, received a degree from Earlham College. She became a concert violinist, a founder of the Society of American Indians, and the Secretary of the National Association of Women. She used her access to national audiences to advocate for American Indian treaty rights, cultural values, and fulfillment of the Trust Responsibility. She even became an administrator in the BIA. Dozens of other Sioux like Charles Eastman and Luther Standing Bear achieved national recognition as educated Indians. Many others used their educations to achieve influential positions within reservations. Lower ranks of the BIA, like teacher, clerk, and farmer's assistant.

The Costs of Colonialism

Despite the growing body of support for changes in the treatment of Indians led by Sioux and others, reservation existence remained bleak. The biggest success of the associations might have been to use public opinion to force the BIA to examine what effects its efforts to assimilate Indians had had. A 1922 study revealed that most of the Indians had lost their land and few families could support themselves either on farms and ranches or through menial jobs on and off the reservation. Many Sioux were, at best, hired hands on their own lands. Alcoholism was epidemic as was tuberculosis and most families lived in severe poverty suffering from disease and malnutrition. Traditional leadership and kinship relations were undermined but alternate institutions did not replace the tribal ones. Individual Sioux were made dependent on often capricious and poorly understood decisions by BIA officials. Several early century studies described Sioux as living in a state of helplessness.

A second study published in 1928, *The Problem of Indian Administration*, also known as the Meriam Report, exposed an infant mortality rate twice that of other Americans, an allocation of about 50 cents annually per Indian for medical care, illiteracy, overcrowded and unhealthy boarding schools, annual incomes that were 20% that of average Americans, and tuberculosis death rates 17 times that of Americans. The report recommended allowing for Indian cultures to be practiced again, more money for education and health, and a measure of self-governance. Unfortunately, the public outcry that was generated was soon silenced by the Great Depression.

United States direct rule of Sioux and other reservations had produced poverty and social distress. The situation was an impossible one because, until much later, Americans insisted on imposing a view of Indians and possibilities that conflicted with reality. Indian resources were continuously reduced as land was placed in the hands of non-Indians, schools were inadequately funded, medical needs were neglected, and jobs did not materialize. Many BIA decisions favored non-Indian interests over Indian interests. For instance, after 1890, the BIA leased Indian land to non-Indians, often at lower than market rates. Just before World War I, the entire Pine Ridge reservation was leased to only three cattle companies which destroyed the nascent Sioux cattle industry.

Assimilation was not really an option for Sioux in an American society that segregated races. Many educated Sioux returned home to find that they were not employable on or off the reservation. Social and political assimilation was prevented by law and custom. Even the BIA hired Indians for only the lower level jobs. Most Sioux did not want to be assimilated and clung tenaciously to their traditional values and identities.

Although the overall picture was bleak for the Sioux and other Indians, some did manage to make headway in spite of the many obstacles. Cattle-raising was an option for some, and a few found permanent jobs with the BIA. Some earned wages as cowboys and farm hands and some women became domestics. A few Sioux managed to start cooperative ranching based on the old tiyospaye kinship organization. Seasonal harvest work became a common family effort for many. However, jobs and health remained precarious for most Sioux. Unemployment was the norm. Kinship patterns did alleviate some of the problems as extended families pooled resources.

New Policies

Unlike most of American society, Sioux communities benefited from the Depression, both politically and economically. The election of Franklin Roosevelt brought new leadership to the BIA and allowed for a major change in American Indian policy. James Collier, a member of the pro-Indian culture and Indian rights American Indian Defense Fund, was appointed Commissioner of Indian Affairs. Along with the support of many reformers, including Sioux like Gertrude Bonnin and Ben Reifel, Collier ushered in a completely new approach to American Indian policy.

The "Indian New Deal" extended the relief projects of the New Deal to Indian communities. At the insistence of Collier , the Works Progress Administration and Civilian Conservation Corps made Indians eligible for work because they were Americans. The Emergency Relief Administration brought farm commodities to the reservation and probably saved many from malnutrition. The programs concentrated on reservation infrastructure and built roads, dams, schools, parks, and wells, and provided anti-erosion landscaping. Before the Depression, Indians were not eligible for federal programs as most states and Americans in general considered them as wards of the federal government. Jobs and income went to the reservations to supplement the economy and staved off starvation.

Collier used his executive power to suspend the laws against being Indian that had anchored the bankrupt assimilation policy. Agents were ordered to allow Indian ceremonies and even to encourage the use of Indian languages. Most Sioux communities were poised to practice their religions openly after decades of doing so in secret. Teton reservations held public sun dances, and Dakota reservations brought out the Big Drums. Sweat lodges dotted reservations, and other traditional ceremonies were conducted.

The 1934 Indian Reorganization Act (IRA) introduced a novel idea—Indian communities were to be asked to vote on whether or not they wanted to have constitutional, representative government. After intense efforts by the BIA to gain support from suspicious Indian communities, referendums were held on each reservation. Nearly all of the Sioux Reservations chose to develop constitutional governments under the terms of the IRA. Those like Standing Rock and Spirit Lake that voted the idea down did so because of internal political divisions and, of course, because many Sioux felt that federal government reform usually meant another disaster for Indian communities. Eventually the pressure of the BIA and desire for a tribal council led to constitutions on each of the Sioux reservations.

Dakota living in Minnesota were recognized as "Indian Communities" and were allowed to purchase land that was in trust. The Dakota Communities were Prairie Island, Lower Sioux Agency, Birch Coulee, and the Upper Sioux Agency. Eventually, Spirit Lake and Standing Rock Reservations added constitutions that were similar to the IRA constitutions.

Once reservations voted to have constitutions, agents convened constitutional conventions on each reservation, and other BIA officials brought standardized templates to assist in the proceedings. Sioux reservation leaders were familiar with American government and legal proceedings and had experience acting in political concert. They amended the templates to meet their needs but did accept them for the most part. Nearly all tribal constitutions called for representative councils elected from districts by men and women over 21. Tribal chairmen and other officers, usually a vice chairman and a treasurer, were elected at large, but there were variations from this norm.

All of the constitutions declared the sovereignty of the "tribe." An interesting aside is that reservation communities declared themselves tribes, as with the Standing Rock Sioux Tribe, the Cheyenne River Sioux Tribe, and the Rosebud Sioux Tribe. The Secretary of the Interior retained the right to veto any tribal ordinance and had to approve constitutions. Membership in the tribe was recognized as a tribal power, but all of the Sioux "tribes" followed the BIA pattern of requiring at least one-quarter blood status from the particular reservation for membership. The term "membership," rather than "citizenship," conveys the dominant idea that being Indian is based on ethnicity/race. Even as late as in the 1930s, most people believed that blood conveyed cultural characteristics and even morals.

Collier was able to move this revolutionary legislation through a Congress dominated by Democrats and willing to introduce novel programs in the midst of the Depression. Even Collier did not expect the tribal governments to continue indefinitely and sometimes argued that practice in government would help Indians merge into American society. Provisions for repurchasing some lost lands and for an economic development fund hinted at the hope that reservation governments would achieve financial independence. The Johnson-O'Malley Act complemented the movement toward integration by allocating funding to states for services and allowing Indians to attend public schools. The Bureau of Indian Affairs retained control of all resources including leasing of Sioux land, jobs, social services, improvement funds, infrastructure, police, courts, and schools. BIA approval was necessary for tribes to employ lawyers. The new constitutions did not change some of the paternalistic restrictions on Indians created since the reservations were established. Thus, BIA agents even continued to control individual Indian bank accounts.

Tribal constitutions did not provide for the separation of powers. Tribal councils controlled both the executive and judicial branch of reservation governments. Even as tribes gained more resources and a tribal bureaucracy from the 1980s onward, tribal councils not only made laws but also could change court decisions, remove tribal bureaucrats, and overrule executives. Checks and balances did not apply to reservation tribal councils except for those imposed by BIA agents. The Secretary of the Interior, advised by the BIA, could veto any tribal legislation and even business contracts.

The Depression, followed by the demands of World War II, limited Sioux government activity and maintained Sioux social and economic status at the same levels as before. Sioux tribal councils did gain experience in legislating and leading campaigns to improve the entire reservation. Councilmen accepted the theory that they represented not only their families but also their districts and their reservation as a whole. This concept of representation led to a growth in reservation nationalism as Sioux came to think of themselves as, for instance, Standing Rock Sioux, rather than simply Sioux or merely members of a particular tiyospaye. Centralization of reservation government replaced politically independent tiyospaye, in theory.

Although reservation Sioux were eligible for the draft, many volunteered. Many were decorated for valor, and a Dakota earned the Medal of Honor. Hundreds left their reservations to work in war industries. Experiences gained by Sioux affected the post-war situation on reservations. Military veterans could join with school graduates to demand a greater voice in their own lives, pursue treaty obligations, and utilize tribal-reservation governments to assert sovereignty. Many of the hundreds of Sioux who had left the reservations remained in cities for the greater number of opportunities there. Although some urban areas became Sioux and pan-Indian communities, they maintained ties to their homelands through kinship, culture, and frequent visits.

Many Sioux joined the post-war college surge and continued the process of developing leadership skills needed for self-government.

As always, trends in American political culture were echoed in the Sioux communities. The larger society moved into the Cold War with an emphasis on rejecting anything deemed communist or socialist. The Cold War brought a reemphasis on assimilation and laws directed against un-American activities. Congress and the administration (first Truman and then Eisenhower) argued that Indians should enter the American mainstream and be released from the socialistic paternalism of the Bureau of Indian Affairs. Indians, it was argued, should be freed to sell their lands and abandon the reservations to participate in the greater economy. American fears and attitudes translated into a new Indian policy that sought to get the government out of "the Indian business."

In addition to the rhetoric about freeing Indians, Congress moved to settle all Indian claims against the United States through the creation of the Indian Claims Commission in 1946. Indian governments and even Indian groups could bring suit against the United States to compensate them for damages caused by "duress, fraud, unconscionable considerations, mutual or unilateral mistakes, [and] claims based upon fair and honorable dealings that are not recognized by any existing rule of law or equity."[4] Once these claims were settled, the path would be clear for Indians to become citizens without the constraints of tribal governments or "federal socialism." The Indian Claims Commission lasted until 1978 when continuing claims were transferred to the Court of Appeals.

All of the Sioux governments filed petitions among the 370 that followed creation of the claims commission. Most claims dealt with land issues. The most famous of the petitions dealt with the taking of the Black Hills from the Great Sioux Nation in 1877. Along with many other Sioux claims, the Black Hills case was decided in favor of the Sioux. The commission was authorized to determine if claims were valid, what the land in question was worth at the time of the taking, how much should be subtracted from an offer because the United States had spent money on the tribes so this should be offset, and what the amount should be. The Commission offered $105 million compensation to the Great Sioux Nation.

Unlike most tribes, the Sioux refused to accept the amount offered because they wanted the land back. If they accepted the offer, they gave up any other claims against the United States about the Black Hills. The Sioux adamantly maintained that the Black Hills were sacred and they needed them returned, not the pittance that was being offered. Although the tribal governments were, and remained, unanimous in rejecting a settlement, there were divisions within the Sioux as was the norm. Some did favor taking the money, but the decisions of elected governments for each of the reservations prevailed. Sioux governments went to court and to Congress to solve the matter, and state governments defended state control and private ownership of the land. In 1980, the Supreme Court concluded that while it was "a rank taking," only Congress could change Indian-related law and authorize compensation other than cash payment. The issue remains unresolved in the twenty-first century.

Congress made termination its clear goal in 1953. House Concurrent Resolution 108 indicated that "it is the policy of Congress, as rapidly as possible, to make the Indians within the territory of the United States subject to the same laws and entitled to the same privileges and responsibilities as are applicable to other citizens of the United States and to grant them all of the rights and prerogatives pertaining to American citizenship . . . [they] should be freed from federal supervision and control."[5]

Sioux leaders, like those of other tribes, knew the resolution was meant to inaugurate a policy of eliminating reservations and the sovereignty of Indian governments. The Trust Responsibility would be canceled. Congress even indicated that the BIA should be abolished and that the states of California, Florida, New York, and Texas should assume control of the former Indian lands while tribes like the Klamath, Menominee, Potatwatomi, and the Chippewa Indians of Turtle Mountain should cease to exist because they were ready to be civilized. Although no Sioux nations were neither on the congressional list nor on a later BIA list, termination was an ever-present threat looming over the Sioux throughout the 1950s and 1960s.

Dakota reservations (called communities) in Minnesota were affected by Public Law 280. Congress delegated its jurisdiction in criminal and civil matters to the states and allowed state law to apply to reservations in Minnesota, California, Oregon, Nebraska, and Wisconsin. The law also offered to let any state assume jurisdiction over reservations. In both Dakotas, a strong state based effort to take control of the reservations failed. Indian lobbying proved decisive in having the states reject the idea, but the possibility remained and, in North Dakota, a few jurisdictions were transferred to the state, anyway. PL 280 reversed the long-established principle that the states did not have any right to make or enforce laws within Indian nations. The application of state laws in one form or another and state intrusion in reservations has continued in various forms.

Relocation

Relocation was another aspect of the Termination policy that affected Sioux nations directly. Congress authorized funding for the BIA to encourage the permanent relocation of Indians from reservations. Indian centers in several major cities were established to assist relocation, and many Indians accepted the urging of BIA officials and moved to major metropolitan areas like Los Angeles, Minneapolis-St. Paul, Chicago, Denver, and Seattle. Funding for on-reservation programs was slashed throughout the 1950s, so moving to the cities had an appeal.

The Santee reservation lost 60 percent of its population by 1960, the Yankton reservation declined to about 1,000, and the Prairie Island Dakota Community lost most of its young people. The western reservations were not as impacted, but they saw hundreds head for the cities. In the cities, Sioux immigrants encountered the same problems that afflict most minorities. They were not prepared to deal with the large society, found that they had skills only for the lowest income jobs, and, as Indians, they lost most BIA services like the Indian Health Service, despite its transfer to the Department of Public Health.

Indian ghettos grew in the urban areas. They were similar to the black ghettos and were often part of them. Problems of poverty were still part of the Sioux experience. In the 1950s and 1960s, minority groups responded to the heady atmosphere of the Great Society and of minority-led civil rights groups. Many urban Sioux also embraced the movement. Resistance to termination policies on reservations, increasing civil rights awareness in the cities, and the crushing poverty of most Indian communities throughout the nation combined to spur a militancy in Indian Country that now included cities.

Pan-Indian organizations grew as well because more and more Indians were aware that they faced the same problems and had the same concerns. Their resistance to termination including the experience of the Indian Claims Commission, the creation of the National Congress of American Indians, and increased lobbying by Indian governments. Many Sioux forged alliances and lobbied for support from Congress and appealed to the general public to challenge colonial control of Indian lives.

During the post-war years, day-to-day changes occurred on the Sioux reservations. Generally, tribal governments became increasingly insistent that they be allowed to realize the intent of the Indian Reorganization Act, that is, that they be allowed to govern according to their own constitutions. Reductions in BIA funding, which were part of the 1950s, placed greater stress on the communities. Elected tribal councils and chairpersons were hampered by a lack of resources and the fact that, in reality, the executive branch for each reservation was the Bureau of Indian Affairs. BIA control of the major decisions continued along with their control of schools, infrastructure, economic development efforts, leasing, and health care. The BIA conducted elections and maintained tribal enrollment lists.

By 1960, BIA control had become somewhat less pervasive, and most agents worked with tribal leadership and accepted tribal leaders' right to establish policies and procedures of governance. Councils made the decisions about the Black Hills litigation, lobbied Congress for changes, and worked to protect their interests. Without access to resources, tribal governments were hampered severely. The agent remained the most important official on each reservation, and individual Indians went to the BIA with most issues.

In addition to the policy of Termination that continued to drain resources and people from the Sioux reservations, several were faced with losing large amounts of the best land on the reservations. Congress authorized building several dams along the Missouri River that flooded reservation land. Although the Three Affiliated Tribes of Fort Berthold Reservation lost the most land and had their reservation divided by Lake Sakakawea, Standing Rock, Cheyenne River, Lower Brule, and Crow Creek reservations lost substantial land to the dams. Tribal governments appealed, went to court, and lobbied, but the dams were built. Once the dams flooded thousands of acres of reservation land, the National Park Service and states used the land for recreation opportunities for non-Indians. Sioux and non-Indian owners were moved from the relatively rich bottom lands to other areas where farming was a challenge. Non-Indians received Fifth Amendment compensation for their lands; Indians received nothing because, technically, the land actually belonged to the United States. Eventually, tribal governments won claims in federal courts for compensation.

GREAT SOCIETY BENEFITS FOR INDIANS

During the 1960s, Americans experienced a major shift in its political culture. This shift is symbolized by the election of John Kennedy and the all-pervasive Camelot atmosphere created by the media amidst the optimism of his election. America moved not only toward acceptance of multiculturalism and economic development for minorities but also to active government intervention to provide the means for minorities to improve their place in America. The Sioux and other Indians benefited from the changes advocated while Kennedy was president, but it was the Great Society of Lyndon Johnson that produced concrete results.

Great Society programs focused attention and funded reform efforts for nearly everything that American Indians needed. Tribal governments, not the BIA, administered Great Society programs that delivered grants to reservations. Initial programs such as the Public Works Administration and the Public Housing Authority bypassed the BIA because astute reformers insisted that reservations be included in the decision-making process and regulations required that reservation governments write and administer the grants that implemented federal funding. Nearly all of the subsequent social service programs such as food stamps were received on reservations either through tribal governments or through required arrangements with state agencies.

These programs were available to tribal governments that had been working on expanding their economic and political bases with some help from the BIA as early as the late 1950s. Significantly, tribal government budgets expanded exponentially with the influx of Great Society funds to set up programs, hire personnel, and provide support for tribal administration of the programs. The Office of Economic Opportunity (OEO) insisted that tribes receive the funds for community action programs, and these became the core means by which Indians gained the experience of administering programs, long-range planning, responding to community needs, and being able to focus on specific reservation initiatives.

Congress laid the foundation for Indians to escape the assimilationist control of two hundred years of efforts to assimilate Indians. The Indian Civil Rights Act provided Bill of Rights protections to reservation Indians. The 1970s witnessed an ongoing Indian effort to practice their religions even off the reservations (freedom of religion on reservations was part of the 1934 IRA). Sioux trekked to the Black Hills, Bear Butte, and Devil's Tower to conduct sun dances, sweat lodges, and other ceremonies.

The Native American Graves and Repatriation Act not only forbade looting of Indian graves but also required museums and other repositories of Indian religious artifacts to offer their return to identifiable tribes. Courts also weighed in with decisions that supported tribal governmental powers. By the 1970s, Indian governments were recognized as having inherent sovereignty and the right to exercise these powers with the exception of those that had been taken away by treaty or action of Congress.

After these advances in tribal government authority and experiments in tribal government, the direct administration of a few BIA programs combined with effective lobbying by tribal governments, staff within various federal agencies, and efforts of senators such as South Dakota's James Abourezk, Congress passed the revolutionary PL 93-638, The Indian Self-Determination and Education Assistance Act in 1975. In a nutshell, the act made it possible for tribal governments to govern themselves because it provided access to the necessary resources to govern. It ended the 200-year policy of attempts at eliminating tribal governments and merging Indians with the rest of the American public. After 1975, it became a given that tribal governments and tribal sovereignty were as permanent and endurable as the United States. It began an era of post-colonialism.

ACTIVISM CHANGES THE SIOUX WORLD

At the same time that most tribal governments and Indian leaders were working to get changes made through congressional, court, and executive branches of the federal government, others were turning to activism to create an atmosphere of change and assertion of Indian culture. The 1960s and '70s witnessed Sioux and other Indians adding confrontational tactics to their repertoire of means to gain public and national attention for Indian grievances. Red Power was influenced by the Black Power movement but had uniquely Indian emphases. Unlike Black and Hispanic civil rights goals, Red Power did not advocate integration; its goals were tribal sovereignty and a revival of traditional Indian cultures as well as civil rights off the reservations.

In 1961, The National Indian Youth Council was formed in Chicago by groups of Indians from many tribes. Gerald One Feather was one of several Sioux who joined in demands for tribal sovereignty and demanded justice for all Indians. Vine Deloria Jr. published the widely read *Custer Died for Your Sins,* and other writers such as the Sioux Luther Standing Bear joined the chorus of voices calling for change and extolling traditional Indian cultures. More defiant actions began in 1964 when Alcatraz was occupied by a group of American Indians, mostly college students. They received mostly sympathetic media coverage. Sioux such as Allen Cottier, Walter Means, Mark Martinez, and Richard McKenzie were among the Alcatraz protesters. In 1969, hundreds of protesters occupied Alcatraz again and managed to sustain their occupation for 17 months.

The most visible of the militant groups was the loosely organized American Indian Movement (AIM) founded in 1968 by three Chippewa in St. Paul-Minneapolis. Russell Means, a Lakota, joined AIM soon after, and many Sioux became prominent in a series of protests that spread across the country. Quite a few of the Indians attracted to AIM were Vietnam veterans and were keenly aware of the activities of the Black Panthers. Originally, AIM concentrated on civil rights for urban Indians and paid particular attention to exposing police brutality in the twin cities. Rather quickly, their goals expanded to include reviving traditional cultures and tribal sovereignty. Treaty rights were a frequent focus of AIM demands.

AIM occupied the Mayflower, demonstrated in many cities, and camped out on Mount Rushmore in the sacred Black Hills. News photographers contrasted them with the presidential faces that adorned the mountain. AIM members and demonstrators all across America adopted a uniform of red berets, often graced with eagle feathers, fringed jackets or vests, and jeans. Demonstrations usually featured drums. They grew their hair long and insisted that they were the warriors defending tribal sovereignty and Indian

Vine Deloria, Jr., who was enrolled at Standing Rock Reservation, but spent his childhood was on Pine Ridge Reservation, was one of the most influential advocates of Indian Sovereignty. He was Executive Director of the National Congress of American Indians, which successfully fought against Termination. His influence was widespread as a writer of the polemic manifesto *Custer Died for Your Sins*, which inspired many American Indians and other reformers. His death in 2005 led to mourning throughout Indian Country. (AP/Wide World Photos)

cultures. Many asked for the help of traditional holy men and sun danced. A Lakota, Leonard Crow Dog, became the spiritual leader of AIM activities on Rosebud and Pine Ridge Reservations. Sweat lodges became a feature of AIM protests and camps. What began as an urban civil rights effort rapidly segued to the reservations and an alliance with traditional opponents of existing tribal governments and those who wanted more control of reservation programs.

The Trail of Broken Treaties began in Indian communities throughout the United States and converged in Washington, D.C. in 1972. Hundreds of Indians followed the leadership of AIM with Russell Means, a Sioux, as the most publicized spokesman. In addition to the AIM involvement, many traditional reservation elders and religious added their prestige to the event. The intent of the Trail leaders was to demand solutions to Indian problems, but frustration with the response of Nixon administration officials led to an

In 1973, Teton/Lakota reformers occupied the community of Wounded Knee. Members of the American Indian Movement (AIM) combined urban style radicalism with an emphasis on traditional Sioux culture. The drum and singers are pictured in the Catholic Church, which was the headquarters of the village occupiers until destroyed by federal agents' gunfire. (Bettmann/Corbis)

occupation of the Bureau of Indian Affairs offices, a standoff with police, and the trashing of the BIA offices. The Nixon administration paid for the demonstrators to return to their homes.

The most spectacular expression of militancy occurred on Pine Ridge Reservation in 1973. After egregious racist incidents occurred on towns bordering on Pine Ridge, opponents of the tribal government led by tribal chairman Richard Wilson, invited AIM to the reservation to help in the struggle for justice on and off the reservation. Birgil Kills Straight, Gerald One Feather, and Severt Young Bear were among the Oglala opponents. They were supported by Frank Fools Crow, a revered holy man, and other traditional religious leaders. Russell Means, an Oglala Lakota from Pine Ridge, was the most prominent AIM leader and his colorful, provocative persona made him the darling of the news media. Wilson had used federal funds to employ a paramilitary group that used violence against his enemies. The tribal council even banned AIM members from the reservation.

During a meeting of the anti-Wilson and traditionalist groups in Calico, some participants suggested that the meeting be moved to the larger community of Kyle, which could accommodate all the people in a meeting space. On the way, they passed through the community of Wounded Knee, site of the 1890 massacre of Lakota by the Seventh Cavalry. A spur-of-the-moment takeover of the trading post by the dissidents led to BIA police and Wilson supporters setting up a blockade around Wounded Knee in order to prevent the demonstrators from leaving. Wilson's idea was to arrest the occupiers. AIM Vietnam veterans quickly established a defense perimeter and used the Catholic church as a quasi-headquarters. Federal marshals were recruited on the reservation to supplement the rapidly expanding federal presence. Armored vehicles arrived, as did supporters of AIM, both Indian and non-Indian, from all over the United States.

The U.S. public was treated to the spectacle of the United States battling Indians for 71 days. Firing into Wounded Knee from the tribal and federal government forces became a common occurrence. Violence flared all over the reservation and even in bordering communities. Some Sioux were adamantly pro-AIM, and others were supporters of the Wilson government. White residents formed militias and many ranches were fortified, but other whites supported the justice of the demonstrators' claims. By the time the federal government agreed to allow the demonstrators to leave, thousands of rounds had been fired into Wounded Knee destroying the Catholic church that stood next to the mass grave from the 1890 Wounded Knee Massacre. Two Indians had been killed, several Indians and one FBI agent were wounded, widespread destruction had leveled most of Wounded Knee village, and millions of dollars had been spent to suppress a demonstration. One tragic aftermath was the killing of two FBI agents in a 1975 gun battle with some AIM members. One man was convicted for the murders, Leonard Peltier. After the occupation ended, sporadic violence continued for several years on the reservation.

It is difficult to assess the effects of the occupation of Wounded Knee and other efforts supported by AIM. American policy had already shifted or was nearly changed by the time of these Red Power demonstrations. Probably, the publicity did help nudge many Americans and Congress toward hastening the reinstatement of tribal governments and the declaration of a new Indian policy. Undoubtedly, Sioux and other Indians see the demonstrations as heroic examples of the tenacity of Indians in defending their cultures and their sovereignty. Wounded Knee II, as many know it, is as symbolically important to American Indians as the Boston Tea Party is for Americans. Red Power provided the foundation narrative for the Indian-directed recovery of tribal self-government and cultural legitimacy.

SELF-DETERMINATION IN A GOVERNMENT-TO-GOVERNMENT RELATIONSHIP

Beginning in 1976, Sioux tribal governments struggled with dealing with the opportunities created by the legislation and decisions of the 1960s and continuing through the 1970s. PL 93-638 provided the opportunity for tribes to contract the administration of BIA programs and committed the BIA to maintaining funding levels for the various programs. The same opportunity was added for the Indian Health Service so that all specifically Indian programs were now eligible for tribal administration. The ever-cautious and paternalistic Bureau of Indian Affairs had opposed much of the move to Self-Determination and continued to exert a braking effect on most tribes. Only gradually was the old guard, consisting largely of Indians, replaced by individuals, mostly Indians, who supported the idea of self-determination.

It is difficult to convey the feelings of optimism that marked Sioux reservations in the late 1970s and into the 1980s as tribal councils and administrators developed the process of self-determination. The problems faced by tribes were similar to those that every ex-colony faced in the Third World. After a century of direct control by the United States, Indian communities did not have the infrastructure, personnel, and governmental structures in place to be effective at self-governing, but they were determined to guard this new power tenaciously. Other legacies included poverty, ill health, community divisions, and the absence of a clear understanding of what was possible within both the Indian communities and the larger society.

The first problem to be solved was how to negotiate contracts that satisfied statutory requirements and were consistent with BIA rules of administration. "Contracting" or "638ing" was a complex process. Tribal councils had to determine which of the many BIA programs they wanted to administer.

A second problem was finding tribal members who could administer the programs as few Indians had any kind of higher education. There were shortages of trained personnel in all areas, a legacy of the colonial past. Members of Sioux communities experienced the heady atmosphere of being able to make decisions for themselves and having funding pouring into tribal coffers. Expectations among Indians were high, but realties soon returned the Sioux to a kind of watchful cynicism.

Most Sioux tribal governments turned to the programs available through the Great Society to fund efforts at improving abysmal unemployment rates (the

Comprehensive Education and Training Act plus OEO funds for targeted efforts), building businesses (programs approved to give tax breaks to businesses that would locate on reservations), health and housing (HUD housing and the Indian Health Service), and dysfunctional aspects of the community (social work, food stamps, and other federal assistance programs).

The tribal governments also created the infrastructure required by the new policy of Self-Determination. Sioux tribal councils and elected leaders needed to create bureaucracies as they assumed increasingly greater control in the nation renovation process. For all intents and purposes, contemporary tribal government did not begin to function until the 1980s. Sioux and other Indian governments had to create governments from the ground up yet within the strictures of federal oversight and historic legacies.

Economic development was a major concern for all of the Sioux nations. Many efforts supported by the BIA and the Great Society did not seem to have much of a positive effect aside from providing temporary jobs and experience in crisis management. Economic development, like so many other aspects of Sioux existence, was development by federal grant. Grant projects had to be tailored to whatever the granting agency required, not to identified tribal needs or to projects compatible with tribal cultures and realities. Jokes abound about how the government provided Pine Ridge Reservation with more trained welders than in any other segments of the American population. Of course, there were few welding jobs on the reservation, but the training did provide income for Sioux people.

There were significant failures on each Sioux reservation that wasted money and deflated expectations. Tourism plans pushed by the BIA often created motels as at Standing Rock Reservation, where there were neither concentrations of tourists nor the need for amenities demanded by tourists. An arrow factory and a moccasin factory on Pine Ridge were undermined by Asian competition that produced goods at a fraction of reservation costs. Although unemployment was extraordinarily high on Sioux reservations (from 35 to 80 percent) in the 1980s, the labor pool was unskilled, so attracting businesses that were willing to overcome the maze of bureaucratic rules set by the BIA and tribes was a major challenge.

Some businesses on Sioux reservations were able to operate effectively for a number of years. Local circumstances, excellent decisions by tribal councils, and external partners have sometimes combined to have a positive impact. Sioux Manufacturing and Dakota Tribal Industries on the Spirit Lake Reservation are examples of tribal businesses that have brought employment to a few. These are based on contracts with the Defense Department which ebb and flow, depending on demand, but some employees have worked at the factories for as long as 30 years. The Santee Reservation developed a ranch; the Sisseton-Wahpeton Reservation manufactured bags. The relatively small scale of the successful businesses leaves high unemployment and the many other problems that accompany long term poverty as a constant on all of the Sioux reservations. Only the casino rich Dakota reservations within Minnesota have escaped poverty for all of its citizens.

The bright light of economic development has been casinos. Federal court decisions recognized tribal sovereignty and precluded state jurisdiction in Indian gambling in 1987. Congress limited tribal sovereignty in the Indian Gaming Act that required oversight through the National Indian Gaming Commission and mandated tribes to negotiate compacts with the states where reservations were located. Despite the regulations and the required role for states, the casinos are tribally managed and they provide funds for other tribal activities.

Most importantly, tribal casinos provide jobs. Unemployment rates decline significantly where casinos operate as they can absorb a few hundred employees in this labor-intensive business. The long-term impact of casinos is to provide capital for other spin-off businesses such as motels, marinas, and grocery stores. Several reservations supplement underfunded federal programs with casino revenues.

Ironically, the most profitable casinos have been those of the Dakota in Minnesota. Once outlawed and existing on postage stamp sized reservations, the Dakota found they were in ideal locations for profiting from American gamblers. Shakopee Mdewakanton Community entered high stakes gambling in 1982 and by 1986 had generated $18 million annually. Mystic Lake Casino replaced the original Little Six casino and now dominates the economy and the skyline not only of the reservation but also of the communities around it. Prairie Island Community's Treasure Island Casino is also near the Minneapolis-St. Paul metropolitan area. Each Dakota tribe has moved to help others through foundations that provide grants, loans, and cultural development projects to other Indian reservations. Their tribal citizens have escaped the poverty that characterized all reservations. Dakota money has gone to many non-Indian public works too like the Twins baseball park and the University of Minnesota. Most of the employees of the Dakota casinos are non-Dakota as casinos employ more people than there are Dakota adults. Casino related businesses have prospered near the casinos and tribal investment in construction of houses has benefited non-Indians. Dakota tribes have provided funds directly to the non-Indian communities around them for charities and other community development.

Casinos on the western Sioux reservations have not been as successful because they are located quite far from metropolitan areas and are not accessible to tourists. However, the casinos do address the most important need of all reservations—they hire tribal citizens. Profits are low but have been used effectively to address many of the needs faced by Sioux people.

The greatest source of employment, aside from the Dakota reservations in Minnesota, is the government. Tribal governments employ the most people, but BIA and even state employees are included in the mix. Requirements for government employment have contributed to a steady increase in the number of tribal members with higher education. Schools require not only certified teachers but also aides, accountants, secretaries, administrators, and specialists with college educations. Tribal government employment also requires special training. Although tribal members' educational levels are lower than those of most other American communities, they are rising.

Given the history of Sioux communities, the tribal governments are the only vehicle for ameliorating Sioux individual and reservation issues. The tribal governments are the only source of capital and delivery of effective services. Of course, much depends on the United States Trust responsibility.

Since the 1980s, each of the Sioux reservations has its own history. Sioux history has merged with all contemporary history as well. Court decisions and acts of Congress are generally directed at all Indians. Executive efforts to reorganize the BIA in order to implement current Self-Determination policy are part of the history of all Indians, not just the Sioux. Anyone wishing to examine reservation histories will find that all of them deal with similar issues but in ways that are specific to the particular reservation.

Notes

1. The Dakota within Minnesota existed on sufferance because all Dakota had been ordered out of Minnesota following the 1862 war. However, some were allowed to stay because they had helped the Americans during the war and some Minnesotans recognized that they had saved lives during the war. These groups of Dakota formed the core of the current federally recognized Indian communities. The Dakota community of Flandreau, which migrated from the Santee Reservation in Nebraska, was federally organized in 1934.

2. President Theodore Roosevelt in a 1901 address to Congress.

3. Quoted in Ward Churchill, *Kill the Indian, Save the Man: The Genocidal Impact of American Indian Residential Schools.* San Francisco: City Lights Publisher, 2004, book cover.

4. Quoted in Francis Paul Prucha, *The Great Father: The United States and the American Indians*, abridged edition. Lincoln: University of Nebraska Press, c. 1986, p. 342.

5. Quoted in Prucha, p. 346.

4

Sioux Religion

TRADITIONAL BELIEFS

IN THE BEGINNING, there was only darkness and *Inyan*. In Lakota, Inyan means rock, and at that time, Inyan's body was full and vibrant. He decided that life was needed on the earth, so he gave his blood to create it, and as he bled, humans and animals and the rest of the universe were created. One can still see the remains of his blood in the red pipestone called catlinite from which the medicine-prayer pipe is still made today. All life and the earth were unfinished, but as indeterminate aeons passed, the proper place and functions of all living creatures. The Sioux call these supernatural Beings, humans other than humans. This is the way one of the Sioux traditions describes life's beginning.

The Sun, the Sky, the Earth, the Rock, the Moon, the Falling Star, and Thunderbird are the most powerful of the sacred Beings. The Four Winds are somewhat lesser in power along with many other sacred Beings. All are imbued with the life force of the universe, *Wakan*. All of these Beings, including animal Beings, have some control over what happens to humans. They can harm humans as well as help them. Some give power to individual Sioux so they can interpret the world to others and that they may help the people with their special power. Often power is given in dreams.

During the period when the universe was young, creation continued, and the proper relationships among all were established. During this mystic past, animals and humans could talk to one another and both talked to supernatural Beings. Everything was in flux. Iktomi, the Spider, was a creator-trickster who roamed the world. Sometimes his actions revealed what was unethical, as when his selfishness harmed himself and others. Sometimes he created roles for animals after they had angered or pleased him, as when a duck was given a red eye forever because he discovered Iktomi killing ducks. Sioux children were taught the stories about Ikotmi as part of their education in the values of their culture.

Star Born was the son of a Dakota woman and a star who was raised by his grandparent the Meadowlark in human form. He traveled to learn and discovered that a giant pickerel was eating the inhabitants of a village; it even swallowed Star Born. He cut the pickerel open and decreed that humans would eat pickerel as a punishment. At another village, he rescued people from a giant owl and punished the owl by making him sensitive to the Sun so that he could hunt only at night. People told him the North Wind was staying so long that winter never ended Star Born fought North Wind, but neither could win. To resolve the problem, they made a treaty that North Wind would visit only half of the year. Therefore, the land and the people have summer and winter. Star Born completed his creations by giving the Sun Dance to the Sioux people so they would respect his parents. In each part of this narrative, humans and supernatural beings interact until, event by event, the world begins to assume its natural state.

Sacred teachings, specific to the Sioux, were brought to the people by White Buffalo Calf Woman. Although her teachings are most closely identified with the Teton/Lakota, the Santee/Dakota and Yankton have integrated them into their own narratives and often recount this version as part of their whole origin tradition. Sioux culture often has adopted beliefs, ceremonies, and narratives from other cultures as well as interchanging them among the Sioux tribes themselves. As with most sacred stories and ceremonies, this cultural genesis narrative has many variations, but its core remains the same.

A simple rendition is: In the distant past, the people were starving and wandered the plains looking for food. One day, the exhausted, pitiful people paused at the base of a high hill that was wreathed in clouds. Two young men volunteered to trek to the top to see if the other side seemed a propitious place to search for food. As they approached the top, a beautiful woman in white emerged from the clouds and walked toward them. One man lusted after her and dissolved into a mist; only his bones remained. The other man respected her as all women should be respected and offered his assistance as men should.

The woman told him that she was bringing knowledge to the people and instructed him to prepare her way. He was to tell the elders to gather the people in the council tipi at dawn and she would join them. The leaders of the people did as instructed because this was clearly the instruction of a supernatural Being. The people waited in their circles within and around the tipi for her arrival. Elders occupied the inner circle and with men, women, and finally, children filling successive concentric circles. The whole nation could hear what the woman had to say and give.

The beautiful woman strode into the council tipi carrying a pipe. She taught the pipe ceremony as the most formal means of communicating with the supernatural. She also revealed all of the cultural norms that were vital to being a Sioux. She instructed women, men, and children about proper behavior and relationships with others. She revealed ceremonies, taught the Sioux to govern by consensus, explained how to respect all living things, and emphasized the reciprocal relationships of the Sioux. Above all she taught that following the norms she revealed would maintain, and restore when necessary, the balance of the universe as it should be. In the world she revealed, she said, "we are all related."

After four days, she left with the promise that she would provide for the people as long as they followed her teachings. As she started up the hill, she became first a red buffalo calf, then a yellow calf, then a black calf, and, finally, a white buffalo calf. The people followed her up the hill into the clouds into which she had disappeared and from the top of the hill they looked out onto a vast plain covered with buffalo. From this time, the Sioux have called themselves the buffalo people because of this sacred relationship. The woman is White Buffalo Calf Woman, the one who gave Sioux their culture.

In addition to White Buffalo Calf Woman's teachings, the Sioux drew upon their earlier ancestors in the Misty Past, influences from other Native American cultures, and changing needs to formulate their view of the world and symbols of their special relationships. The circle offers a proper view of life and symbolizes Sioux existence. Life is an endless circle, the Sun and the Moon are circles, and the tipi is a circle. The human life cycle progresses from childhood to adulthood, to elder status, and back to childlike status again, in a circle. The Teton bands camp in a circle with each band having its prescribed place. There are endless examples. A circle has no beginning and no end—it is the *Oceti Sakowin,* the Sioux.

Other symbols that were received and remain important in Sioux religion include the Sun, Moon, the directions of the compass, the sacred colors (red, black, white, and yellow), eagle and raptor feathers, white buffalo, and special sacred places such as the Black Hills, Devil's Tower, and Bear Butte. The most sacred of Sioux symbols is the pipe, and, in particular the White Buffalo Calf Pipe, which is still cared for by the Looking Horse family; Orval Looking Horse is the nineteenth Keeper of the Sacred Pipe. The pipe carries Sioux prayers, needs, and gratitude to the heavens-to the supernatural Beings. According to the Sioux, humans have to persuade supernatural Beings that they are respected and should help humans maintain a balance in the world. Persuasion is expressed through praying, dancing, sacred singing, and the

A posed picture of a Teton/Lakota performing the pipe ceremony in 1907. (Library of Congress)

pipe. Sacred Beings appreciate sacrifice, and humans can emphasize their pitiful, weak state through fasting, weeping, and sacrificing for the good of the whole. Humans can receive special powers from supernatural Beings, particularly through visions/dreams. Individual humans can be afforded special protections and guided in their life choices in visions.

Some humans are more attuned to the powers of the universe than others and therefore are able to help others through healing, interpretation of dreams, revelations, prophecies, and conducting effective ceremonies. These specially gifted humans help all of the people with prayers and appeals to the supernatural. Anthropologists refer to these holy people as either shamans or priests. The Sioux call them *wicasa wakan,* holy men. Men and women alike received special powers from dreams and training, but men's powers were generally the ones that enabled them to exercise priestly roles for the whole community. As with many of the roles in Sioux society, demarcations among specific roles were not rigid, and even children could be especially inspired and provide guidance.

BASIC WORLDVIEW AND CEREMONIES

Sioux basic beliefs are derived from the revelations of supernatural Beings to the people through direct teachings and dreams. They can be summarized in the following:

- All existence, and the universe, is filled with power—*Wakan*—that can be good or evil and that humans can influence through proper behavior.
- Everything, animate and inanimate, is related and interdependent.
- Each person must worship every day through prayers, rituals, songs, dances, ceremonies, expressions of gratitude, and humble acknowledgement to maintain balance throughout the universe and to assure that supernatural Beings use their power to help people.
- Those who have supernaturally granted wisdom are expected to use that wisdom to teach and guide others. People with power are holy people and have received a special calling that is their destiny. Power often comes in dreams.
- Human weakness often leads to foolish behavior and must be countered with appropriate use of prayer and ritual lest it endanger the whole. What one does affects the whole.
- Violations of prescribed behavior can result in the punishment of individuals or of the entire people by offended Beings.

These basic religious beliefs are similar to those of other American Indian cultures. Perhaps a similar worldview might well have originated in a common Misty Past, but like so much in religion, this connection cannot be proved empirically. The Sioux act upon their beliefs in ways unique to their culture that have evolved (been given to them) over centuries.

Parenthetically, the Sioux do not see their religious beliefs and practices as exclusively right and those of others as wrong. Again, like other American Indian cultures, the Sioux feel that their religion was a special gift to them. Other cultures have different gifts from supernatural Beings that are right for them. For instance, the Manda Okipa Ceremony is theirs, and the Sun Dance belongs to the Tetons-Lakota. Both are ceremonies are "right."

Acceptance of validity of other religions also allows the Sioux to borrow ceremonies from other religions and incorporate them into the Sioux religion. For instance, Midewiwin is a healing society/religion most closely identified with the Chippewa, but the Santee have a similar society. The Ghost Dance was developed in Paiute culture but adopted and adapted by Sioux holy men. Traditionally oriented Sioux see no contradiction in being both Christian and Traditional, nor do they hesitate to participate in ceremonies of other Indian tribes.

Each of the Sioux subcultures expresses its cultural unity in the practice of common ceremonies. Ceremonies, in the Teton rendition, emanate from the teachings of White Buffalo Calf Woman and from additional, received, visions. Each combines specific sacred songs, prescribed actions, and words. The Seven Sacred ceremonies are:

- *Sweat Lodge.* The sweat lodge is the basic purification ceremony of the Sioux and most other Native American cultures. It begins and sometimes concludes most other ceremonies or can be performed as a ceremony on its own. Some describe it as symbolic of Mother Earth's womb, as its physical appearance is a dome formed by branches, preferably from the willow, and covered with hides. Today, most use canvas to cover the framework. Rocks are heated in a fire and then ritually placed in the lodge where water is poured over them to create steam. Holy men and, today sometimes women, conduct the ceremonies, songs, and prayers. Purification and openness to supernatural power, supplications, and prayers for the good of all are the focus of the ceremony.
- *Vision Seeking (vision quests).* Part of the rite of passage from boyhood to manhood includes the guidance of young men by holy men. After a sweat lodge ceremony and instruction by the holy man, a boy who is deemed ready is isolated in a place identified as having powerful properties. For instance, some Sioux will go to Devil's Tower or other sites in the Black Hills. Each reservation has places where the power is greater than other places. The boy remains without food for several nights (usually four) and prays for a vision that will reveal his particular destiny and his unique relationship with a supernatural being. The supernatural Beings take many forms—thunderbirds, bears, lightning, etc. Often the boy is taught songs that can invoke his particular supernatural assistance. After the quest, a holy man interprets the dreams for the boy, and the boy often receives a new name to symbolize his revelation.
- Adults seek visions in order to receive specific revelations. For instance, Sitting Bull experienced a vision prior to the Battle of the Little Big Horn that predicted soldiers falling into the Sioux camp. Others seek visions for major decisions affecting family and community. In recent times, women seek visions in formal vision quests, although this practice was not traditional. Sioux religious ceremonies are adaptable to new needs and circumstances.
- *Sun Dance.* Historically, this ceremony was developed by several plains tribes. Culturally, some say it was brought by White Buffalo Calf Woman. It is a ceremony of cultural unification in that it brings together large numbers of Teton Sioux in a multiband gathering. Traditionally, the Sun Dance was held around the summer solstice and, ideally, included the entire Teton nation. One of the largest Sun Dance ceremonies on record prior to reservations occurred near the Little Big Horn River in 1876 and included about 6,000 participants. Individuals vow to Sun Dance in return for a specific form of assistance such as sparing the life of an afflicted relative or finding buffalo in times of scarce buffalo or success in war. Today, the assistance sought or the gratitude expressed may be modern, but the goals are the same. Preparation includes the entire family of

each Sun Dancer; family members provide assistance and encouragement throughout. Sun Dance leaders are trained holy men. The multiday ceremony, ideally lasting seven days, begins with the cutting of a Sun Dance pole by a virgin, its ceremonial erection, and a sweat lodge ceremony for participants. The heart of the Sun Dance is the piercing of the dancers' pectoral muscles or back muscles and the insertion of a peg that is attached to the top of the pole by a rope (originally, buffalo hide). Some men are attached to buffalo skulls, which they can drag behind them. Some, particularly women, will offer up slices of their flesh. Dancers dance forward and back, leaning against the thongs, until they break free. Throughout, families and tribal members sing their support, offer encouragement, and feed those who attend. This ceremony is a visual sacrifice for the good of the people. The ceremony was performed in secret from the 1880s to the 1930s because participation was a federal crime, but after 1934, the law allowed public Sun Dances.

- *Hunka (adoption).* This ceremony generally includes an older man taking a younger man under his protection and offering to treat the younger man as a son. It also is used to cement a close relationship between two men and indicates that they will sacrifice all for their special *hunka*, or relationship. Occasionally, the ceremony also is a means of adopting nontribal members into a family. This was an important traditional ceremony that reinforced intertribal alliances and personal friendships in embattled times and provided family/patron support for individuals.

- *Buffalo Sing.* This puberty ceremony generally occurred at first menses. Girls were isolated and supported by older women who reminded them of the virtues necessary for womanhood, such as modesty, supporting male relatives and husbands, generosity, and child bearing. Girls were given an eagle plume and had their hair braided like a woman and the part was painted red. This ceremony is not practiced much today because gender expectations have changed.

- *Spirit-keeping Ceremony.* This ceremony is marked by a series of specific prayers and songs that keep a deceased relative's spirit in place because they are too precious to be given up. After a year, the spirit is released, and a commemorative banquet and gift-giving ceremony are held. The one-year commemoration remains a common ceremony today.

- *Throwing the Ball.* Speculation by Sioux scholars is that this began as a puberty ceremony that included the entire tiyospaye. Today, it is sometimes used as a healing ceremony for a stressed community, perhaps after a series of tragic deaths or some other community trauma. Essentially, the ball is passed from person to person amidst emphatic statements of unity and reinforcement of the idea that we are all relatives.

There are numerous other ceremonies and special occasions, such as naming ceremonies. In most ceremonies, prayers emphasize the relationships of humans to the supernatural and dependence of humans on sacred assistance.

The vibrancy of traditional religion continues in Sioux culture. Although traditional religion never disappeared, the removal of restrictions on Sioux religion by the United States in 1933–34 and subsequent revival of Indian cultures in the 1970s are major factors leading to the public display and widespread practice of Sioux religion in the twenty-first century.

"Traditional" is the term used today for the practice of Sioux religion that developed in the Misty Past, before the reservations were established. In a way, it is the fundamentalist expression within the many religious options in Sioux Country during the twenty-first century. Traditionalists are a minority within any Sioux reservation, but their beliefs and ceremonies are known and sometimes participated in by the majority. Nearly all Sioux know the general outlines of traditional beliefs and accept them in a modern context. Most Sioux have probably participated in one or more of the ceremonies, even if they are not regular practitioners. Essentially, contemporary Sioux beliefs exist along a spectrum from most fundamentalist to non-practitioner.

THE SIOUX AND CHRISTIANITY

The Sioux have been exposed to Christianity since their first contact with Jesuit priests in the late seventeenth century. The major influence of Christianity began in the 1830s when Protestant missionaries arrived in Minnesota. Catholic and Episcopal religions took root among the Teton-Lakota, and Presbyterians carved a niche too. American policies favored and encouraged conversion to the point that Christian converts among the Santee received more rations and other preferential treatment. Even on the Plains, the Tetons had brief exposure before they were on reservations. Father DeSmet and a few other Catholic missionaries, in particular, were recognized as holy men and respected. Christian missionaries ranged from those who were convinced that the Sioux were devil worshippers to those who were appreciative of Sioux culture and flexible about religious views. Sioux individuals were concerned with the spiritual and were willing to listen. Many sincerely converted to Christianity because the teachings and inspiration were convincing.

After reservations were established, American policy moved from encouraging Christianity among the Sioux to outlawing Sioux religious practices. At the same time, many missionaries set themselves the task of protecting their converts, potential and real, from indifferent or outwardly hostile American officials and settlers. In the melee of dispossession, the Dakota War, the Plains Sioux Wars, the establishment of reservations in all of Sioux country, and forced disintegration of Sioux societies, many Sioux embraced Christianity, and many others tacitly accepted it.

By 1860, many Santee in Minnesota had formed separate communities of Christians, mostly Congregational and Episcopal; these flocks were tended by white missionaries. However, several Santee were in the process of becoming ministers, a pattern that continued among the Protestant denominations as they spread westward into Teton reservations. In the 1890s, ordained Sioux ministers became missionaries to their Yankton and Teton relatives. Tetons were receptive to Catholic missionaries for historic reasons—because the Catholics established schools brought nuns and monks to teach in them and because the religion was appealing to an intensely ceremonial people. Presbyterian Christianity was particularly attractive because it provided for meetings that brought Lakota together in church leadership roles; the Niobrara Presbyterian annual meetings were well attended. The Protestant churches still exist but are not as well supported by the mainstream denominations as in the early twentieth century.

Roman Catholicism was reinforced by Catholic schools that were a vital part of Catholic missions. Sioux parents knew their children needed schooling and accepted that Catholicism was part of the adjustment to the dominant society that they had to make. As early as 1878, Catholics built a school on Standing Rock Reservation, and it was followed by, among others, Holy Rosary Mission on Pine Ridge Reservation, St. Stephan's on Lower Brule, and St. Francis on Rosebud Reservation. These schools are still in operation and have educated generations of Sioux. Parents generally chose to send their children to Catholic schools in preference to the BIA schools. Sioux parents and leaders recognized the need for American education as a tool for survival despite insistence that Sioux culture was a pagan culture on the part of the nuns and priests and despite the use of corporal punishment. Catholic rituals were appealing to Sioux as they were familiar with the use of ritual, incense, and purification ceremonies. Many Sioux leaders in the twenty-first century are Catholic school graduates. Many Sioux consider themselves Catholic; in fact Catholicism is the most popular of the Christian faiths on the majority of Sioux reservations.

In the twenty-first century, Sioux reservations have several Christian denominations, and even Ba'hai congregations, but usually one religion predominates on each reservation. For instance, Catholics are the most numerous on Standing Rock Reservation, while Congregationalist are the majority on Santee reservations. Since the 1970s, most Christian religions have incorporated more and more traditional aspects into their services, creating a syncretism reflective of both Christian and Sioux roots. There are some Christian fundamentalist congregations that continue to reject Sioux culture entirely. Most Christian churches, particularly the mainstream ones like the Catholics, Presbyterians, Episcopals, and Methodists have become more ecumenical which has made Christianity more palatable to the vast majority of Sioux. It has become common to have both Christian and traditional holy men conducting prayers at weddings and funerals. Some Christian churches are decorated with Sioux motifs to emphasize the acceptance of Sioux culture.

Traditional religions have never died out. Daily prayers and most ceremonies continued even when the Bureau of Indian Affairs directed its power toward suppressing traditional religion. In the period roughly encompassing 1870 to 1920, traditional practitioners were imprisoned, fined, had their rations cut, and were discriminated against for employment. The Sioux religion and tribal culture was ridiculed in BIA and public schools. Students attending BIA and parochial schools were even required to attend Christian services as part of the school curriculum. One result was that, for many, traditional ceremonies went underground, and Christian beliefs and ceremonies were adapted to be compatible with traditional religion, thereby making Sioux Christianity a syncretic religion with various Protestant and Catholic emphases. Another result was that some Sioux did abandon traditional beliefs to become fundamentalist Christians, rejecting Sioux tradition totally.

WACIPI WANAGI (THE GHOST DANCE RELIGION)

Loss of independence, war, and reservations traumatized Sioux societies. As in many other stressed societies, many Sioux turned to an intensified focus on religion. One manifestation was the adoption of the Ghost Dance as revealed to the Paiute Prophet, Wovoka. He had a vision that if Indians adopted the dance revealed to him, abandoned American-introduced goods particularly liquor, and prayed intensely, then the buffalo would return, and the White people would disappear. Ancestors would return from the dead and be reunited in an ideal world with the present generation. Americans called the new religion the Ghost Dance because dancing it was intended to bring the dead back to life and most saw Indians as worshipping false spirits. The Sioux named the new religion Wacipi Wanagi and this lends itself to the term ghost.

The Teton Sioux sent some of their holy men, like Shortbull, by train, to learn of the new religion. These Sioux holy men altered the basic message to fit their needs. They added the idea that special symbols worn on shirts could deflect bullets if the Americans tried to suppress the religion. Many Sioux withdrew to remote parts of their reservations, such as the stronghold on Pine Ridge Reservation, and began to dance. Many Americans feared that the new religion was a prelude or incentive for a massive rebellion against colonial rule. Responses by the Americans included efforts to make the new religion illegal, withholding rations of the dancers, and moving more troops to Pine Ridge and reinforcing troops already stationed on different Sioux

This painting shows people gathered for a ghost of spirit dance ceremony. The Ghost Dance Religion promised a reunification of the living and the dead on a renewed earth. Misinterpretation by BIA agents, reporters, and non-Indian settlers, led to a tragic slaughter of Lakota by the U.S. Seventh Cavalry at Wounded Knee. (James Mooney, *The Ghost Dance Religion, Fourteenth Annual Report of the American Bureau of Ethnography,* 1896)

reservations. In 1890, Agent James McLoughlin sent BIA police to arrest Sitting Bull because the agent felt that he was fomenting rebellion by not opposing the dancing. Sitting Bull was killed by the police as federal troops encircled Sitting Bull's camp. Many Sioux interpreted the killing of Sitting Bull as a declaration that the United States intended to kill all of the Sioux.

After Sitting Bull was killed by Bureau of Indian Affairs police on Standing Rock Reservation, one of the itancan, Big Foot, led his tiyospaye to Pine Ridge Reservation from Cheyenne River Reservation because he believed the cavalry were going to use his band's Ghost Dancing as an excuse for killing all Indians. Other bands and individual families scattered to seek safety as well. When Big Foot's tiyospaye reached Pine Ridge Reservation, they were intercepted by the Seventh Cavalry and surrounded at a creek called Wounded Knee.

The Wounded Knee Massacre ensued. Big Foot and about 300 men, women, and children were killed, some as far as two miles from the site. One of the many Pine Ridge Lakota, Black Elk, remembered this as the "breaking of the circle" and the end of the free Lakota. Many historians note that the Wounded Knee Massacre ended the plains wars. One famous Lakota Holy Man, Black Elk, concluded that the circle which was the Sioux nation was broken at Wounded Knee—the nation was shattered, the universe was unbalanced. Wounded Knee remains a symbol of traditional religion, and its commemoration annually is widely observed and respected throughout Sioux communities.

The most prominent commemoration of the massacre and its consequences for the Sioux nation is The Big Foot Ride. It was inspired by Lakota leaders, many of whom are descendents of Big Foot. As a prelude to observance of the Massacre's centennial Sioux and others gathered at Cheyenne River Reservation and rode the route followed by Big Foot. Arvol Looking Horse, hereditary Keeper of the White Buffalo Pipe joined the riders. The ride was marked by ceremonies designed to heal the nation and began four years before the 1990 anniversary of the massacre. The ride has continued into the twenty-first century. The Ghost Dance was revived during the 1970s, and some participants still dance. Most see the Big Foot Ride and revived Ghost Dancing as an assertion of traditional culture and of Sioux sovereignty.

THE NATIVE AMERICAN CHURCH

The Native American Church was another reaction to the trauma of confinement to reservations and policies that sought to eradicate traditional religion in all of Indian Country. Like the Ghost Dance, the Native American Church was given to the Sioux from another tribe. It was carried by a Yankton holy man, Sam Necklace, from the southern plains where peyote ceremonies were common for generations. Various ceremonies with obvious Christian influences had evolved into an eclectic religion that blended Christianity with traditional values.

Its tenets emphasized peaceful acceptance of the world and preparation for heaven with the help of various spirit Beings including Jesus. Visions were sought with the assistance of mildly hallucinogenic peyote. Members were required to abandon alcohol, a particularly pernicious problem in the stressed reservation cultures, to be monogamous, and to live according to the traditions of their traditional cultures. For instance, the Sioux pipe ceremony and sweat lodges were appropriate. An appealing feature was that services were conducted in the language of the reservation.

Quanah Parker, a former Comanche war leader, even had the Native American Church incorporated in Oklahoma in the early twentieth century. Indians from throughout the Plains and the Southwest journeyed to Oklahoma or invited its priests to their reservations to learn the religion, and it spread from its Oklahoma base.

Reaction against the Native American Church was emphatic and according to some historians, hysterical. Christian ministers, members of Congress, and agents of the BIA fulminated against the religion as they did against all Indian religions with the added concern about peyote as a drug. Although there was no evidence, many considered use of peyote as dangerous and as an expression of primitive religions that needed to be stamped out. Eventually, peyote was placed on the federal prohibited drug list. Members of the church were jailed and harassed by BIA agents on the reservations. Even into the 1930s, tribal councils passed laws outlawing the Native American Church. They have since been rescinded, and the Indian Civil Rights Act extended freedom of religion to the reservations.

The church was introduced to the Yankton and spread to some of the other Sioux reservations. It remains a minority religion amidst the amalgam of religions in Sioux societies but is no longer outlawed. The use of peyote is legal for its members and has been shown to be mildly hallucinogenic at most. Many members consider the church a Native creation and an assertion of Indian freedom of religion.

PUBLIC TRADITIONAL RELIGIOUS REVIVAL

After 1934, American Indian policy changed, and the Bureau of Indian Affairs prohibitions on practicing traditional religion were lifted. Many ceremonies, including the Sun Dance, became a public feature of reservations, although some of the practices were muted.

In the late 1960s, a renaissance of Indian culture not only increased participation in traditional prayer and ceremony but also became a feature of nearly all public gatherings. School graduations, powwows, organizational meetings, and sporting events feature opening prayers by elders. Prayers are usually in Lakota or Dakota. Funerals often have a Christian minister and a traditional holy man presiding jointly. Vision Quests, Sweat Lodges, and Sun Dances even moved beyond reservation boundaries. The 1968 Indian Religious Freedoms Act made it national policy for the National Park Service to provide access to sacred places like Devil's Tower for Indian ceremonies.

On Sioux reservations, most school systems now teach tribal culture and encourage respect for traditional religion. The 1968 Indian Civil Rights Act specifically excludes separation of church and state as a requirement for reservations. Most tribal governments sponsor tribal cultural education as part of their school systems, and Indian school boards insist that tribal cultural education is integrated within the required curriculum. Holy men and women are often called upon for their teachings and their prayers at public events.

Sioux traditional religion adapted to the relative powerlessness of the Sioux societies after the 1890s. New visions brought a new message to the Sioux. Religious leaders emphasized the harmonious facets of religion by stressing avoidance of conflict and even a message of inclusion for non-Sioux and non-Indians. Commonly, prayers were said for the poor, the afflicted , and the downtrodden and to show for pity upon the people. War was not emphasized in what might be seen as a retreat to traditional religion for the solace of the Lakota. Four Lakota holy men illustrate the emphasis that has come to dominate traditional religion: Black Elk, Fools Crow, Leonard Crow Dog, and Arvol Looking Horse.

Black Elk (ca. 1863–1950) became widely known after John Neihardt published *Black Elk Speaks*. Black Elk was a boy at the Little Big Horn and was at the Wounded Knee Massacre. His visions and teachings stressed the importance of traditional values, the seven ceremonies, and the need for peace and harmony among all peoples. He emphasized that even non-Indians could benefit from Sioux values and sacred knowledge. Black Elk's publicized teachings rode the crest of interest in Indian spirituality that was part of American and European cultural trends in the 1960s and 1970s. Black Elk, like many Sioux, saw no conflict in accepting Catholicism; he was baptized and became a catechist while remaining a traditional religious leader.

Many Americans and Europeans know about Sioux religion because of the popularity of works by John Neihardt in *Black Elk Speaks,* which popularized the Rainbow vision including the teachings of the Six Grandfathers of Black Elk, Joseph Epps Brown's *The Sacred Pipe,* which spread Black Elk's description of the seven sacred ceremonies throughout the world, and Raymond DeMallie's many scholarly studies of Black Elk's teachings and Teton-Lakota religion. Thousands of high school and college students read *Black Elk Speaks* into the 1980s. New Age practitioners have latched onto Black Elk and Sioux religious ceremonies to blend them into their eclectic spiritual messages of harmony in the universe. Sioux religion, like Sioux images, is the epitome of what Indians are supposed to be like according to popular stereotypes in the United States and Europe.

Images of Sioux religious wisdom were reinforced in the non-Sioux world by the holy men who, in some senses, succeeded Black Elk. Leonard Fools Crow (ca.1890–1989) was a disciple of Black Elk and was seen by Teton-Lakota as his successor in the role of preeminent holy man. Fools Crow introduced the idea of allowing non-Sioux, even non-Indians to participate in Sun Dances. He also collaborated with a writer-photographer on a detailed book about the Sun Dance. These decisions were controversial and many Sun Dance leaders did not follow suit but Fools Crow's right to make these

Frank Fools Crow, the leading holy man of the Teton/Lakota, is receiving a copy of
the letter from the White House that agreed to investigate conditions on Pine Ridge
Reservation. The letter symbolized the end of the 1973 Occupation of Wounded
Knee. (AP/Wide World Photos)

decisions was not doubted, just criticized. Sioux religion does not have prescribed, canonical ways of believing or practicing. Some non-Indians were
allowed to Sun Dance and many participated in other ceremonies. Fools
Crow reached national prominence during the 1973 siege of Wounded Knee.
He provided the moral support for the occupiers and was instrumental in
negotiating the end of the occupation. Most other Sioux holy men acknowledged Fools Crow as their mentor. Thomas Mails has written a biography of
Fools Crow and published, with his permission, a study of Sun Dancing.

Leonard Crow Dog (1942–) is a third-generation holy man who became
the spiritual advisor to the American Indian Movement. After Wounded
Knee, he was indicted for resisting arrest and served a federal sentence. As
with many other traditional leaders, Crow Dog blended non-Lakota elements
in his teachings. He was a leader of Native American Church services and
revived the Ghost Dance during the 1970s. Crow Dog's international reputa-
tion was enhanced by the popular *Crow Dog* written with Richard Erddoes.
He has a Web site.

Arvol Looking Horse (ca. 1940–) is the nineteenth-generation Keeper of
the White Buffalo Calf Pipe, which is the pipe that marked the beginning

Arvol Looking Horse is the nineteenth hereditary keeper of the White Buffalo Calf Pipe. It is the symbol and power of the creation of the Sioux nation and is brought out only if the Sioux nation is in danger. His ritual position makes him the symbol of Teton/Lakota culture and a spokesman for Sioux values. (AP/Wide World Photos)

of Lakota culture as revealed by White Buffalo Calf Woman. He travels the world from his base on Cheyenne River Reservation to convey the message of world peace. He has predicted on his Web page and in speeches that the twenty-first century will be a century either of international harmony or the end of the world. Most throughout Sioux Country respect Looking Horse for his responsibility for the symbol of Teton-Lakota culture, the White Buffalo Calf Pipe.

Although these religious leaders, or *Wicasa Wikan* (holy men), are widely known and were instrumental in spreading the teachings of Lakota religion widely, they are only four among many. Throughout Sioux Country, reservations and communities have elders who perpetuate and personify the traditional Sioux religion. They conduct most of the ceremonies brought to the Sioux, pray at public events, and offer healing to many. Dakota and Yankton join these Lakota in perpetuating a vital spiritual world of the Sioux.

The current religious life of Sioux communities is quite eclectic. Most Sioux blend Christianity, traditional religion, and secularism in their lives.

Although these elements are difficult to measure, the impression of Sioux and other scholars is that nearly all Sioux have a reverence for traditional religions, accept some elements of Christianity, and tolerate other's religions. Most Sioux are married in Christian churches and have Christian services at funerals, but many also introduce traditional elements. Children are usually baptized, but many ceremonially receive Indian names. The result is that funerals and marriages, for instance, often combine elements of both Christian and traditional religion. Generally, Sioux accept that this eclectic mix is normal and acceptable.

5

Government and Economy

TRADITIONAL GOVERNMENT

SIOUX GOVERNMENT was based on consensus. The actual structure of government was relatively straightforward because it flowed from kinship obligations into a band/village council formed by the male elders of each family. Men who had survived beyond approximately the age of 40 had acquired the knowledge to make decisions for the good of the community, according to traditional values. Day-to-day governing was mainly a matter of following tradition with most decisions made under the jurisdiction of families. When something of import for the whole town or band needed to be weighed, the leader (*itancan*) called upon prominent men who made up a band council together, and they decided a common course. Everyone was welcome to attend and voice their recommendations, even the young men, and deference to the council elders was the norm.

Itancan positions were usually hereditary as each itancan was succeeded by the most capable adult in his family, usually a son. New itancan often took the name of their father and predecessor. For instance, there were at least four itancan named Little Crow in the nineteenth century. The most famous led the war against the United States in 1862. Each itancan was bound by the consensual decision of the council of elders, according to tradition. Orders of the council were enforced by military fraternities or warrior societies (*akicita*) when necessary. Itancans were called chiefs once Europeans and Americans arrived, and their roles became more authoritative as Europeans and Americans insisted on a single voice through the chief.

War leaders were chosen or recognized by acclaim, and their authority lasted only during military operations. Blotohunka, war leaders, relinquished the status that went with being a war leader and returned to being just a band member. Some war leaders became itancan especially as pressure from other tribes, like the Chippewa, and from the United States mounted. A band nearly constantly at war had to accept more centralized authority for obvious reasons. Crazy Horse was a famous war leader who was also an itancan for tiyospaye including around 1,000 men, women, and children by the time he surrendered in 1877.

Other band decisions were made by those who had the expertise to make them. Women's societies or elder women made decisions about the farming and gathering ripening wild produce. Religious leaders decided when joint ceremonies would occur. Some bands chose leaders who were particularly knowledgeable about mass hunts and they then organized them with the assistance of the warrior societies. Whenever the band carried out collective action, the akicita enforced order according to tradition.

The Yankton pattern was similar to that of the Dakota. Although they had left the woodlands to build earth lodges towns surrounded by palisades and had replaced an annual deer hunt with an annual buffalo hunt, the Yankton still had village elders' councils, itancan, and military societies. Various other associations fulfilled their specialized roles just as they did among the Santee council fires.

The Teton-Lakota are more widely known than any of the other council fires because they assumed a major place in the American imagination and their wars with the United States drew journalists, dime novel writers, photographers, and scholars to produce copious amounts of information and myth. The Teton/Lakota captured the imagination of an American public. To the Americans and even European visitors, the Teton were adversaries whose military prowess had made them the perfect light horse cavalry and whose defeat of Custer represented the last gasp of a savage, noble culture. They were so colorful in their war bonnets and on their painted horses! During the latter nineteenth-century salvage anthropology turned out reams of studies of the plains Sioux and the Sioux cooperated in recording their culture for posterity. Even in the twenty-first century, the Teton/Lakota continue to attract the attention of novelists, scholars, documentary film makers, and movies. The plains Sioux were the focus of the 1990 epic, "Dances With Wolves" and the stereotypes of the noble savage continue to wear Teton/Lakota war bonnets and speak Lakota.

Lakota governance was governance was similar to that of the Santee/Dakota However, it was based on the mobile tiyospaye rather than villages. At different times in the year, community size ebbed and flowed as necessitated by the high plains environment. Virtually from the time that the Teton acquired horses in the late 1600s or early 1700s they pursued what can be termed imperialist as they steadily expanded westward and wrested land from other tribes like the Crow, Pawnee, Cheyenne, and Mandan. Near constant war required a government flexible enough to make decisions involving several tiyospaye and to provide for a nomadic buffalo hunting economy. By 1840, Tetons had made the necessary adjustments to accommodate the needs imposed by the high plains environment.

As with the other Sioux council fires, kinship was the basis of all organization as it defined one's relationship with not only human beings and with all living things. The Teton insisted that one was either kin or an enemy. Enemies were the natural prey of the Tetons because they were part of the world as revealed by the White Buffalo Calf Woman. In an idealized sense, a group of related families were a tiyospaye, the equivalent of a band in the other council fires.

Ideally, a tiyospaye had to be large enough to have a council consisting of an itancan, a *blotahunka* (a war leader), headmen for each extended family, a few warriors, and a few holy men as well as a camp administrator who coordinated all joint actions. This arrangement required at least seven husbanded tipis (a husbanded tipi is the people associated with one man and his wives, even if there are in actuality more than seven tipis). The arrangement provided all of the decision makers necessary for the tiyospaye to survive and to live according to the teachings of the pipe as conveyed by White Buffalo Calf Pipe Woman. When the Americans began negotiating treaties with the Tetons, they tried to get all of the tiyospaye leaders to sign because they realized that agreements required the consent of all of the bands. An itancan who had not signed a particular treaty did not feel committed to its terms.

Multi-tiyospaye organization was the next larger level of governance. It was implemented when several bands gathered for a common purpose such as hunting, planning a war, or responding to an American initiative like that held at Ft. Laramie in 1851. It replicated the tiyospaye pattern but with additional formal positions and a council comprised of several itancan. This council was known as the Big Bellies or Silent Eaters, indicating that the councilmen were elders who had earned hefty reputations and, sometimes, were equally hefty in size. Decisions were made by consensus, as was always the ideal in Sioux governments. If there was a need to present a common front within the tribe or to outsiders, the council chose a spokesman to convey its decision.

These multiband organizations included the itancan recognized by tiyospaye leaders, and he had two assistants. The rest of the council consisted of a mix of senior renowned individuals as shirt wearers. Shirts were fringed with human hair to signify that this wearer represented the people and was a paragon to be emulated; each of these council members was expected to embody the virtues of a Teton male and use his prestige to settle disputes.

The akicita enforced decisions and punished malefactors. By tradition, the akita could not be resisted. For instance, if the multiband gathering was to carry out a joint buffalo hunt, and a man jumped the gun to shoot buffalo before the other hunters, the akicita could destroy the man's wife's tipi, kill his horse, whip him, or even send him into exile. There were several akicita societies, and membership was by invitation. The main societies were *tokala* (kit foxes), *kangi yuha* (crow owners), *ihoka* (badgers), *chante tiza* (brave hearts), *sotka yuha* (plain lance owners), and *wacinska* (Packs White). Membership was expensive because continuous demonstration of generosity was required the heroic success of one who counted coup and acquired booty, like horses.

Once decisions were made by the council, usually after much caucusing among constituents, these were announced by camp criers throughout assembled camps. Throughout traditional Teton history (roughly from 1700 to 1880), the multiband organization was sufficient to bring together enough Teton bands to maintain successful wars against numerous tribal enemies and even to defeat the United States in Red Cloud's War, 1866–68. The Ft. Laramie Treaty that ended the war had the signatures of multiband spokesmen, with Red Cloud being one of the last signatories.

Regardless of the structure of the government, the ideal for Teton decision-making was consensus within a traditional context. Although the councils were dominated by senior men, even senior women were allowed to speak if they chose to do so. Warriors were expected to watch and support their elders, but they too could speak to the council. Once consensus was reached, if there were some who could not abide by the consensus, they were free to move with their families to other tiyospaye. No one was coerced, but peer pressure in a small community was great.

Readers should note that this apparently ideal government was possible because each tiyospaye was small. If there were 300 people in a tiyospaye, this meant that 75 or so were men. They knew one another, and everyone in the tiyospaye was aware of the abilities of others. Additionally, most of the members were kin. Volatile meetings were common, sometimes part of the tiyospaye left to join or create another, and sometimes there was bullying. However, Sioux governments worked well enough to allow the Sioux to survive as a tribe for 700 years before the United States imposed a new form of government.

Several external factors influenced changes in Sioux governance during the nineteenth century. The fur trade brought wealth to itancan who established

Red Cloud, first a war leader of the Oglala Teton/Lakota, achieved prominence in American eyes for having been the dominant leader of the 1866–68 war against the United States. He signed the Fort Laramie Treaty only after the Americans abandoned their forts. At first, an agency was named for him, and then, he was instrumental in securing Pine Ridge Reservation and lobbying for Oglala Lakota survival and rights. He was renowned throughout Sioux Country. (National Archives)

kinship relations with traders. This led to more power for itancan who distributed the gifts involved and who negotiated trade deals. Pressure for decisions related to American expansion also tended to make some itancan quite powerful decision makers. Negotiations in treaties, the need for centralized, quick decisions by bands, and increased warfare made it necessary for Sioux tribal members to modify consensus-style government. Both war and commerce led to larger and larger towns and bands that were concentrated more often as the century progressed. Decision-making fell to respected itancan and war leaders. Americans, whether fur traders or government officials, pressured the Sioux to adopt the practice of choosing a single spokesman who could control others and make decisions for others. For instance, in 1851, American negotiators insisted that the Teton choose a single leader for all of the Teton/Lakota. The Sioux did respond to this pressure in various ways.

The Dakota, Little Crow in 1862 had more authority than his grandfather, also named Little Crow, in 1812 because the Americans gave him more attention and Dakotas who wanted good relations acquiesced. Sheer force of personality gave power to Teton/Lakota like Crazy Horse, Sitting Bull, and Red Cloud. Little Crow was dominant among the Dakota. The Charger had power beyond just his tiyospaye for the Yankton.

TRIBAL GOVERNMENTS TODAY

Even after reservations and American colonialism removed the forms of tribal government, the ideas of political consensus remained. Consensus decisions are still preferred, even in tribal councils elected under the American style of representative governments that are institutionalized in tribal constitutions. Kinship continues to be a major factor in the outcome of tribal elections and leadership. Reservations encompass more bands than any former single band or village did, but reservations still reflect the values of traditional times.

Tribal governments have operated under congressional legislation that facilitated Self-Determination since the 1960s and through organic laws and constitutions that were first adopted by the tribes in the 1930s. Most tribes have an elected tribal council representing electoral districts, and an elected tribal chairperson, secretary, and treasurer. Representative government is firmly established as a principle, as are the civil rights of individual tribal members.

The political infrastructure generally includes a tribally created court system, tribal police, and a government bureaucracy that administers various programs like social services, roads and maintenance, taxation, realty and property, tribal enrollment, economic development, cultural affairs, and grants. Most schools on reservations have their own school boards and are public schools, but some are also contracted from the BIA and operated according to federal and tribal requirements. Several of the Sioux reservations have created tribal colleges, and these are independent of the tribal government but interact with it just as state higher education institutions do with their state governments.

TRADITIONAL SIOUX ECONOMY

The Sioux did not accumulate wealth in the same way that American and European society did. The most important reason for having wealth was to be able to give it away, which increased the reciprocal relationships with Sioux society. For the Lakota, wealth was measured in horses, and these became the chief way to display generosity. Banquets and distribution of goods like horses, beadwork, guns, food, blankets, leatherwork, and other valued possessions were held by the families of individuals who were being honored. The worst thing that a Sioux could be called was selfish, and peer pressure promoting generosity was a constant in all Sioux societies. Itancan were expected to share all that they possessed and not be richer or have more goods than their band members.

Several factors discouraged accumulation of material goods and even the development of a money economy. The nomadic Lakota, for instance, could not carry much as they were in constant motion. Even the relatively more sedentary Dakota and Yankton moved with the changing seasons as they interacted with their environments. Given that storage of goods, including food, was difficult, all of the Sioux societies had a boom and bust kind of economy. Hunting and farming were precarious, and shortages were common. If there was food, everyone ate; if there was none then everyone starved.

Europeans and Americans did not understand the absence of private property and a society that preferred to give things away. Sioux had trouble understanding an economy of supply and demand. For instance, when a fur trade glut led the French to suspend trading, the Sioux and other Indians saw this simply as an example of selfishness and of French disrespect. Set prices based on demand were another area of difficulty in the intercultural exchange.

The subdivisions of the Sioux tribe traditionally derived sustenance from the bounty of whichever region they lived in. Dakota communities' harvests of deer, fish, and wild rice combined with wild fruits and herbs provided their basic needs. As Dakota towns were relocated southward and westward, buffalo were added to their diets. Supplementary food came from farming of corn, beans, and squash but was not a major part of the traditional economy. Females typically worked the farms and did the gathering in groups and men hunted in groups as well.

Yankton communities farmed extensively, as did other tribes located along the rivers of South Dakota. They even produced surpluses for sale to nonagricultural tribes. Fishing and buffalo hunting as well as gathering of wild products supplemented the Yankton larders. Gender division of labor, with extended families forming the core economic units, was traditional.

Lakota tiyospaye were entirely nomadic. They followed patterns dictated by the movement of buffalo and the ripening of wild plants. Large horse herds also determined living patterns that required movement every few weeks for much of the year. Mobility was the key to their economy and to survival.

Each of the Sioux subdivisions formed part of intricate and extensive commercial networks even before contact with European and American traders. Sioux regularly participated in trade fairs, usually directed by Mandan and Hidatsa along the Missouri and its tributaries. Later, the Teton were integrated into the Shoshone trade networks. European and American merchants were integrated into these networks and gradually came to provide important hubs of trade themselves. Sioux communities encouraged Europeans and, later, Americans to build trading posts because they provided goods that Sioux wanted.

The Sioux saw the fur trade as, primarily, a means to reinforce good political and intercultural relations. The goods were symbols of a symbiotic, respectful relationship among peoples. Europeans and Americans grasped the essential elements of the idea of trade as part of sociopolitical interdependence, and they utilized Sioux protocols in the trade. Trade began with an exchange of presents, smoking, and discussion. Trading followed with bartering based on perceived value. As time passed, Europeans and Americans were able to convince Sioux traders that certain goods had specified prices. The Hudson's Bay Company even published a price list based on the cost of beaver. Completing the deal meant that presents were again exchanged. American and European merchants were considered wealthy, so they were expected to provide the bulk of the gifts.

Harvesting beaver and other furs in the eighteenth and nineteenth centuries was a key part of Dakota and Yankton economies. They changed many of their patterns of living in order to produce furs for market. These changes affected women's roles as they were the ones who had to spend more time processing the furs because men spent more time trapping. The fur trade gave rise to ancillary industries as well. The traders needed food, clothing, and other assistance. Dakota and Yankton communities were happy to produce provide them. Many worked with the traders in collecting furs, interpreting, and manufacturing products.

On the plains, Lakota increased their harvest of buffalo for their hides and for food sold to the new traders. Pemmican manufacturing became a subsidiary industry in many tiyospaye. Possibly, the need in the nineteenth century for preparing more hides supported an increase in polygyny because the household was the basic unit of production and more wives were needed as husbands became more efficient at killing buffalo. Tetons also sold horses by the hundreds for the eastern American market in the nineteenth century.

The fur trade brought luxuries to the Sioux. Guns, powder, blankets, iron pots, needles, pins, axes, coffee, sugar, beads, body paints, cotton and wool clothing, and many other items were added to the material wealth of the Sioux. Unfortunately for the Sioux, the world market for luxury furs declined in the 1830s and '40s, which created an economic void, particularly for the Santee. Buffalo hides remained a vital part of the market for the Yankton and Tetons until the 1870s. Sioux sold thousands of buffalo hides annually from the 1830s through the 1860s.

Collapse of the fur trade market in Santee-Dakota country coincided with the steady expansion of American desire for land in the 1830s and beyond. Dakota leaders were reduced to selling the only commodity they had, land. Needs had to be met, and the Dakota were convinced to sell land in return for the goods and funds they needed to survive in the world. The first sale was in 1805, and others followed in 1837, 1851, and 1858. By 1858, the Dakota had only a small strip of land on the Minnesota River and their economy was, essentially, based on treaty annuities.

Yankton leaders made the same decision for the same reasons. The 1851 Treaty of Washington replaced the fur trade with annuities, and the Yankton surrendered nearly all of their land to the United States. For example, the town of Yankton became an American, not a Sioux, city. The Teton economy remained stable until after all Tetons were restricted to reservations in the 1870s.

From about 1880 onward, the Sioux adjusted to an entirely new economy. Santee, Yankton, and Teton alike were dependent on the United States for basic needs. Rations were part of Sioux life nearly until the onset of World War I. As settlers moved into Sioux Country, many Sioux became hired hands, while a few were able to make the transition completely. Lakotas had some success as ranchers, while some Dakota were able to support their families with farming. However, most of the land was controlled by non-Sioux.

THE SIOUX ECONOMY TODAY

Tribal income is derived from multiple sources. Much depends on tribal tax codes and tribal legislation. Although all reservations do not have the same sources, such as casinos, for instance, all do have some type of income. Tribally owned enterprises such as logging, land leasing, motels, and casinos provide profits for each reservation. Tribes receive taxes from many sources, although they cannot tax trust land (this is an old policy—technically trust land is owned by the United States, so just like army bases, the local government cannot tax it), but sales and use taxes are common. Leasing fees also provide income for tribal governments. Sometimes, tribes receive settlements from federal courts that determine that money is owed for illegal taking of lands. For instance, Standing Rock, Yankton, Lower Brule, Cheyenne River, and Crow Creek reservations have received compensation for land taken by the United States to build dams and reservoirs.

A major portion of tribal income flows from the United States through the BIA as part of the Trust Responsibility and treaty rights. According to U.S. law, the federal government is the guardian of Indians, their governments, and their resources. This translates into the government using tax revenues for education, social services, and other needs of federally recognized Indians. Also, funds received by some of the tribes are required by treaty law as compensation for the lands acquired by the federal government.

The issue of taxation in Indian country is perplexing to many Americans. Stereotypes about Indians not having to pay taxes are common. The truth is that Native Americans pay all of the taxes that other Americans pay if they do not live on reservations. If they earn their income on reservations but live in a nearby town, they pay state taxes. If they live on Trust land and receive all of their income from earnings on the reservation (working for a tribally owned business, for instance), then they do not pay state taxes but do pay federal taxes. If an Indian's income is entirely from Trust land (income from leasing his or her land, for instance), and the person lives on Trust land, then the income is not taxable. This complicated situation makes it difficult for tribal governments to collect taxes, but some do so. For instance, sales taxes are sometimes collected in an arrangement with states and sometimes gathered by the tribes themselves. Use taxes for land are another approach.

Tribal governments are eligible to receive federal funds as a part of special grants passed by Congress to help reservations, and they are able to receive the same federal grants that states and municipalities receive throughout the United States. Funds for public housing are an example; they are received by states like North Dakota and by reservations like Standing Rock. Environmental impact and economic development funds are other examples.

The nearly complete absence of a private sector is an obvious feature of reservation economies. This fact is a legacy of the enforcement of federal policy on reservations which led to reservation land and resources being exploited mainly by non-Indians. During the period from 1887 when the Dawes Allotment Act was passed in 1934 when allotments and forced removal of Indian land from trust status were halted, Indian owned land in the United States was reduced from approximately 138 million acres to around 40 million acres. Many non-Indians acquired land within reservation boundaries and this land is not subject to tribal jurisdiction. Indian land owners cannot use their land as collateral for loans because it cannot be foreclosed by banks as it is in trust; this keeps more Indian land from being lost but it also prevents a landowner from getting capital to acquire land. The solution of the BIA is to simply lease Indian land to non-Indians.

Trust status for land includes extensive regulations enforced by the BIA governing businesses that operate on trust land. These regulations are particularly onerous as entrepreneurs try to start businesses. The rules make it difficult to acquire capital, to incorporate, and to hire and fire workers. Permission is required from multiple layers of bureaucracy from the tribal governments to Washington, D.C.

Generally, the private sector that exists on Sioux reservations is non-Indian owned and even many of the businesses are really farm-ranch operations or "mom and pop" operations that have little impact on the entire economy. Some studies have indicated that the multiplier effect of wages and profits on reservations is one. In other words, the money leaves the reservation immediately and multiplies off reservation economies.

Some scholars have concluded that the persistence of kinship based sharing is an obstacle to economic growth. They indicate that any profits are expected to be shared among all relatives, a practice that allows survival but not the accumulation of capital. Others point to the generations of unemployment that have prevented individual Sioux from developing the skills to enter a work force if there were jobs available. Other obstacles include distance from markets, absence of infrastructure, low educational levels for much of the population, and the size of reservation markets.

Despite the numerous impediments to economic development, particularly in the private sector, each reservation has a few Sioux who operate small businesses. Some are involved in cottage industries like fixing cars, tribal crafts, and other services. A miniscule few do manage to do well. Some are successful cattlemen on the large western reservations and others operate gas stations, convenience stores, and even franchises like Taco Bell or Pizza Hut. An outstanding example is Big Bat's on Pine Ridge Reservation. It evolved from a propane distributor to a gas station to a convenience store that includes a large restaurant that serves three meals daily, retail art featuring Sioux artists, and other spin-off businesses. Another successful venture is the White Buffalo grocery in Fort Yates. Each of these businesses employs more than just immediate family members. As an indicator of the enormity of the private sector problem, each of the stores is the second or third largest employer in the private sector. Other Sioux reservations have similar "success" stories but they do not dent the 35 to 45 percent unemployment statistics.

Sioux reservations, excluding the casino rich communities within Minnesota, are rural. Just as in the non-Indian rural communities, economic development does not seem to be a real possibility on the scale necessary to even maintain community size. On reservations, the populations continue to grow and they already are too large for any possible economic growth on a scale to alter the economic facts of poverty and unemployment. These denser populations are dependent on government employment, federal or tribal. In part, this explains why more than 50 percent of Indians do not live on reservations. A common remark on reservations is, "it is hard to be Sioux."

6

Traditional Sioux Society

THE OCETE SAKOWIN (THE SEVEN COUNCIL FIRES)

HISTORICALLY, Sioux society, as a distinct culture, has existed for about seven hundred years. Sioux country has ranged from their original homeland in northern Minnesota eastward to Lake Superior, westward to the Big Horn Mountains, and southward into the Minnesota-Iowa-Nebraska triangle. Over time, groups of Sioux moved into different ecosystems and developed economies and social organizations responsive to different environments. Sioux societies evolved differences in dialect and modified and borrowed oral traditions and ceremonies from other tribes to add to their own. Europeans and Americans influenced massive changes variations in Sioux societies from the seventeenth century onward.

Traditional Cultures (Roughly from 1700 to the 1870s)

Describing Sioux cultures is a complex undertaking. Sioux society was never static, yet any description has to "freeze" cultures in place in order to provide a coherent narrative. Readers should remember that a "typical" Sioux community in the fourteenth century was quite different from one in the sixteenth century, and it would be unfathomable to a Sioux from the twentieth. Every aspect of Sioux society was in flux, and even the most basic of ideologies were adjusted in response. Despite the constancy of change, it is possible to describe general aspects of Sioux society that apply to the whole because there were basic foundation beliefs and responses that held more or less true throughout a long period of Sioux history.

A further complication to keep in mind is that, until quite recently, Sioux society was described by only a very few outsiders, and this makes it more difficult to provide complete descriptions. It was not until the late nineteenth century that ethnographers made any systematic effort to describe the various Sioux societies. Many bands were not described at all, while others were visited by a single ethnographer. Of course, Sioux oral histories describing the Misty Past related after the reservations were established painted a halcyon past focused on life the way it should have been. These limitations mean that we can create only a clouded, somewhat selective, picture of Sioux society over the centuries.

It is certain that, by 1700, the Sioux included named, identifiable subdivisions that had been developing since around 1500. In Sioux metaphor a major subdivision, sometimes called a tribe by Europeans and Americans, is symbolized as a council fire. The Sioux envisioned their nation as the Seven Council Fires. The Santee-Dakota were a woodlands society with four separate council fires the Yankton had adopted the life style of Arikara and other prairie neighbors, and the Teton-Lakota had created a culture based on war, horses, and buffalo hunting similar to other plains tribes. The Yanktonai are often lumped together with the Yankton, but they blended so many different characteristics from their Lakota and Dakota relatives that they are an anomaly. Despite the anomaly, the Yanktonai saw themselves, and other agreed, as a distinct council fire.

Despite the fact that each subdivision's appearance and way of life resembled their neighboring tribes more than each other, the Sioux subdivisions retained an affinity for one another and maintained that they were one people (the *Oyate*) whose seven major subdivisions were each a council fire (*Oceti*). "Council fire" is a common metaphor in American Indian cultures and signifies an identified tribal subdivision. For example, the "Three Council Fires" were the Chippewa, Potawatomi, and Ottawa. The Sioux Council Fires are: the Mdewakanton, Sisseton, Wahpeton, and Wahpekute fires, collectively called the Santee-Dakota; the Yankton and the Yanktonai fires; and the Teton-Lakota fire. Together, all Sioux had a common language, considered themselves one culture and one kinship group that had been created by supernatural Beings. Collectively, they call themselves Oyate, the people.

Europeans recognized the unity of the Seven Council Fires by calling them, collectively, the Sioux tribe. Their subdivisions have been called bands or tribes depending on the definition of tribe at a particular time period or the precision of the person using the term. The United States continued the idea that the Sioux were a single tribe as a legal fiction in treaties and laws as well as in practice. Until the latter twentieth century, Americans even substituted Dakota as an all-encompassing term for the Sioux.

KINSHIP: THE BASIS OF SIOUX TRIBAL ORGANIZATION BEFORE RESERVATIONS

Kinship relations provide the organizing principle for each of the Sioux subdivisions, the Dakota-Santee, Yankton, and Teton-Lakota. In traditional Sioux society, either you were a relative or you were an enemy. Loyalties were focused on relatives, and in fact, to be a good Sioux was to be a good relative. Relatives included the brothers and sisters of parents who were often referred to as "father" or "mother" by Sioux boys and girls. The children of each "father" were called "brother" and "sister." Descent was traced through both parents, although the male line was the dominant source of family identity. The Sioux did not have clans like their Algonquian neighbors, but they might have had them in a time beyond memory.

Sioux kinship identified the place in society of each person. It was so central to Sioux social organization that most people were known to one another through terms for kinship rather than by their given names. For instance, the first-born female was always called *winona* while the oldest son was *chaske*. Each term made it clear to any Sioux what the relationships were between people and what their reciprocal obligations were.

Anyone called "father" was expected to care for and indulge anyone called his son or daughter. Father's brother was usually expected to be the one who taught boys the skills of adulthood. Of course, others also played a role in teaching the young. Children belonged to extended families and the tiyospaye, not just to the biological parents. Families and bands were organized for hunting, gathering, craft work, residence, and even war, around brothers, their wives, their children, and their grandchildren. Children belonged to the family, and a common statement by Sioux today is that, in traditional times, no orphans existed because a child had many fathers and mothers.

Kinship was so much a part of the fabric of Sioux existence that they described diplomatic protocols in kinship terms and developed ceremonies and practices that allowed outsiders to be incorporated as fictive kin. Other tribes were called "brothers" if they were allies, "little brothers" if the Sioux considered themselves dominant, or "women" if they wanted to indicate a subservient relationship.

From earliest times, the Sioux referred to the president of the United States as "father" and, to them, this explained what the relationship should be. Sometimes, the president was called the "Great White Father," and such other Americans as treaty commissioners were referred to as "father." The idea was to establish reciprocal relationships. The "father" was expected to share his wealth and bounty with his children, the Sioux. Sometimes kinship metaphors caused difficulties because Americans heard "father" as a dominant relationship according to which children were to obey; Sioux heard "father" in their way; "fathers" did not order their "children" about.

When European merchants arrived in Sioux country, beginning in the seventeenth century, they had to adapt to the realities of kinship if they were to do business with the Sioux. French and, later English and American, merchants married Sioux women for mutual benefit. Sioux families added rich relatives through these marriages and the traders now had kinship obligations. In return, the merchants received protection for their goods and brothers-in-law who could collect debts from other Sioux. Family members traded with family members. Merchants and the mixed-blood children of Sioux-European marriages were important in traditional Sioux societies.

The Sioux referred to these traders and, sometimes their children, as "kinsmen of another kind." They were expected to be interpreters and cultural brokers, as were their children. In only a few generations, these children and their parents developed a different kind of Sioux grouping within the bands. By the 1870s there were mixed-blood tiyospaye in the Dakota and Yankton tribes. These mixed blood Sioux and their families became a new category or class within the more traditional social organization. They served the community and their other relatives by being trading families and, often, as interpreters for councils with the Americans and as treaty deliberations. For instance, the interpreters hired by the United States for the treaty council in 1868 and who signed the treaty were Lakota mixed bloods whose descendents are still part of the Teton/Lakota reservation communities. Their children often married one another which maintained their status as an integrated merchant class. Other mixed blood children married what is called full bloods and their children followed the traditional rearing of Teton Lakota children. Some of the itancan in the 1880s and beyond were mixed bloods. Americans were not comfortable with mixed bloods because they did not fit into the neat racial categories nineteenth-century Americans preferred. Many American authors and politicians considered these "half breeds" as neither Indian nor White and were never sure how they should be treated, legally. In time, those who remained as participants in reservation society were enrolled officially, as Sioux.

Courtship and Marriage

Marriage was seen as a means to unite families if the marriage was with another Sioux. It was also used to cement alliances between Sioux and other tribes just as it was used to incorporate the non-Indians. Dakota marriages with Chippewa were so common that many leaders of both tribes had one parent from each tribe. The Dakota itancan Wabasha and Red Wing had Chippewa mothers. Also, captive women could become wives and were sometimes stolen specifically for that reason.

Within Sioux societies, generally, a young man would court a woman and secure her consent. Courtship typically included the couple playing the flute and talking while wrapped in a single robe or blanket. If the young man had proven himself as a hunter and warrior, then he might ask his father or brother to talk with the woman's family. The discussions began with presents to the woman's father and family; often the presents were provided or supplemented by the male's extended family. Ideally, the woman's kin would decide that the man came from a good family. If the presents were accepted, then the marriage could proceed with an elaborate exchange of presents from family to family. Despite Hollywood imagery and contemporary Sioux practice, there was no specific wedding ceremony. Sometimes, however, the village herald would announce the new arrangement. Once families accepted that the marriage had taken place the couple took up residence together.

Generally, the bride's family provided the tipi and most household goods, which remained the property of the woman. Women usually married when they were 15 or 16, and men married in their early twenties. Residence was a flexible decision, as were most other aspects of family life. The Sioux did not have rigid requirements, but usually, the bride lived with her husband near his family. If the bride was from a different band, then the couple almost always lived with the man's family, sometimes even in the same tipi.

Many European and American observers falsely assumed that the woman had been bought and paid for with the presents. They also assumed that women had no say in the matter. These observations were wrong. A woman could refuse to marry a man proposed by her father and family, and the presents indicated both respect for the woman and her family and the ability of the man and his family to provide for her and other relatives. Of course, young women and men tended to follow the wishes of their families because they respected the wisdom of their elders and they had been raised to consider family wishes. Also, in small communities like the Sioux tiyospaye, everyone knew everyone else, and the formal proposals were preceded by informal agreements between courting couples. Even when inter-tiyospaye marriages were arranged, perhaps at one of the multiband gatherings, the likelihood is that the spouses were known to each other and had been checked out thoroughly before gifts were exchanged.

Polygyny (marriage of one man to more than one woman) was a common feature of Sioux society. Men who had acquired wealth and status needed more than one wife to provide the support necessary for carrying out the duties of generosity and leadership. Often the first wife would encourage her husband to marry a second time. This was both practical and prestigious because it solidified status while lessening the burdens of being married to a leader. Most men had one wife. Divorce was fairly common whether the marriages were polygnous or monogamous.

The practice of multiple marriage is hard for most twenty-first century Americans to understand because it is so contrary to American views of the way marriage should work and there are laws prohibiting bigamy in the United States. All of the Sioux governments prohibit polygyny too. However, cultures change. Perhaps the best approach is to remember that multiple marriages worked for centuries as an effective means of organizing society.

Sioux tiyospaye did not exist in isolation from other tribes and certainly not from their trading partners. Exogamy (marriage outside one's society) was a feature of Sioux society from its beginnings. Marriage between Chippewa and Dakota men and women is noted repeatedly in the oral histories of both tribes. Cheyenne and Lakota families considered intermarriage good for providing the kinship support that reinforced their military alliance. After the arrival of fur traders in Sioux Country, many marriages created the bonds between the traders and Sioux communities that were necessary for good interpersonal relations. Throughout Sioux Country, the initial marriages were usually between Sioux women and French-descent men. These marriages provided living evidence of kinship relations.

The children of these marriages were called *iyeska* (literally "talks White"— usually translated as mixed blood), and they occupied a somewhat separate existence within Sioux society, but they were relatives. Commonly, mixed-blood women married mixed bloods, while iyeska men could strengthen kinship ties with marriages to "full-blood" Sioux. These individuals grew up as Sioux, but with multilingual skills and as part of the larger trading firms like the American Fur Company. Iyeska often acted as interpreters and intermediaries with traders and American officials. One of the Dakota leaders who signed the first treaty with the United States was a mixed blood. Red Cloud, the famed Oglala leader, pointed out that the Treaty of 1868 needed to include specific clauses to assure that would "take care" of his mixed-blood relatives. The United States often provided for iyeska to receive allotments from tribal lands when treaties were negotiated.

A pattern of marriage to non-Sioux continued throughout the reservation period into the twenty-first century. In general, American Indians have the highest out-marriage rate of any American ethnic group. Boarding schools, Pan-Indian gatherings, urban Indian communities, the military, and colleges provide intertribal and non-Indian courting opportunities. Most Sioux in the twenty-first century have some non-Sioux ancestry. Of course, given the fact of centuries of intermarriage with other tribes and four hundred years of intermarriage with people of European ancestry, the idea of "pure blood" is merely a concept, but on a human level, it has real-life effects. The continuing idea that race can be measured in blood quantums clung to by both non-Indians and Indians remains a divisive issue in the twenty-first century.

Gender and Traditional Marriage Customs

White Buffalo Calf Woman instructed the Tetons about the roles of women and men when she instructed them in Teton culture. The other six council fires also knew that the place of women and men was supernaturally assigned gender division of labor and roles in the symbiotic Sioux culture. Throughout the traditional era of Sioux history and well into the reservation era, women and men remained unequal in that their functions were determined by gender. However, the place of women in an idealized tribal culture was quite different from that of the "weaker vessels" envisioned in American Victorian society, for instance.

Simplistically stated, women gathered/farmed and men hunted. However, gender roles were much more complex than this simple formula. Women and men alike had responsibilities and functions that went beyond merely duties to ensure basic survival. Some women were healers with knowledge of the homeopathic medicines given to them by women teachers and through dreams; women were expected to influence men's governing decisions, and women were the carriers of culture. A supernatural woman, White Buffalo Calf Woman, had taught the Teton to be Teton. As Lakota tradition would have it, according to the holy man, John Lame Deer, women are "part of ourselves, part of our souls."

Women had rights in traditional society that reflected their value. Women owned the homes and everything in them except for a husband's personal property. They had the right to initiate divorce. Women were protected from abuse throughout life by their brothers. Such rights guaranteed a measure of status that women in most non-Indian cultures did not have. They belonged to societies that celebrated the skills of women to the point that revered women had an equivalent prestige with men who had accomplished war honors. Women elders became medicine women through the power of dreams and their use of herbs for healing.

The ideal Sioux woman was modest, virginal, and respectful. When a woman reached puberty, she was instructed in the place of women in perpetuating Sioux culture and in the role she needed to play in supporting the males in society. She celebrated their prowess in battle and supported her husband's needs. All women were expected to marry, as their main function was also their blessing and the source of their power—bearing children. Sioux society recognized that women ensured the survival of the people.

Fathers were granted the right to pick a daughter's husband but were not supposed to insist if the daughter strongly objected, and of course, divorce was her right. Generally, marriage was arranged as it was in societies throughout the world; marriage was a uniting of families, not just a bond involving two people. A young man talked to his relatives about his intention, and if not dissuaded, he sent a brother to talk to the girl's family. If his family were deemed worthy by her family, then he would send presents and show, in other ways, that he was capable of supporting her and her family, if necessary. In Teton society, the ideal gift was horses because they were laden with cultural significance, but other presents were also given. Usually, the perspective groom's family provided presents to show their support.

If the presents were accepted by the woman's family, her family would send presents, and the marriage was contracted. Contrary to Hollywood renditions, there were no formal marriage ceremonies as there are now. Essentially, the woman's family provided a tipi or house, or the couple moved in with the family of the groom, there was feasting within the community, and the couple cohabited. Everyone recognized that the two families were now kin.

One concept that is difficult for modern cultures to understand is the practice of giving presents to the bride's family. This "bride price" was often negotiated to assure greater honor for the woman's family and for her, but often, Europeans and Americans thought that the daughters were bought and sold like any other commodity. Understanding that Sioux culture was based on generosity and that giving large presents was both an honor to the recipient and a gesture of generosity and reciprocal gift exchange expected of all Sioux is difficult to reconcile with American culture which tends to see three horses given to the father and then the daughter marries the donor. In traditional times, it never really was this simplistic. The process might look like a purchase to an American, but it is not. It is an illustration of cultural difference.

Another area of difficulty in cross-cultural understanding is the concept of equality between the sexes. Sioux women had importance parallel to that of men in Sioux culture, but each had specified roles that were necessary for survival, spiritually powerful, and honored. Women were expected to be subservient to men in political matters and were for the most part simply supportive and influential in these areas. Many outsiders commented on the use of physical force against women by husbands, for instance, but this practice has to be understood in the cultural context. A practice accepted in a culture, and supported by the women as well as the men, does not have the same impact as it would in a different culture. We can never know the place of women and their response to it when we are looking through either the idealized lenses of contemporary Sioux or the biased lenses of Victorian Americans who interpreted what they saw without understanding what they were actually seeing.

Children

Sioux children grew up surrounded by relatives. Although they knew their biological parents and were expected to respect them, other relatives were often just as important. Uncles taught boys the skills of manhood, and aunts taught girls. Families worked together according to gender, so education and enculturation were the responsibility of the community. Teaching styles combined lectures in which children merely absorbed the wisdom of the elders and experiential learning of specific skills. Children's play was often consisted of their efforts to act out adult behaviors.

Sioux children were rarely physically punished. Until they were around ten or so, children moved freely throughout the community and were able to intrude on adults because children were not expected to understand all of the rules. Teasing was the primary means of control. Children who misbehaved, for instance by being disrespectful, were teased about their behavior and gradually learned the proper way to behave. In small communities, ridicule is effective. Generally, the Sioux attitude was that children should be allowed to learn through experience what was right and wrong as well as the reciprocal relationships necessary to be members of a tiyospaye. Children who misbehaved were teased, and this ridicule generally was effective.

Religious and cultural education was imparted to children by elders and reinforced with stories and traditions told and retold by adults. If a child wanted to, he could move to the household of an uncle, an aunt, or even a friend. Community size allowed this, and it proved to be no problem. Children who showed particular talents could live with a religious leader to begin the process of being a holy man.

Children were also expected to work, assisting their relatives. For example, Teton girls gathered wood and buffalo chips and drew water, while boys controlled the horse herds, which included moving them from place to place, driving off predators, and watching out for human thieves. Above all, children learned to emulate adults and were incorporated into the community through examples and stories that explained Sioux culture and values.

TRADITIONAL CUSTOMS AND LIFESTYLE

Children and the entire community played games and sports in their leisure times. Some of the common games were shinny, stick ball (similar to lacrosse), horse racing, running, target contests with available weapons, throwing spears at rolling hoops, and pretending to be adults. Girls had dolls,

Stick ball or lacrosse was a woodlands Dakota game and was not played by the Lakota. It often involved inter-village competitions as fiercely contested as any modern sporting event. *Ballplay of the Dakota on the St. Peters River in Winter* by Seth Eastman, 1848. (Library of Congress)

and boys had bows and arrows. Girls played house, and boys played war and hunting.

Adults often played variations of games of skill. Dakota stickball was an especially popular game and offered a way for communities to compete with one another. The games were so fiercely contested that some tribes called the games "little wars." Trade fairs often featured stickball tournaments, horse and human racing, archery contests, and other games of skill. Games of chance included the moccasin game, which required guessing which moccasin hid an object, hand games where teams competed in discovering which way hands held objects, various dice games, and of course racing and competition in skills like shooting. Adults gambled quite a bit, and many non-Indian observers concluded that the Sioux would bet on anything.

Frequent feasts marked nearly every occasion in Sioux communities. Music and dancing accompanied feasts too. Generosity was one of the cardinal values of Sioux culture and was displayed frequently. Marriages, funerals, successful military expeditions, naming ceremonies, births, successful hunts, harvests, particular ceremonies, and other commemorations led to feasts. Often feasts were accompanied by the giving of gifts from the sponsor to those attending.

Dancing was considered a means of homage and expression of community exuberance so they were part of feasting too . . . the greater the wealth and prestige of an individual, the greater the feast and the more valuable to gifts.

Tragedy and death were also experienced communally. The average life expectancy of Sioux in the pre-reservation period was about 35. Death in childbirth claimed many women and children. Men died in war and hunting. Cholera, measles, smallpox, and influenza stalked Sioux communities. Deaths were occasions for self-mutilation by relatives and for tiyospaye-wide mourning and lamentations. Ideally, one year after the death of a relative, the family held a ceremony to release his or her spirit. One can imagine that many Sioux communities quite nearly alternated happiness and mourning.

Children were pre-adolescents. After puberty, both girls and boys vaulted directly into young adulthood with the duties and roles of adults rather than moving gradually toward life as a teenager. Girls became wives, and young men set out to prove themselves at war, hunting, and the tasks of men. Although there was a kind of apprenticeship, there was no extended in-between status as is common in societies today.

Adults progressed through the stages of responsibility as given to them by White Buffalo Calf Woman or explained by other Beings. Labor and most other activities were gender driven. Work often was communal. All of the women of one family and their friends worked side by side to perform the ongoing chores even after reservations were established in the mid-nineteenth century. Women and girls gathered wood, tanned hides, prepared food, sewed, beaded or quilled, went for water, maintained the tipis or lodges, and supported the men in feasting and ceremonies. They also danced and played games. Groups worked together.

Women moved through different stages of life from girl to wife to elder. Some women received accolades because of their artwork, chiefly in the beading and quillwork that decorated so much of their work, and there were women's societies that required a mastery of skills for a woman to be invited to join. Some women became revered as particularly powerful in assisting at births and teaching girls. Others became important healers known for their ability to combine prayer and homeopathic medicines in helping the sick and injured. A few elders joined the small group of wise male elders in providing wisdom to the entire community and received the respect due their wisdom.

The primary function of men was war and hunting. Honor and success began with warfare for most Sioux. Warfare was particularly prominent among the plains societies of the Yankton, Yanktonai and Teton-Lakota. Boys trained for war through practice with weapons and mock wars and caring for horses. Young teens accompanied military expeditions as helpers and eventually were allowed to join adult men as they attacked other tribes for horses, territorial control, women, and glory. Young men sought spiritual guidance and protection in vision quests to prepare them for war. Individual achievements began the process of accumulating wealth and prestige for men, and such achievements were recognized by the entire community.

Although Sioux men killed enemies in battle, and sometimes women and children, for the individual, the most important aspect of war for the Sioux was to demonstrate bravery through a reckless dependence on their received spiritual power to protect them. They taunted enemies and courted death. For the Teton, Yankton, and Yanktonai, the bravest act was to touch a living enemy, called "counting coup." Some even carried special staffs, or coup sticks, with which to touch their enemies. Others used their hands or bows. Killing and scalping were secondary to these displays of bravery.

Crazy Horse of the Oglala had such powerful spiritual protection that he and other Oglala believed he could not be shot. According to oral tradition, Crazy Horse would ride from one side to the other across the front lines of an enemy force—daring the enemy to kill him. He charged into enemy villages ahead of other Oglala to taunt enemies as he took their horses. He led the detachment of Lakota and Cheyenne who tempted Lieutenant Fetterman into an ambush in 1867. Crazy Horse was at the Little Big Horn Battle and charged the Seventh Cavalry with disregard for the bullets flying about. This kind of fame and glory was the dream of every Sioux boy.

When a man returned from war, the entire village turned out to celebrate the victors and to mourn any losses. Mothers, sisters, and wives sang the praises of their men and even paraded scalps about the village to show all how brave their men had been. Celebrations included feasting and dancing where each man would be able to recite his war honors, give presents of captured horses to others, and bask in the respect earned. Of course, not all expeditions were successful, and the arrival of the nonvictorious was marked by subdued receptions.

After men achieved a measure of success, they could be invited to join one of the akicita (warrior or police) societies and begin the process of contributing to their communities in other ways. Some became shamans and some concentrated on hunting and trade. Eventually, they could move to positions of leadership in the tiyospaye and societies.

Most social decisions were made within extended families, not by a formal government as they are today. Marriages, criminal justice, divorces, social services, and economic organization began with the family and included others only when the joint action of several families or even the whole community was needed. Families met regularly, discussed issues, and handled their own decisions, but always with a consideration of the impact on the band community. Sioux children grew up and lived as adults surrounded by their relatives, were taught what was right by their relatives, and were supported by family. Disputes within the family or outside the family with other Sioux involved family action to resolve them.

In the Sioux view, violations of the law threatened the entire community, and reconciliation was necessary. For instance, in the extreme case of murder, compensation was required of the criminal. Taking a man's life was considered an extreme act and simply deprived the community of another productive male. Compensation in horses, services, or accepting responsibilities for the victim's family were the preferred ways to handle such a situation. However, the victim's family could exact revenge if they insisted. Killing the murderer or a member of his family was the right of the victim's family, but usually, the itancan and council argued against a response that furthered the disruption of the community. Lesser offenses were handled for the most part through compensation. This ideal approach, compensation rather than retaliation, was not always followed, as Sioux men were warriors and tempers did flare. The guiding principle of Sioux culture and of its justice system was that the community is more important than the individual.

Sometimes, the entire community would need to be involved in dealing with threats to the community. If an individual violated the rules of hunting by killing buffalo before the signal was given to the entire band, he endangered the community's food supply. In cases like this, the akicita (warrior/police societies) punished the culprit by whipping him or killing his hunting horse or destroying his tipi. People who violated the rules of the road when the band was moving from place to place could be punished by the akicita. Endangering the whole society was the greatest wrong a Sioux could commit.

Polygyny was frequent in Sioux society. Wealthy and important men often had more than one wife because women were necessary to receiving guests, running large households, and even preparing furs and hides for trade. Often men married sisters, as sisters already knew how to get along. Usually, if there were problems within a marriage, appropriate members of the extended families would try to mediate. Divorce could be initiated by women as well as men and required a simple change in residence. Scholars have concluded that divorce was common, particularly in marriages with three wives.

When the tribe was first developing, a community consisted of an extended family, but as time progressed, groups of families joined to create bands. The Santee and Yankton chose to organize in town or village bands united by kinship and affinity under the dominance of a particularly influential leader. After the Europeans arrived, they often named these towns after the dominant leader. Wabasha, Mankato, and Red Wing in Minnesota were Santee towns named for prominent leaders.

The Teton lived in extended family groups augmented by families that were attracted by leaders who were particularly effective. *Tiyospaye* is the Teton word for these bands and translates roughly as "home community." By 1750, the Teton had altered their former woodland culture to become a nomadic, buffalo-hunting, tipi-dwelling, horse culture. Tiyospaye in particular areas of the high plains formed bands and then shared multiband identity.

The band, whether within a village or in an association of tiyospaye, was the focal point for Sioux society. Each band was an autonomous part of the tribe and not bound by decisions made by any other band with regard to war and peace, moving from place to place and maintaining commerce, hunting, and relations with other tribes or the Europeans and/or Americans. The political structure for decision-making began at the band level. Bands varied in size depending on the time of the year, external threats, or the effectiveness of leaders in attracting or repelling band members. Santee and Yankton bands ranged from a few hundred to a thousand or so by the 1850s; Teton bands could reach several thousand during the buffalo hunting seasons or for purposes of religious or cultural gatherings. In the winter, the bands separated into family groups because resources were scarce and dispersal of extended families and their friends was the logical way to survive. In the spring, the families joined their tiyospaye again and they, in turn, merged with other tipospaye to form bands.

The Sioux developed a variety of ways to reinforce their identity as a tribe and to act jointly. Men's societies, tribalwide religious ceremonies like the Sun Dance, joint hunting and military expeditions, and frequent interband visits helped cement Sioux culture. As one might expect in a society where kinship is so important, marriage was another means to reinforce interband unity and identification. For instance, Little Crow, a Santee leader in the 1850s and '60s, had wives from the families of other Dakota band leaders, and this allowed him to call on his in-laws and their bands for support.

Ideally, the entire tribe would gather annually. However, no oral history record exists of whole gathering at once but large numbers did gather on various occasions. The Battle of the Little Big Horn involved up to 3,000 Teton men because they and their families had just finished the annual sun dance. Apparently, the Seven Council Fires was a theoretical construct that never really met. On the other hand, the concept of all Sioux as related meant a common identity, and any of the Sioux, whether Teton, Yankton, Yanktonai, or Santee-Dakota, were welcome in any of the other communities. Although the Battle of the Little Big Horn involved mainly the Teton, other Sioux were there too. All Sioux are kin.

A modern rendition in traditional style of a buffalo hunt. It is a portion of the mural that depicts Teton/Lakota historic life—the center is in Eagle Butte, Cheyenne River Reservation. (Nativestock.com/Marilyn Angel Wynn)

ANNUAL CYCLES

By 1750, the Sioux had established themselves in three different ecosystems, and their annual activities reflected the resources and locations of these ecosystems. The Santee-Dakota had remained woodlands-prairie communities located particularly along the Mississippi and Minnesota rivers. The Yankton had moved to a prairie-plains environment and established large earth lodge towns where they combined buffalo hunting with farming. The

Sun Dancing was one of the major ceremonies of the Sioux. Although it is mainly a Teton/Lakota ceremony, the Dakota also held Sun Dances. The purpose was for individuals to sacrifice on behalf of the tribe or to fulfill a vow. *Worship of the Sun, Dakota Dancers* by Seth Eastman, 1852. (Library of Congress)

Teton-Lakota had acquired horses, which gave them a nomadic range on the northern plains.

The Dakota began their year in the spring as they sallied forth from their towns for collective deer hunting, harvesting the bounty of spring—maple sugar and herbs, and fishing. The summer was the time for planting, war, ceremonies, and trade fairs that attracted participants from many towns. Inter-town marriages were a part of each summer. Multicommunity towns also encouraged leaders to meet on tribalwide decisions such as the best way to deal with the Chippewa or with European merchants.

The end of the summer led to large, collective deer hunts, harvesting wild rice, collecting fruits, and gathering corn, beans, and squash, which were the commonly planted crops. After the 1750s, many of the Dakota substituted buffalo hunting for their deer-hunting expeditions. The Red River Valley and much of eastern South Dakota teemed with buffalo. Winter led to hunkering down in the towns with men leaving periodically to hunt and trap. Trapping demanded more and more time as the fur trade expanded throughout the eighteenth and most of the nineteenth centuries. Women processed the furs that were trapped and also trapped smaller animals such as mink. Aside from local trade, the long-distance fur trade was with first the French and then the English merchants sent out from Canada.

A typical Yankton year followed a similar pattern. The year began in the spring with planting, and then most of the Yankton left their towns to hunt buffalo and harvest wild plants. Horses had been acquired by 1750, which allowed large-band movement and hunting over a large area. As with the Dakota, war expeditions were common in the summer, as were ceremonial activities that included Yankton as well as other Sioux. It was not uncommon for Dakota families to join Yankton communities for part of the year, and Teton visitors were frequent too. Fall buffalo hunts provided winter food, particularly pemmican. Pemmican is dried buffalo mixed with tallow and dried fruit stuffed into buffalo intestines. This sausage-like food was a staple for winter and a major trade item. Buffalo hides were prepared by women for trade, along with beaver and other pelts. After 1760, Yankton commerce was mainly with Spanish and French traders from the St. Louis area.

The Teton-Lakota were a rapidly expanding subdivision in 1750. Their territorial expansion reached the Black Hills, according to one winter count, in 1760. In the process, Tetons fought nearly all of the tribes that preceded them. Lands formerly of the Kiowa, Pawnee, Mandan, Hidatsa, Arikara, Crow, Ponca, and Cheyenne fell to Teton conquest. Expansion was facilitated by the smallpox epidemics that were so devastating on the plains, especially to the urban Mandan, Hidatsa, and Arikara whom many consider to have been blocking Sioux expansion. Ironically, the diseases that weakened American Indian communities for American imperialism also aided Sioux imperialism.

The Teton year began in the Spring when the tiyospaye emerged from their sheltered winter camps to fatten their horses on the plains, locate and hunt buffalo, harvest wild flora, and launch attacks against their enemies. Buffalo and horses required a nomadic existence, but usually around the summer solstice, many of the Teton bands gathered for a sun dance. Other occasions such as joint tiyospaye war expeditions brought Teton together, but the sun dance period was the time when they gathered in the largest numbers and for an extended amount of time.

After 1830, many of the Teton bands used fur trading—later army—posts as nearly permanent homes. Fort Laramie and Fort Pierre were built where Tetons had gathered regularly for a few generations, and after the trading posts were built, they continued as centers for Teton commerce and residence. During the period following 1854, wars with the United States meant that the Sioux multibands grew ever larger as a matter of self-defense. For instance, when Crazy Horse surrendered in 1877, "his" band had more than a thousand members with several other war leaders and itancan who had joined.

After the fall buffalo hunting ended, the bands moved to wooded, sheltered locations to endure the northern plains winters. Tipis were typically scattered along creeks and rivers where cottonwoods could provide fodder and wood for fires. Pemmican, dried fruit, and the spoils of short hunting expeditions carried the Teton through the winters.

Reducing the dynamics of Sioux society to the same annual pattern for two hundred years or so poses the danger that readers might picture Sioux life as a static, unchanging existence. The descriptions above should convey some sense that change occurred. Not only did the pattern vary somewhat each year for all of the Sioux, but it also varied from town to town and tiyospaye to tiyospaye. War could threaten some when it did not threaten others. Disease had different effects from community to community. Some of the vast Sioux land could experience drought when other parts did not. Some bands spent most of their time near trading posts, creating a multiband town, while other bands stayed as far away as possible. The Sioux were interwoven with the outside world always, and that outside world was larger and larger as Europeans and, later, Americans joined it.

The Teton Sioux warrior of Hollywood, dime novels, and the American imagination was a product of change. His war bonnet was made of locally obtained eagle feathers and trimmed in fur, but it was decorated with beads made in the Netherlands. His horse was descended from those brought by the Spanish. His weapons included guns and metal-tipped arrows. He used steel knives, and his wives used needles and thread. His wife wore a wool blanket, beaded her clothes with European and American manufactured beads, and even wore a cotton dress. All of these goods were purchased with the profits from selling buffalo hides and other Sioux made products. Sometimes, these items were acquired through war. Change was constant.

7

Sioux Customs

TRADITIONAL SIOUX CULTURE and customs were similar to the tribal cultures found near each of the major subdivisions of the Oyate Sakowin (Seven Council Fires). Each subdivision was situated in the heart of different cultural-ecological zones. The Dakota bands mirrored the culture of their woodlands neighbors like the Ho-Chunk (Winnebago), the Chippewa, and the Menominee. Yankton communities were similar to their neighbors like the Arikara who lived in large towns anchored in riverine agriculture. Nomadic Tetons resembled the Cheyenne, Blackfeet, and Crow especially after the horse culture began in the 1700s.

MUSIC AND DANCE

Perhaps the most ubiquitous characteristic of the Sioux societies was the constancy of music and dance. Songs, accompanied by drum, permeated daily and ceremonial life. They were sung for all religious ceremonies, to praise individuals, to lull children to sleep, to express sheer exuberance, and to pray. Large drums accompanied by several male singers/drummers were, and are, roughly the size of bass or timpani drums. Women sometimes complete a drum group by singing while standing behind the men. Traditionally, women did not sit at drums. These were particularly used for large ceremonies and are featured in contemporary powwows and for sacred occasions like sun dances. Small hand drums, usually about or foot or so in diameter, accompanied individual songs and healing prayers by a holy man. The Sioux also used rattles and flutes. Women did play hand drums. Flutes were used for courting.

The Sioux did not separate religious from secular activities as done in contemporary American society. For instance, drums were sacred objects treated with veneration because they were gifts of supernatural powers and echoed the heartbeat of the people. Songs were given to individuals or social/military/craft societies by supernatural beings. Sacred songs came from divinely inspired dreams and belonged to particular individuals or groups. They were property, and permission to use them was required. On the other hand, they were also used on social occasions. Some songs are quite playful and some are even used to tease. Drums were used for social dancing. The divine and secular were intermingled throughout Sioux culture.

Dancing was ubiquitous also. It was one of the aspects of Indian life that most non-Indian visitors mentioned repeatedly about the first contacts through the reservation era. As with songs, there were dances for celebration of events and particular religious ceremonies, and for just about every event that people celebrated. There were even dances for funerals, just as there were songs of mourning too.

Drumming and dancing were particular targets of missionaries and the American government as they ruled the Sioux after the reservations were established. American policy was to forbid traditional religion and the "savage, licentious" dancing that characterized tribal culture. However, Indian agents on Sioux and other tribal reservations found that dancing and singing were so ingrained in Sioux culture that laws could not eradicate the practices. Gradually, a kind of cautious tolerance allowed for Sioux to dance from time to time as a reward for good behavior.

Ironically, the tension between American goals and Sioux realities led to the creation of today's most characteristic expression of American Indian traditional cultures—the powwow. In Lakota, it is *Wacipi*. Briefly stated, the Sioux were able to take advantage of two desires of Americans to create the powwow. Agents needed to demonstrate that their charges were learning to farm and can vegetables and behave as civilized Americans. So agents decided to have the equivalent of county fairs where Indians would display their agricultural progress. At the same time, American communities wanted to feature Indians in their traditional regalia and dances at American celebrations like the Fourth of July parades and Wild West Shows. Sioux leaders agreed to participate as long as they were allowed to wear traditional clothing and dance. The Sioux got what they wanted in the guise of cooperation, and the *Wacipi* became a feature of Indian life from then until today. One of the largest Sioux powwows is the Rosebud Fair, an echo of its early reservation origins.

Wacipi (Powwows)

Powwows are the central feature of all Sioux people today. No matter how nearly assimilated to American culture or to Christianity or to secularism, almost every Sioux "powwows," as the saying goes. This does not only mean dancing in traditional regalia or drumming; it also means attending and socializing and absorbing the ambience of traditional cultural expression. Powwows are announced and songs sung in one of the Sioux dialects. Individuals are honored for their outfits that reflect traditional values and are often inspired by dreams. Contests stress doing dances the traditional way. The event is all one vast expression of Sioux traditional culture.

The basic powwow format that exists today is universal in Indian country and, to a large extent, was developed in the Southern Plains with particular contributions from the Kiowa and other southern plains cultures. However, the Sioux style has come to dominate powwows throughout the country, as many of the standard powwow songs are sung in Lakota, the regalia is borrowed from the Lakota example, and the preferred dance styles of the Lakota appear in powwows throughout America. Sioux and plains culture is so dominant at powwows that anyone who attends a powwow anywhere can understand it and find it familiar. One can see Indians in Virginia dressed as Plains Sioux as they powwow to the accompaniment of Sioux songs and Sioux-style drums.

Wacipi are either traditional or contests. Traditional powwows highlight the enjoyment of dancing and community participation. They are usually small, community events mainly attended by Sioux. Contest powwows are deliberate extravaganzas that seek to attract contestants from far and wide. Contestants vie for money, and many follow the intertribal powwow circuit throughout the season (lasting roughly from April through October). For the Sioux, the season often begins with the University of North Dakota Wacipi around the first of April and ends with the United Tribes Technical College Powwow the week after Labor Day. Nearly every Sioux reservation government funds a large powwow sometime during the season. Spirit Lake Nation wacipi takes place during the Fourth of July celebrations and Rosebud Fair is in August.

Powwows begin with a grand entry when all of the dancers, in regalia appropriate to their style of dancing, enter the arena. They are led by military veterans carrying the traditional eagle staff of the Sioux, the American flag, and often specific reservation flags as well as state and even Canadian banners. After dancing into the arena, the grand entry continues with a prayer in one of the Sioux dialects and the posting of the colors.

Dance categories include men's and women's Traditional Dance, Jingle Dress, Grass Dance, Men's Fancy Dance, and Women's Shawl Dance.

The Fancy Dance is a major style of dancing at powwows. It was adapted from southern tribes and is for young, vigorous men who celebrate Indian cultures through dance. (Nativestock.com/Marilyn Angel Wynn)

Sometimes there are other categories, but all powwows have the main categories. Categories are further subdivided into age groupings for competition. Large powwows start with a grand entry on Friday evening, two grand entrys on Saturday, and one or two on Sunday. Obviously, this configuration allows for the modern workweek. The social aspects of the powwow are enhanced by camping near the grounds by families and dancers and those just wanting to powwow. Audiences include both Indians and non-Indians. Contest powwows, in particular, are usually advertised. Vendors offer goods from the traditional Indian tacos (fried bread and taco fixings) to Hmong craftwork, but the emphasis is on Indian-related craftwork, music, and clothing.

Many other cultural events have been folded into the powwow time periods, particularly those on reservations or within an Indian community in urban areas. Giveaways, feeds, naming ceremonies, rodeos, athletic tournaments, road runs, college graduations, courting, and even wellness activities are often part of the general powwow activities. In the late evenings, socializing and often spontaneous dancing to "forty-niner" songs like "John Wayne's Teeth" are common throughout the camps that surround powwow grounds. Forty-niners are playful party songs often in English but the music is Indian. Songs are sometimes graphic expressions of courtship styles or parodies of nearly any subject.

Giveaways

Generosity is one of the cardinal virtues of Sioux culture as it is with other American Indian cultures. Giveaways are public demonstrations of generosity. They provide a means of honoring an individual's accomplishments, the important stages in a family's history, and respect for community. For example, when a student graduates, the family will often give away items such as blankets, beadwork, food, and many others. Sometimes specific people are recipients, and other times, the family will simply invite any attending the event to select items that have been accumulated by the family and displayed in the powwow arena. Giveaways usually occur in the mornings and during breaks in dancing. Sometimes giveaways are stand-alone events, invitation gatherings of community taking place when someone wants to honor an elder or a graduate or a returning soldier.

Naming Ceremonies

Naming ceremonies have become popular additions to powwows, but, as with giveaways, these can be events for just family and friend too. Until the 1930s, these ceremonies were prohibited by the BIA, and so a hint of defiance of the larger society is an underlying theme. Most Sioux parents who wish to see that a child receives "an Indian name" will offer tobacco to a traditional elder who will seek spiritual guidance in selecting a name. Naming is done publicly and is usually accompanied by a giveaway because the event marks an affirmation of traditional identity. Traditionally, Sioux had several names during their lifetime; at least one was somewhat private and one was of general usage, so a legal name and an Indian name are consistent with Sioux culture. Some Sioux will change their names legally to affirm tribal nationalism.

Feeds

"Feeds," a reservation usage derived from feast, are another expression of generosity combined with respect and honoring. At various times, sometimes for powwows, families will invite community members to come and eat. As with other modern events, feeds are rooted in traditional culture. Anytime an event needed to be celebrated, the family provided food for guests, and special celebrations meant feeding the entire community. Today, the most common vehicle are the "feeds" at powwows. Generally, a family pledges to provide a meal for all that attend a powwow.

Feeds are also common during many other ceremonies. Another variant of the feed is the banquet that is part of the commemoration of the death of a member of the family. Usually, after one year, mourning is completed with a memorial dinner. Sometimes these are punctuated with Give-Aways too. Frequently, a son or daughter will sponsor a feed to honor a parent or a grandparent. Just as with other ceremonies, these commemorative and celebratory meals are not observed by every Sioux nor by every Sioux family, but they are common features of contemporary Sioux culture.

Most feeds include traditional foods as a reminder to all that there is continuity over the generations and that the family sponsoring the feed is connected with the traditional culture. As is customary, food is set aside as an offering to supernatural Beings before it is distributed to people.

OTHER HOLIDAYS AND CELEBRATIONS

Sioux societies readily participate in holidays common to all Americans. Labor Day, Veterans Day, Thanksgiving, Christmas, New Year, Easter, Memorial Day, and the Fourth of July are usually noted with appropriate festivities. Some reservations also mark special holidays that are part of one religion or another. Specific Sioux observances that are analogous include the anniversary of the Battle of the Little Big Horn for the Lakota and the anniversary of the Executions of Dakota patriots at Mankato. Since 1996, an annual Big Foot Memorial Ride retraces the route taken by Big Foot in 1890. Horseriders begin on Big Foot's Cheyenne Reservation and ride for several days to Wounded Knee, Pine Ridge Reservation, arriving on December 29, the date of the massacre. This memorial event is marked by pipe ceremonies to renew the Sacred Hoop of Lakota culture that are held at the site of the massacre.

RECREATION AND GAMES

In traditional times, Sioux adults and children played numerous games. Much of the play consisted of gender-specific imitations of adults. Girls played house and crafts, and boys played grown-up hunters and warriors. Some of the specific games were shinny, snake, double ball, lacrosse, hoop and pole, and ball juggling. Shinny is similar to field hockey and was played by children and adults of both genders. Snake was a winter game that included sliding a long stick across the snow by tossing it underhanded. The winner sent the stick the farthest. Lacrosse, or ball, was played by the Dakota and is similar to the game of the same name played today. Lacrosse matches were played with large teams and often featured one Dakota community against another or as a competition with teams from other tribes. Hoop and pole was played with a hoop made from willow and leather webbing. The object was to cast the hoop and then throw a wooden shaft at it. Ball juggling is similar to hacky sack but used a hide ball stuffed with fur or grass.

Gambling accompanied games, and many observers described high stakes games where individuals bet nearly everything they owned, including horses, tipis, guns, blankets, and so on. Bets were especially high in dice games, moccasin games, and hand games. These games were played by all, but the serious betting was when adults played each other and even teams from other communities. Dice games used carved bone or marked stones. Generally, these were cast in an effort to create patterns. Those familiar with craps would quickly understand the dice games.

Moccasin and hand games involve hiding tokens and guessing where the tokens are hidden. One person would hide a marker in a moccasin and play a game similar to three-card monte. Hand games were played by teams of designated hiders of the object and designated guessers. As with all other facets of Sioux life, games involved prayer and religious ritual. For instance, there were hand game songs accompanied by hand drums that were sung to provoke opponents' confusion opponents and help one's team. Often shamans used special prayers to gain an advantage over the other team.

Although most of the games have been replaced by computer games and other outdoor games common to all Americans, the gambling games maintain their place alongside bingo, poker, and blackjack. The high plains cultures, in particular, features hand game tournaments that last for days and include most of the tribes. Woodlands cultures still feature moccasin games more often but all of the Sioux play each of the games.

Sioux reservation cultures have absorbed the larger American interest in sporting events. Not only do tribal schools compete in high school conferences and for statewide titles, but post-school athletic events are common too. The most popular sport is basketball, and "rezball," as it is known today, is played and followed by all. All-Indian tournaments bring competing teams together, often at a major off-reservation venue like Rapid City. Fans of high school teams are as rabidly enthusiastic as any in the larger society. Whole reservations seem empty when tribal schools are participating in district, regional, and state playoffs or tournaments.

Outdoor activities included demonstrations of horse riding, horse and foot races, target shooting (both arrows and bullets), and wrestling. Today, many Sioux cowboys and cowgirls are rodeo devotees. Many have become world champions and are members the Rodeo Hall of Fame. Phil Baird, a Lakota, is a well-known supporter of rodeos as well as the Hall of Fame. On Pine

Ridge, the Herman family has produced renowned rodeo competitors. The Valandry family from Rosebud Reservation raises rodeo stock.

CLOTHING

During traditional times, each of the Sioux subdivisions wore clothing that resembled that of the tribes in their areas. Buckskin was a primary material for the Dakota, while bison provided hides for the plains Sioux. Elk and antelope hides were used by all of the tribes, as were beaver, marten, ermine, fisher, muskrat, and feathers from many different birds. Dyed quillwork decorated leather clothing. Dakota were likely to quill in the same style used by the Chippewa and Winnebago, and plains tribes used motifs similar to the other plains tribes. Tanned hides were often painted and might include pictorial representation of a man's deeds on his buffalo robe, for instance. Tipis were decorated similarly for the Teton-Lakota and Yankton.

Sioux men, in particular, added personal embellishments to the standard clothing of long fringed shirts, breechcloths or kilts, leggings, and moccasins. Women demonstrated their skill in decorating their men's clothing and accoutrements. Painted shields, pipe bags, and decorated quirts were additional artifacts that lent themselves to decorations. Sometimes men wore special painted designs that had been revealed to them in dreams and "become" part of the individual's power. Women operated in more restrictive styles distinguished by personal beading or quilling. Of course, all of the ceremonial clothing was not worn all of the time. There were work clothes and special occasion clothes.

Dakota women wore shoulder straps, and Yankton women used side seam dresses. Lakota women wore two skins sewn together and then added a third to provide a cape-like yoke. For special occasions, the yokes were decorated with quills, elk teeth, and dentalium shells. Even after blue wool and cotton cloth were introduced, the styles that had been produced in leather were maintained. Blankets came from the Hudson Bay Company and its imitators, like Pendleton. Hairpipes were used after about 1800 by most of the Sioux after they made their way westward from where the New York Dutch had first invented them.

Sioux clothing styles experienced a florescence of creativity when European and American goods were added to indigenous materials. European wools using commercial dyes became common attire for dresses, shirts, leggings, and the ubiquitous blankets. The use of European-manufactured beads allowed for more creativity than quillwork and the Lakota, in particular, became famous throughout the plains for their colorful geometric designs that decorated nearly everything from saddles to quivers to articles of clothing to moccasins.

As with all other facets of Sioux culture, religion played a role in clothing. Eagle feathers were sacred and wearing them in the traditional headdresses indicated a man's status, and decorations like ermine skins and beadwork demonstrated a woman's skill. Interestingly, the iconic war bonnet of 30 or 40 eagle feathers, featured in all stereotypes, probably was created by Crow and Missouri Valley tribes about 1800 or so. During the nineteenth century, a kind of heraldry developed to signify different war honors. The Dakota eventually adopted the war bonnet, but in their Minnesota homeland, they wore feathers attached to a band so they would stand upright. Male warrior societies had special items of clothing or decoration that marked them as members.

Although reservation restrictions encouraged Sioux to "dress white," as BIA agents stated in their annual reports cataloging their success at getting Sioux to assimilate, the skills involved in making traditional clothing did not disappear. Fortunately, one can attend any powwow and see the pre-reservation styles as well as the adaptations that modern materials make possible. Women's shawl dancers, for instance, wear colors never seen by their ancestors and clothing made from materials like Lycra. However, the traditional men and women dancers try to re-create the styles of the past and usually use materials that their ancestors would have recognized.

When away from powwows, Sioux dress in the styles that are common around them. On the plains, jeans, cowboy boots, and cowboy hats are favored, along with western shirts. Buckles on the boots might be beaded, but they are still cowboy boots. Many Sioux simply wear whatever the chain stores are featuring, however. Sweats and running shoes are very much in vogue. Women usually wear clothes that resemble male clothing, only in more feminine variations. Dresses and formal attire are not common . . . just for special occasions as in the larger society.

FOOD

The Sioux traditional diet was similar to their neighbors. One difficulty in reconstructing traditional recipes is that commerce has continuously introduced new foods and condiments. For instance, fur traders brought sugar, salt, and coffee to the Sioux diet. After the reservations were established, canned goods and flour joined the buffalo, venison, prairie turnips, wild rice, and berries as food. Beef and pork replaced wild game as staples by the twentieth century, although the Sioux continued to hunt and fish up through the present. In the twentieth century, most Indians were eligible for commodities from the U.S. Department of Agriculture. Commodity foods such as cheese became popular throughout Indian country. Canned ham, beans, butter, lard, canned fruit, and other high-carbohydrate, high-fat foods made up most of the commodity foods. Since 2000, the federal program has sent fresh vegetables and fruits in an effort to reduce obesity.

Traditional cooking was limited by the absence of stoves, so pots were used to provide a basic soup to which many ingredients were added. The Dakota used birchbark containers before pots were available. As long as there is water in a birchbark container, it will not burn. The Lakota often used buffalo stomachs for cooking.

During the pre-reservation days, the main Sioux food was soup. Nearly anything could be cooked in birchbark dishes, buffalo stomachs, and the trade pots that arrived with the fur traders. Sioux preferred to keep the pot on all day and to eat when they were hungry. Traditionally, any successful hunter's wife served feasts for a few or many depending on how much meat was available. Visitors were always fed. Generosity was expected of all. For the Sioux as with other tribal cultures, when some ate, all ate.

The Dakota ate venison as their staple meat but added any other animal to the larder as available. Fish, ducks, other birds, beaver tails, and whatever else could be trapped became ingredients in soup. The Dakota added the local roots, berries, and wild rice that were common. They joined their relatives in eating buffalo as they moved west, particularly after the 1863 Dakota Wars. The Yankton and Dakota ate fish, grew corn, beans, squash and sunflowers. Lakota foods included bison tripe and edible parts of the buffalo plus prairie dogs, antelope, deer, and elk. They also gathered fruits such as buffalo berries and added prairie turnips and other vegetables from the seasonably available cornucopia.

Sioux also ate dogs in their regular diet and for ceremonial purposes. Another staple was dried meat (*papa*) and pemmican. Pemmican was a mixture of dried meat and fat enclosed in a case. It was a basic food for traveling and storage through the winter. Fur trade companies bought pemmican in large quantities from Sioux and other tribal manufacturers.

The fur trade introduced sugar, coffee, candy, and even canned food by the end of the nineteenth century. The Dakota were the first to combine native farm products with wheat, chicken, eggs, pork, and beef. Aside from a food obtained through a continued effort at hunting, fishing, and gathering where land was still available, Dakota diets resembled those of the American immigrants.

After the reservations were established, buffalo and large quantities of other game animals were no longer available. The Sioux were reduced to eating cattle and pork and other rations provided by the United States as part of their trust responsibility. Rations were eliminated before World War I. United States Department of Agriculture commodities arrived on the reservation and became the source of most household foods after World War II. Many researchers have concluded that diets high in fat, sodium, and starch have contributed to the many health problems on Sioux reservations. Grim jokes about "commod bods" are common throughout Sioux country.

Commodity foods and earlier flour rations accompanied by lard enabled widespread development of frybread. Indian tacos, essentially fried bread with added baking power in some recipes, have become a pan-Indian food. Every reservation, none more so than the Sioux reservations, has frybread and Indian tacos. Other staples of modern Sioux diets include *wojapi,* which is a kind of fruit pudding and many kinds of soups. The traditional foods are available now that buffalo herds are common on reservations. However, they are available mainly for such special occasions as funeral wakes, feeds, pow-wows, giveaways, and other ceremonies. Other than at special occasions, Sioux eat the same foods as most Americans. Some fast food chains have even reached reservation communities directly.

Sioux Recipes

Wild Rice

This was a staple product for the Dakota but not available to the plains-dwelling Lakota and Yankton unless they bought it. Boil one part (a cup) of wild rice, after rinsing it, to four parts of water. The rice should boil about 45 minutes. Some put salt in, and others wait until the cooked rice is served to add salt. Generally, wild rice is served in a stew.

Frybread

After reservations, Sioux received large quantities of flour from which they crafted the basic food for all Indian country. Frybread in many different forms are featured at powwows as well as in any feed that purports to be traditional Indian. Basic ingredients are 3 cups of flour mixed with 1 tablespoon each of sugar, salt, and baking powder. After blending the ingredients, knead $1^1/_2$ cups of water into the mix. After allowing the mix to set for about 25 minutes, roll the dough out to about $1^1/_2$-inch strips, with a hole punched in the middle. Boil $1^1/_2$ cups of lard or butter with 3–5 cups of cooking oil. When the oil is hot, cook the dough like a doughnut. Drain each piece and serve.

Indian Tacos

Make larger pieces of frybread and then add chopped tomatoes, lettuce, cooked beans, and tomato sauce along with commodity cheese and sour cream. Many like to add hot sauce to taste. Indian tacos became widespread after World War II and are now a common meal at homes and occasions such as wows.

Blueberry Wojapi (Sometimes Called Pudding)

This is a post-reservation dish that harkens back to traditional fruit soup. Put blueberries in a saucepan and add 3 cups of water, 1 cup of sugar, and 3/4 cup of flour. Boil. Can be eaten hot or cold and is often dipped up with frybread.

Chokecherry Pemmican

Take one pound of dried meat (buffalo, moose, venison, elk), wrap in a canvas cloth, pound with a rock until it is has powdery consistency. Add chokecherries (or other fruit) to the meat and pound some more. Add 1 cup of sugar and 1 cup of lard and knead until you get a the meat has the consistency of ground beef. Roll into balls and eat with fingers.

Pemmican and Wild Rice

Cut pemmican (dried meat—usually buffalo) into half-inch strips. Put the strips in a pot with salt and spices, cover with water, and simmer. Add rice and use the liquid to cook it. Then add cattail shoots and stems or prairie turnips.

Buffalo Stew

Fill a large pot with water and drop prairie turnips (*timsila* in Lakota) into the simmering pot along with chunks of buffalo meat. Season with whatever spices are available.

MEDICINAL HERBS

In traditional times, Sioux healers were keenly aware of the medicinal value of many plants. As with all of Sioux culture, use of homeopathic medicine was imbued with religious-sacred meaning. Generally, the properties of herbs and the ceremonies that activated them were passed on from one healer to another. Sioux belief held that herbs did not work unless the proper prayer and ritual was done. Healers, called medicine men by Americans, were *wakan wicasa* (holy men) in each of the Sioux dialects. Women were also healers. In addition to learning through apprenticeship, holy men's and healers' dreams conveyed healing powers and, often, instruction on how to use particular plants. Some plants were widely used, and others were restricted to use by the person who dreamed of them.

Sage is used in most ceremonies today as well as in traditional times. It grows throughout the western reservations. It is burned like incense and helps in purification and clearing of the mind. For medicinal purposes, Sage leaves are boiled to ameliorate upset stomachs and cold. Sweet grass is also used for purification when burned. Sweat lodge, Sun Dance and Yuwipi ceremonies feature sweet grass, and it is used to purify or "smudge" areas and even rooms where bad things have happened. Some do use it like incense, just because its odor is pleasant. Most Sioux get their sweet grass from Montana, Wyoming, or Canada.

Mint tea alleviates colds and makes a pleasant tea. Puffballs serve as a styptic for wounds, and its spores were used as diapers for infants. The purple coneflower, echinacea, is an antidote for snakebite, and its roots to alleviate toothaches. Other uses of the coneflower include washing away poison ivy skin eruptions.

Sioux healers used hundreds of plants, but they also were aware of other means to care for wounds, broken bones, and other common ailments. Today, most Sioux utilize hospitals and drugs like the rest of Americans but often add a Sioux variation. The Indian Health Service (I.H.S.) first rejected all of the Sioux and other Indian treatments but has come to respect the knowledge, including the validity of prayer, as a means to treat the whole patient. Holy men (medicine men) are commonly available in I.H.S. facilities and usually are treated somewhat like chaplains. Many Sioux prefer to consult traditional healers first, and many others reject the old ways altogether.

Turn of the century portrait of Fool Bull, a Sioux medicine man holding a medicine shield and wearing a bear claw necklace. (Library of Congress)

Traditional healing emphasized the whole person and his or her community when determining a treatment. Drawing on this idea, treatment programs with specific traditional ceremony and values have been developed. One program of treatment for alcohol or drug abuse that has been widely adopted is the Red Road Approach developed by Gene Thin Elk. Thin Elk uses traditional teachings and ceremonies to convince addicts to move away from their addictions through traditional prayer and help from extended family members. The White Buffalo Calf Woman Society, which helps women who have been abused, also incorporates traditional ceremonies and beliefs in an effort to restore the balance of life for these victims of abuse.

Unfortunately, Sioux societies of today are plagued by ill health. Even before the reservations, pandemics introduced by Europeans and Americans devastated many Sioux communities. Even the Lakota Winter Counts picture smallpox and cholera. After the reservation, poor rations and miserable living conditions led to epidemics like tuberculosis and, today's epidemic, diabetes compounded by obesity. Traditional and modern health practices are hardly able to reduce the effects of generations of poor health.

STORIES AND ORAL TRADITIONS

The Sioux provided education and entertainment for adults and children through storytelling. Some stories were just about the community and what happened. Others were stories about heroes, particularly warriors, and others were told just for entertainment. Collectively, stories are a way to explain the world, educate the young, and provide a common background for all Sioux.

Sacred stories related how the supernatural worked and how cultural creation occurred. These were told only at night and after the first frost because the words themselves were powerful and if evil Beings such as snakes overheard them, this could endanger the community. Today, these stories, like that of the White Buffalo Calf Woman, are written, and Sioux culture no longer maintains prohibitions about when to tell sacred stories. Given contemporary availability through books, movies, and recordings, stories are not told the same way or as frequently as they used to be. Children are more likely to read them in school than they are to hear them in community story sessions.

There are numerous collections of Sioux stories dating back to pre-reservation and early reservation collectors. Authenticity is a problematic concept because the very nature of storytelling demands variations depending on the time available, the purpose for telling the story, the band whose version is being collected, and the culture of the collector. For instance, many Americans who collected stories as well as the Indians who wrote them down had to amend the somewhat earthy, frank stories to conform to the sensibilities of Victorian prudishness. Another problem is that the Sioux had a different narrative style than Americans, so direct translations sometimes do not sound like narratives. For this reason, they were modified to comply with American ideas of how a story should be told. Problems of style and sensibility can be overcome, and oral traditions remain an important vehicle for understanding traditional Sioux culture.

Other stories are instructional, serving as reminders to adults and education for children about how to behave, how things came to be the way they are, and what is proper cultural behavior. Often, these stories are about Iktomi (the Spider) who is a supernatural Being who exhibits the follies of selfishness, disrespect, pride, and the like. His failures in the story come about because he violates cultural values. Iktomi is what anthropologists call a Trickster figure. Most cultures have Tricksters in their own oral traditions. Iktomi is sometimes a creator of good things too, and sometimes he benefits the Sioux people. Most often, he is an example of what not to do.

The stories below are the author's versions borrowed from various collections and adaptations. They are far more fun when told aloud with proper voices and gestures to enliven them.

Sacred Stories—Two Examples

After, or perhaps before or at the same time, that Inyan created the earth and humans and White Buffalo Calf Woman brought Sioux culture to the people, Buffalo ate people and the various four-legged and two-legged creatures did not know how they were to behave—which creatures would be food for the others or which creatures would support the others. Much remained to be determined in the new world where animals and people could talk to one another.

The Great Race

Creator noticed confusion, so he sent Crow to summon all living creatures to the Black Hills. The Creator said that a race would decide whether buffalo or humans were to serve the other and become food. He had Crow summon all of the living creatures to the Black Hills and decreed that if buffalo won the race around the Black Hills, they would rule humans. The Sioux picked a young man who was strong and fast, while the buffalo chose a young cow who was the swiftest of all of the buffalo. The other living creatures chose representative fast runners too. All of the four leggeds joined the buffalo's side, and the birds aligned with the humans because both were two legged. Wolf signaled the start of the race, and hundreds soon churned up enough dust as they ran to create the Milky Way. Magpie immediately landed on buffalo's back while the others ran on and on. Gradually, all dropped out because they were distracted, like rabbit when he saw coyote running close to him, or because they grew too tired, like meadowlark. No one noticed the magpie. Gradually, the man dropped behind and it appeared that the weary buffalo would win. Within sight of the finish line, Magpie, who was fresh, soared up toward the sun and dived across the line just ahead of the buffalo. Magpie's reward for winning for the two leggeds was to have the sun's light embedded in his feathers, and this is why today all magpies are iridescent. The race determined that man would be the hunter while buffalo supplied food, clothing, shelter, and many other helpful things. Other animals would also provide materials for the Sioux. Humans would always respect the animals for their sacrifices. This was the way it would be because it was meant to be. (Thos narrative is adapted from Paul Goble's *The Great Race of the Birds and the Animals,* which is also an adaptation of several recorded versions of the Lakota story.)

The Origin of the Medicine Dance

The Creator noticed that people were sick and dying because they had no way of healing themselves, either of physical ailments or spiritual illnesses. He descended on a rainbow to create, from part of his body, two underwater monsters (*Unktehi*), one male and one female. These monsters floated on an endless sea, but the female, who seemed smarter than her male counterpart, decided to create the Earth. First, she sent Loon to dive for earth but Loon died. Then Otter and Grebe failed as well. Muskrat dove for the bottom and then, after a long time, floated to the top. He was clutching earth, which the female underwater monster turned into the Earth. The two monsters breathed on their sacred roots and brought the dead animals back to life. The monsters then summoned all of the animals and birds. They taught them the sacred Medicine Dance and songs and the use of shells to inject magic into the bodies of the afflicted. The birds and animals then taught the humans. Ever afterward, the people who danced and sang would be able to heal the dead and ill. The monsters settled into the earth and healing herbs grew from their bodies. (Adapted from a retelling by Amos One Road in *Being Dakota.*)

Iktomi Stories—Two Examples

The Trickster is the subject of hundreds of stories that illustrate creativity and larger-than-life human foibles. Sometimes, he even committed the most grievous violations of Sioux values. There are stories of Iktomi marrying his mother or his sister or his sister-in-law. His reward is to suffer untold pain and to be banished from the people. Iktomi is always alone, always hungry, always selfish, always cheating. Two of the more popular stories today have Iktomi displaying foolishness and pride.

Iktomi and the Boulder

One day Iktomi was walking along (all Iktomi stories begin this way). He was dressed in his finest clothes. Beadwork decorated his vest and moccasins and fine quillwork gave color to his shirt, which was done in the finest of elk skin. His buffalo robe was so white that it was almost like cotton, and it was painted with Ikotmi's imagined glorious deeds. His hair was braided with otter skin tails hanging from the braids, and his headdress was covered with eagle feathers signifying the great deeds he thought he had done. His face was painted with the shiniest of paints. Iktomi looked beautiful as he walked toward the next town. Along the way, he noticed animals watching him and thought to himself how envious they must be (they were actually making jokes about this silly, vain man). But soon it grew hot, and Iktomi wondered why he had brought his blanket. He noticed a great boulder alongside the trail and said, "Little brother boulder, you look exposed, so I will give you my blanket to give you shade." As Iktomi walked farther, clouds appeared, and the wind increased the chill in the air. Iktomi decided he had made a mistake, but what was he to do? A gift cannot be taken back—that is too disrespectful. Iktomi returned to the rock and took his blanket back, but Rock growled at this show of disrespect. As Iktomi walked away, a storm came and with it a great rumbling like thunder, but Iktomi looked back to realize that Rock was chasing him. He ran and he ran and he ran, but no matter how fast he ran, nor how many streams he jumped, Iktomi could not get away. Finally, Rock caught him, rolled on top of Iktomi, and stopped. No matter how much he squirmed and wriggled, Iktomi could not escape. Soon he called to a passing buffalo, "Little brother" (a sign of disrespect), come and help me! The buffalo had better manners than Iktomi, so he tried to push the boulder away, but neither the buffalo nor other animals could free Iktomi. As night fell, the animals abandoned Iktomi because they had to go home. Bats arrived, and Iktomi thought of a plan. "Little brothers," he called, "This boulder has been saying you are not sure whether you are an animal or a bird—he called you a furry bird! He said you're so stupid that you sleep upside down! I tried to tell him he was wrong, so he got angry and rolled on top of me." The furious bats gathered in the thousands and dashed their noses against the boulder. Each time a bat's nose hit the rock, a small piece was chipped off until all that was left of the boulder was pebbles. Iktomi was freed at last. The weary Iktomi looked at his torn and bespattered finery and trudged homeward. Pride, arrogance, and disrespect led to his humiliation and injuries. You can still see that bat has a short, square nose and that

Boulder is now scattered across the plains. (Adapted from an adaptation by Paul Goble).

Iktomi and the Ducks

One day Iktomi was walking along and he was hungry. He heard a great commotion and peeked over the hill to see ducks gathered near the lake but too far away to shoot with his bow. So he came up with a scheme. Iktomi left his bow behind but brought a bag with him. He walked up to the ducks who watched him warily even if he was unarmed—after all, he was Iktomi. As he walked, Iktomi hummed quietly to himself, and the ever-curious ducks wondered what he was singing and what he had in the bag. "Just some new songs— you know, I could teach you, but these songs require a special dance too. First, you need to form a circle and then close your eyes while I play and sing. If you open your eyes, the power will be lost, and your eyes will turn red." The ducks, always looking for a new ceremony, followed the instructions and, with their eyes closed, they danced to Iktomi's drum and song. As each duck passed in front of Iktomi, it was strangled and stuffed in the sack. Soon a loon who had joined the dance grew suspicious and opened his eyes. His alarm sent the ducks scurrying away, but Iktomi had already captured some ducks. Later, Iktomi roasted the ducks in the ground, went to sleep, and woke to find that Fox had stolen his ducks. Iktomi was still hungry. (Based on a Dakota story collected by Amos One Road and many others.)

ART

Most cultures that are as mobile as the pre-reservation Sioux concentrated their artistic endeavors on beautiful decorations of functional artifacts. Pipe bowls were carved into many sacred shapes, clothing was quilled with dyed porcupine and bird quills, dressed skins displayed art, and many, particularly buffalo and elk, robes were painted. Tipi covers were decorated with the war accomplishments of the husbands and sons of the woman who owned the covers though men did the actual painting. Women earned honor and membership in beading/quilling sororities as they established their art. Almost everything was turned into a work of art for special occasions and to honor the people to whom they were given. When the Europeans brought new goods like dyes, face paint, and wool along with their demand for beautifully made products, the Sioux responded. Men decorated their horses and used them to display their military accomplishments in pictographs. However, the Sioux did not make a distinction between artifacts and functional craftwork as opposed to creative art in the same way that Westerners did.

High Hawk, a Brule Sioux historical authority, wears ceremonial warrior dress: scalp shirt, leggings, moccasins, and pipe bag—all embroidered with porcupine quills—and an eagle feather war bonnet and stone-headed war club. Photo taken by Edward S. Curtis, ca. 1907. (Historic Print & Map Company)

Once the reservations were established and the Sioux had to live in fixed houses, art was evolved that reflected the influence of Americans and Canadians. Many objects were made specifically to sell, but since most non-Indians wanted authentic work to serve as beautiful souvenirs, Sioux artists tended to portray pre-reservation styles. Of course, those Lakota who went to art schools or who were exposed to European-American art education did utilize new media. Sculpture, oil painting, watercolors, leatherwork, and abstract designs appeared in the twentieth century. Quilting was introduced to Sioux women by wives of missionaries and teachers and the Sioux used traditional Sioux motifs to make quilts. Today, star quilts are seen as expressions of traditional culture and are often given away to commemorate major events or to honor someone like the teacher of a school graduate.

Portrait of a young Teton/Lakota woman dressed in deerskin embroidered with beads and porcupine quills. Photograph by Edward S. Curtis, ca. 1907. (Historic Print & Map Company)

Generally, traditional artists did not identify themselves. There were women's societies that invited accomplished artists to become members because of their demonstrated skill in beading, quilling, and tanning. These women were respected and well known throughout their communities. Since art critics and collectors have come to value traditional arts, some have made names for themselves in the larger society. Alice New Holy Blue Legs is widely praised for her quillwork, and she creates it with traditional colors and styles. However, many who preserve the old ways continue to be known only within their own communities.

Today, there are many Sioux artists who have national and international reputations. Oscar Howe was the first famous Sioux artist, and his work is a staple in any collection of Indian art. He pioneered a new school of Indian art and was criticized for deviating from the established norms of picturesque Indian art. He even provided the designs for the Corn Palace in Mitchell, South Dakota, where he was an art teacher at Wesleyan College for decades.

A modern rendition in the traditional style of a buffalo hunt. It is a portion of the mural that depicts Teton/Lakota historic life. Arthur Amiotte is one of the leading Teton/Lakota artists and an historian of culture and art. His works are internationally collected. (The Art Archive / Buffalo Bill Historical Center, Cody, Wyoming / NA.302,102)

Daniel Long Soldier's murals and paintings of traditional scenes were funded by the Works Progress Administration, and he is one of a long line of traditional style successful painters.

Just as Oscar Howe was faced with conforming to others' expectation of what Indian art must be, Sioux artists in the twenty-first century have a problem becoming fully recognized artists in their own rights. The American art world, and Americans in general, expect Sioux artists to express themselves through traditional Sioux subjects. They are not supposed to simply paint a landscape . . . it is expected to have a tipi in it or an Indian maiden. Portraits are supposed to have subjects adorned with feathers and beads. Even as early as the 1920s and 1930s, Oscar Howe was roundly criticized for not drawing according to American perceptions of what Indian art should look like. His sweeping, modernistic stylings were not well received until quite a while after his death. These expectations keep successful artists like Martin Red Bear painting two-dimensional figures like buffalo hide or ledger art. Typically, Sioux with an artistic bent learn that they should paint traditional scenes if they are to be accepted, even by other Sioux.

Arthur Amiotte has become not only a well-known artist whose style provides a twist on the traditional while remaining recognizably Indian, but he has also become an art historian. Vic Runnels has had a successful career using art to illustrate Oglala Lakota values. Rick Red Owl and Dwayne Wilcox are among many others who have achieved recognition in Indian art circles. Sioux artists are well represented at the South Dakota Art Museum in Brookings, south Dakota, at Akta Lakota Museum in Chamberlain, South Dakota, and the Journey in Rapid City, South Dakota. Reservation museums at St. Francis on Rosebud and Red Cloud School on Pine Ridge contain art ranging from the collectible to that designed to be souvenirs. Perhaps the largest collection of Sioux art from the traditional to the contemporary is found at the two sites of the National Museum of the American Indian's sites in Washington, D.C. and New York City.

8

The Sioux and Contemporary Issues

GENERAL OVERVIEW

FIFTEEN SIOUX RESERVATION governments with about 75,000 Sioux citizen-residents are joined in the twenty-first century by another 75,000 citizens who live off the reservations. Sioux nations clearly reflect the effects of history and legacies of past American policies. Traditional cultural patterns are ever present in modern Sioux communities, but these communities have adapted to the larger society as well.

Striking contrasts exist along the Sioux community spectrum. Casino-rich Dakota communities within Minnesota are challenged by cultural issues compounded by an urban setting, while economically poor Lakota societies are anchored in large rural reservations that offer an environment suitable for maintaining much of the traditional culture. Reservation populations range from a few hundred to thousands.

Despite immense variations from reservation to reservation, twenty-first century Sioux and their governments have to deal with the same basic issues. Some will do this more successfully than others, but the issues remain the same. Tribal people and governments have inherited the history of federal Indian policies that created the status of both reservations and people. Sioux reservations' issues are essentially the same as for all reservations.

Among the legacies are the Trust Responsibility of the United States toward Indian nations, the plenary power of Congress, the laws and regulations remaining from earlier times, incomplete sovereignty that perpetuates non-Indians ownership and exemption from tribal government for a significant portion of each reservation, and generations of poverty and unemployment. Other legacies that appear to be systemic are population growth that taxes limited resources, a brain drain similar to that experienced by rural areas, racism, and poverty.

Individual Sioux deal with the same questions that all American families and individuals do, but with the added concern of being Sioux and what that means to them. Religion, education, values, residence, career, marriage, and what it means to be a good, contributing member of society are decisions each Sioux and his or her family must make in every generation.

One decision that most Americans do not need to face is whether or not to practice traditional culture as well as one can in this century. Should one learn the ancestral language, believe in and practice traditional religion, live on the reservation where choices are limited, and remain distinct from the larger society? Alternatively, should one abandon the past as irrelevant and assimilate? The answers to these questions vary widely as each Sioux negotiates the present. Most occupy a kind of middle ground, partially faithful to tradition in beliefs and values and partially reflecting the values of the larger American society and the twenty-first century.

All tribal governments face the same issues, whether they represent wealthy or poor constituents. Perhaps the most obvious issue is sovereignty and jurisdiction. Others include economic development, effective governing, the legitimacy of tribal governments, state-tribal relations, Sioux cultural preservation and enhancement, the many dysfunctions induced by poverty, education, and quality of life for citizens. Sioux governments, like individual Sioux, are profoundly affected by the attitudes and expectations of the larger, dominant society.

American Indians make up only about 1 percent of the American population and reservations cover about 4 percent of the land mass within the United States. The Sioux constitute about .06 percent of the U.S. population, and they are scattered throughout more than 20 reservations and nearly every major city in the United States. Given the relatively small size of the Sioux population, it is obvious that continued political existence for the Sioux tribe is dependent on actions taken by the United States and greatly affected by public perceptions. American recognition of tribal sovereignty and interpretation of the Trust Responsibility is a precarious situation for all of Sioux country.

Most research concurs that most Americans picture the Sioux and other Indians as minority groups similar to African Americans or Mexican Americans and do not consider that they have real governments with real sovereignty. Sioux and Indians in general are expected to look like Indians and to act like Indians if they are to remain entitled to the unique status embodied in U.S. law. Many feel that if Indians "lose their culture," then they are not "real" Indians. This attitude revolves around a view of Indians as exotic—"not like us"—and discounts the constant changes taking place in Indian societies. These attitudes continue to affect the actions and possibilities for Sioux and their governments.

FACING STEREOTYPES

American Indians are described in stereotypes by many Americans. These stereotypes sometimes contradict one another, but they remain prevalent, clouding not only dominant society-Indian relations but inter-governmental relations as well. Some of the stereotypes are those applied to most ethnic minorities, particularly those with a high level of poverty, and some are uniquely related to the idea of Indian. Ironically, one of the stereotypes is that all Indians were like the Sioux—they wore feathered headdresses, fought valiantly against the United States, and lived on the plains where they hunted buffalo and lived in tipis while being one with nature.

It does not seem to matter that most of the stereotypes are easily refuted. People cling to them, anyway. The list below is based on the author's research among non-Indians over the past decade and draws upon several thousand samples. Stereotypes about Indians in the twenty-first century are mostly negative. Indians get a check each month, just for being Indian. The government gives Indians everything. Indians are poor because they are too lazy to work. Indian reservations are dangerous, lawless places. Indians do not have to follow "our" laws. Indians have special privileges that other Americans do not have. Indians have lost their culture and are just a bunch of whiners. Most Indians are not even really Indians—they have very little Indian "blood."

There are some stereotypes that reflect positive attitudes even if they are wrong.

- Indians have a special relationship to the earth and were the first ecologists.
- Indians are a very spiritual people, and Americans should be more like them.
- Indians have a special wisdom that allows them to tell the future, heal the sick, and change the laws of physics (they can make it rain).

Whether positive or negative, persistent stereotypes help shape federal legislation, actions by non-Indians, misunderstanding of reservation government actions by the general population, and even the actions of tribal governments. If present-day Indians do not act the way Indians acted in the nineteenth century, are they Indians? Many Americans would say no.

Blood Quantum

Attitudes, stereotypes, misinformation, and romantic views of Indians provide the framework for tribal government actions in the twenty-first century.

An example of the intermingling of dominant society beliefs about Indians and tribal government decisions is "blood quantum." Many Americans, including many Indians, cling to blood as a determinant of behavior and identity as an Indian. Until recently, even most scholars accepted the idea that somehow one's "blood" or phenotype determined one's behavior. Culture was believed to be conveyed to an individual through his or her genes; therefore, Indian blood determined what an Indian was. The idea of inheriting one's culture through bloodlines has been a dominant idea in most cultures for centuries, so its application to Indians was not surprising.

Americans as far back as Thomas Jefferson debated how much Indian blood one needed to be Indian. The belief was that it was difficult for "White" blood to overcome the dominance of Indian blood. Jefferson and others decided that 1/8 Indian blood could be overcome by 7/8 White blood to make a person White. By the early nineteenth century, government policies and treaties began to use 1/4 Indian blood as the smallest amount to make one Indian. Although this whole idea is scientifically unsupported, ignores the realities of historical intermixing of genes, and makes for really bad recordkeeping, the idea is buried deeply in American and American Indian assumption.

In the twenty-first century, Sioux constitutions require 1/4 Sioux blood quantum in order to be enrolled as citizens of the tribes. The Bureau of Indian Affairs accepts 1/4 as the necessary quantity for eligibility for Bureau services, unless a person is enrolled in a tribe. The catch is that all of the Sioux tribes require 1/4 blood. This racism ignores science and the reality that culture, phenotype, and legal status are mutually exclusive categories. If your parents are citizens, should you not be a citizen?

The blood quantum debate poses a major problem for Sioux governments. One scholar has estimated that the number of Sioux of 1/4 Sioux blood will be only about 40 percent of the population by about 2050. American Indians have the highest rate of marriage outside of their ethnic group of any American ethnic group. Since Sioux tribal constitutions include a blood quantum requirement, reservation governments will have to address this issue or watch as they are bred out of existence. The accompanying question is will the American government and American public accept a tribal solution based on something other than race?

JURISDICTION

One of the more pernicious colonial legacies is that tribal government jurisdiction is limited by the presence of large numbers of non-Indian landowners within the boundaries of reservations; these residents are not subject to tribal government law, and the privately owned land is almost entirely beyond the control of tribal government law. States have jurisdiction within reservations for instances in which illegal actions occurring on nontribal land (non-trust land) include only non-Indians, even if an incident occurs within the reservation.

Put another way, if a non-Indian commits a crime, his or her crime will fall under the jurisdiction of the state. Even if that non-Indian commits the crime on Indian land or against an Indian, he or she will be subject to federal, not tribal, jurisdiction. Tribal governments are not even in control of what happens within their own boundaries. This situation is a legacy of the Allotment Act and of federal court decisions denying tribal court jurisdictions over non-Indians.

State governments have consistently tried to control reservations because the states believe that the reservations are part of the state and because all Indians are citizens of the state in which they live. As one bumper sticker puts it, "This land is your land, this land is my land, that is why we spend so much time in court." Federal courts and Congress have not been able to avoid conflicting jurisdiction; in fact, they have often contributed to it. For instance, Dakota communities in Minnesota are subject to state law because Congress delegated responsibilities to the communities mainly to the state back in 1953.

Clouded and disputed jurisdictions among the tribes, the states, and the federal government affect tribal efforts to maintain effective government. If a tribe needs to raise revenue through taxation, do non-Indians living or working on the reservation have to pay them? Can a zoning law passed by a tribal council include non-Indian owned property within the reservation? How can law enforcement be effective when tribal police cannot investigate some people and enter some property? These kinds of questions often have to be answered in federal courts. Sioux governments spend a disproportionate amount of money on legal issues involving jurisdiction over land or people.

POVERTY AND HEALTH CONCERNS

Poverty is the dominant feature of Sioux reservations. Tribal governments are faced with the reality that their populations require a major commitment on the part of social services, in the short run, and economic development as a long-term solution to the problems caused by pervasive poverty. All but the casino-rich reservations have unemployment rates that range from 35 percent to as high as 65 percent. Generations of Indian adults grew up without the opportunity to work because reservations had no private economy. After the 1960s, opportunities arrived on the reservations through Office of Economic Opportunity programs, and an economy that was federal grant driven offered employment. As more Indians received higher education, jobs opened in the Bureau of Indian Affairs and in education, but overall employment remains high (35–45%) because there are more Indians than jobs.

Poverty has led to broken families, alcoholism, drug addiction, violence, high crime rates, and a constant struggle to be able to live a good life. A comparison to the larger American society is to areas like Newark, New Jersey, or the Appalachian region. The difference is that Sioux reservations are entire societies and not "just" pockets of poverty amidst states that have greater resources. Also, most of the productive land and what private economy exists typically belong to non-Indians who do not contribute to Sioux societies—their taxes go to the state or to the United States.

American Indians, including the Sioux, have a life expectancy of about 10 years less than the general population, and this has been an improvement during the last 20 years. Health problems associated with poverty not only produce individual tragedies but also drain resources from each reservation. Diabetes is an epidemic, as is obesity. Funds for Indian health care are less than what the United States pays for prison inmates' medical needs. Suicide rates are twice that of the general population.

In response, tribal governments are using casino and other tribal income to supplement appropriations for the Indian Health Service, a division since 1956 of the National Health Service. Many of the Sioux reservations have also contracted to administer their own programs and have collaborated with Public Health to focus more on prevention. Social services provided by tribal governments are part of U.S. public policy. For instance, assistance to elders (senior citizens), the new food stamps, public housing, commodities, and other federally funded programs are administered by tribal governments according to federal guidelines. Social workers operate on reservations as they do in the rest of the United States.

Since the 1970s, non-government organizations have been developed to work with social agencies and organizations such as the Casey Foundation to provide services. The White Buffalo Calf Woman Society now operates on many Sioux reservations. Its purpose is to assist abused women and children. The Society also tries to use Sioux values and religion to provide a foundation for healing. Society members contribute to public information campaigns that use the message "Abuse is not traditional" to frame their work in traditional ways. The Red Road approach to dealing with alcoholism, drug abuse, and other dysfunctional behavior was developed by an individual but has blossomed into a widely used approach, particularly on the Lakota Sioux reservations. In the Red Road approach, individuals and their families participate in ceremonies of restoration and purification such as the sweat lodge in order to try to use family values to make a family's world whole. The Red

Road is seen as the path of living in a good way as described in Sioux oral histories.

Social needs are far greater than the available funds. Tribal governments cobble together funds and programs to meet community needs. These needs remain a constant challenge because most of the Sioux reservations are impoverished. More than half of all Indians, including Sioux, live below the poverty line. Sioux tribes and the federal government have tried to deal with poverty through economic development. The federal programs of the 1970s and 1980s were failures.

Some scholars indicate that the federal programs tried to use "one size fits all" approaches and were directed by bureaucrats who did not understand economic development. Tax breaks to businesses don't work either in the face of an undertrained labor force that is more expensive than Taiwanese workers or in areas without infrastructure and housing for managers and specialists. Federal program impacts were limited by assumptions that reservations were like state economies, and the implementation of grants only provided a year or two of funding after which the tribal government was supposed to pick up the funding. Tribal governments did not have revenue for picking up start up businesses. Although Sioux reservations were soon littered with closed arrow factories, electronic assembly businesses, and motels without any draw for tourists to use them, some businesses did develop and continue to help specific reservation economies. On Sprit Lake Reservation, within North Dakota, the tribe and a private business developed a factory that was able to tap into military contracts. Sioux Industries began as partially owned by the tribe and was gradually bought out by the tribe. Today, military contracts for body and other kinds of armor keep the plant operating. Some Sioux workers have had careers with Sioux Industries. The tribe also used profits to fund its casino. Cheyenne River Reservation operates telephone and utilities for the region, not just the reservation.

ECONOMIC PROBLEMS

Some individual Sioux have been able to develop and maintain small businesses that serve the community. On Pine Ridge Reservation, for example, a Sioux entrepreneur began with a propane supply business and has expanded it into several other businesses that employ not only his relatives, a traditional Sioux practice, but also others. Most reservations do have numerous informal businesses where individuals and families exchange labor and make enough to provide some income. These household industries make and sell quilts, traditional bead and quillwork items, and even special powwow regalia. Others operate car repair shops at their homes. One family on Pine Ridge specializes in carving and painting "horse sticks," traditionally used at give-aways to indicate that a horse is given to someone, for sale at powwows and tourist shops in Rapid City and the Black Hills Horse sticks are now considered to art and no longer signify the gift of a horse.

Any major economic development, however, requires that the tribal government provide ownership and capital. Few individual Sioux have access to bank loans and other sources of capital for developing businesses. The most obvious example of tribal economic development is the casino industry. The Dakota governments within Minnesota have lucrative casinos that have been used to eliminate poverty on these reservations.

Casinos are regulated through the National Indian Gaming Commission that was created by Congress in 1988. The casino movement began in Florida and California, where they were started offering high stakes bingo, to meet Indian needs for revenue. Individual states and the Bureau of Indian Affairs challenged the tribal initiatives in court. Several cases reached the Supreme Court, and in *Cabazon Band v. California* (1987), the court ruled that states could not regulate Indian casinos and that sovereign tribes could initiate economic development if there was any gambling in the states. Congress responded to the state and congressional concerns that unregulated Indian casinos would have negative effects with the National Indian Gaming Act (NIGA).

Congress requires that Indian casinos have to be more than 50 percent owned by the tribal government, be located on Indian Trust land, devote a portion of its income to the good of the community, and have a state-tribal compact that prescribes a complex relationship of regulations, gaming types, size, and jurisdictions. States are required to negotiate in good faith with the reservations. In order to sign a compact, most states have required tribes to pay the state to compensate for state permission. The law also created the National Indian Gaming Commission and led to a large regulatory bureaucracy.

The state of Minnesota negotiated compacts with Dakota and Chippewa governments that are considered by most scholars as the most fair to the tribes. Also according to most analysts, Nebraska has been the least supportive of tribal casinos. The Dakotas and Montana fall somewhere between these. Generally, although the state compacts require a large payment to the state for operating and compliance with some state jurisdiction, most of the regulation is left to the federal government and the tribal casino operating staff.

Most of the Sioux reservations consider the requirements of the Gaming Act a violation of tribal sovereignty and a breech of the constitutional law that declares that states do not have any jurisdiction on reservations. No tribe can operate a casino without state approval. Tribes have agreed to the limitations because they must have some form of economic development.

The Dakota communities in Minnesota have been highly profitable because they are near urban locations. Most casinos on Sioux reservations make little profit but do reduce unemployment and provide spin-off capital for economic development. (AP/Wide World Photos)

The impact of casinos is now apparent since many have been operating for over 20 years. The results have been positive for Sioux reservations and communities. Casinos have provided jobs for tribal members and many non-Indians as well. A Sioux managerial class has developed, and many families have had steady employment for nearly a generation. Unemployment rates have declined along with public assistance rolls. Capital generated from the casinos has allowed tribes to develop other businesses such as motels, marinas, and grocery stores, and even other businesses not related to tourism and gaming. Profits have been used to supplement social services and even to provide individual profit sharing for tribal members on some reservations, for instance, the Dakota within Minnesota. Crime rates and welfare rates have declined.

State and non-reservation communities have profited from the Sioux casinos. State taxes for employees living off the reservations or who are non-Indians have grown. Nearby towns have also added motels and supply companies for the casinos. Casinos need soft drinks, towels, machines, electricity, water, construction, and workers. The non-Indian communities have these for sale. Nationally, about 70 percent of Indian casino workers are non-Indians.

Sioux governments face the need for strategic planning about business profits. Most scholars recommend that they be used to generate other businesses and create long-term infrastructure—not to use profits for short-term solutions to needs. However, many Sioux pressure councils to simply share out the money on a per capita basis. Per capita payments reduce the amount of money that can be used for meeting the need for roads, social services, education, and others that affect the whole reservation. Should profits be only for reservation Sioux? Many Sioux do not live on their reservations, so what is fair? How much should be invested and in what? What happens if the casinos stop making profits? Are casinos mainly for making profits or for employment?

Politicians have the ever-present temptation of using profits from casinos to curry favor with voters. Another temptation is to use jobs at casinos as a means to reward supporters and as a source of personal income. Research has shown that the most effective way to manage tribal enterprises is for the tribal council to charter the businesses, provide for a board of directors, and establish clear goals for the business, and then not interfere on a day-to-day basis by mixing political priorities with business priorities. Some Sioux reservations have managed to follow this pattern, and others have created turmoil through excessive political interference.

It is noteworthy that the Dakota reservations within Minnesota have been making their capital available to other tribes, particularly Sioux reservations. Shakopee, the owners of the immensely profitable Mystic Lake Casino in the Minneapolis metropolitan area, have established a foundation to provide grants to other Indian entities. Spirit Lake, a Dakota reservation within North Dakota, has received both grants and loans from Shakopee. Most of the Sioux reservations have chosen to use what profits there are to build infrastructure and subsidize tribal government operations. As profits are so low for most Sioux casinos, this use will probably continue for decades.

Casinos and other tribal enterprises have made life better in measurable ways on the Sioux reservations. Poverty remains a reality however because the population is growing rapidly and the demand for more and more development continues to increase. Tribal governments have enacted business codes, made decisions that increase revenue, worked with the federal and state governments to continue to provide programs that tribal governments determine are needed, and improved infrastructure. Despite improvements, poverty and economic underdevelopment remain very real concerns.

PROVING TRIBAL GOVERNMENT STATUS

For a government to be legitimate, it must be accepted by other governments and, most importantly, be considered legitimate by its own population. Tribal governments are new as far as governments go because they have received effective power, recognition by state and federal governments, and resources only since the 1960s and 1970s. Many Americans still do not see tribal governments as "real" governments and demand to know why they are considered sovereign and expect them to be subservient to state governments. This ignorance of the legal status of tribal governments has a negative effect on the way tribal governments are treated by state legislators, municipal governments, and the public.

Many Sioux governments are still trying to prove themselves to their own people. Part of the problem lies in the history of federal control until the 1970s. It was the BIA that made governmental decisions; naturally, many Sioux still look to the BIA to solve their problems and even overrule decisions made by tribal governments. Sioux individuals see the BIA/federal government as having all of the power, so they just go over the head of the tribal government and contact the BIA in an effort to reverse tribal government actions or to solve some other problem. In the past two decades, the BIA has pursued a pattern of non-interference in internal reservation issues which has reduced the end runs of discontented Sioux. Some Sioux see the tribal governments as mere puppets of the BIA and not truly legitimate because of their dependence on federal decision making. There is even an association of descendents of treaty signers that holds that no tribal government decision is legal or binding. Most Sioux simply accept the government they have and follow the patterns required whether or not they are tribal or federal or even state requirements.

The goal of all tribal governments is to establish and maintain the support of their citizens. This requires demonstration of fairness, absence of corruption, a predictable set of services, and efforts to make sure that all identify with the government. These are not easy tasks when governments do not have enough resources. Another exacerbating factor is that tribal officials reflect the value of family and there is a strong tendency to hire one's relatives when jobs are available. This practice creates distrust in a government that is not "fair."

During the last quarter of the twentieth century, many of the Sioux reservation governments were challenged by dissidents. Rosebud and Pine Ridge reservations were particularly subject to demonstrations that included occupations of tribal buildings and other forms of protest. Maintaining legitimacy is hard for long-established governments like the United States, but it is harder for new governments like the Sioux reservations.

SUPPORTING SIOUX CULTURE

All of the Sioux governments declare their support for Sioux culture. With this, tribal people convey that they support and want to replicate the practices of pre-reservation Sioux culture. Tribal governments insist that reservation schools teach Sioux culture and history. Tribal funds support powwows and various other public displays of tribal culture. Various organizations from local powwow committees to veteran's organizations to the Gray Eagles Society of elders on Pine Ridge Reservation devote much attention to making the practices of the past available. In addition to powwows, Sun Dances have proliferated since the 1970s with some reservations experiencing as many as twenty or so in a single summer. Other commemorations, like the Big Foot Ride that memorializes the trek of Big Foot and the massacre at Wounded Knee of 1890, are held annually.

Some Sioux question the effectiveness and even the advisability of an emphasis on cultural practices that are frozen in time or even whether the "old time religion" is valid, but these reservations are a distinct minority. Others point out that traditional practices are losing ground to modern ones. Many Sioux never attend powwows, although most do, fewer and fewer speak their dialect, and some are exclusively Christian. Even if they are living on a reservation, Sioux youth are more likely to imitate urban styles, beliefs, and practices than to follow the old ways. Materialism is often a part of Sioux modern culture just as it is in the larger society, and debates about materialism are common on reservations too.

The twenty-first century will see the challenge of maintaining a unique status tested even more than ever before. Tribal governments will reflect these struggles and are aware of the seeming contradiction between wanting to operate as modern self-governing nations and supporting a pre-reservation traditional culture.

EDUCATION

Formal education provides an arena where all of the forces that have formed and challenged modern Sioux societies converge. Statistics might mask the roots of the issues, but they establish what all Sioux deem is a problem. Remember that statistical generalizations do not apply to every instance. Many Sioux students do equally as well other students from ethnic groups. However, collectively, Sioux children's performance consistently mirrors the pattern of other communities of poverty. They test below the levels of the larger society. In the ratings of No Child Left Behind requirements, it is usual for schools with Indian majorities to be sanctioned. Only about 65 percent of Sioux children finish high school, and even these have test scores below the norm. By the fourth grade, Sioux children's performance is consistently below grade level. American Indians are less likely to finish college. Indians are underrepresented in all of the professions that require higher education,

A Sioux girl, age 10, waves a U.S. flag during an annual Fourth of July parade in Arlee, Montana. Whether or not to assimilate, and how much traditional culture to retain, remains a question to many contemporary Sioux. (Nativestock.com/ Marilyn Angel Wynn)

particularly the sciences, business, computer science, engineering, and the medical professions.

Although poverty is a key factor in the explanation of educational issues, the history of Sioux education is compounded by the problem of poverty. Education was a tool of conquest and forced assimilation in the memory of Indian communities. Schools were places where children were taught that being Indian was wrong and that the accumulated wisdom of their communities was nothing more than savagery. For much of reservation history, schools were divorced from the community and seen, in reality, as wrapped up in the control of the BIA. Indian children were rounded up for school, torn apart from their families, and sent to boarding schools. Although this description could be a bit exaggerated, it is the picture held by many.

In addition to being the instrument of an alien culture, schools were underfunded, and the curriculum was devoted to making Indians into a kind of "colored" class of subservients. A typical boarding school day well into the 1950s was a highly regimented schedule in which children had to attend classes for half a day and then work at growing food, tending cattle, sewing and cleaning, and doing maintenance work. Graduates, as a result, were not

A third-grade student reads a textbook in class at the Pine Ridge Elementary School on the Ogala Sioux reservation in South Dakota. Most schools on reservations are now governed by local school boards, which add courses in Sioux culture to the required curriculum. (Time & Life Pictures/Getty Images)

as well educated as might be expected. Teacher administered discipline reflected the harshness of nineteenth century American schools, and abuse was common enough to be remembered by many with horror. Speaking Dakota was punishable, and attendance at Christian services was mandatory. Reservation-based schools followed the same pattern, but children were allowed to return home daily so they were known as "day schools" in contrast to "boarding schools."

Many of the incentives for getting an education that lured immigrants into striving for educational achievement did not exist on reservations. After completion, jobs on reservations were few, and until the 1950s and 1960s, higher-level jobs were reserved for non-Indians, with few exceptions. Teachers were white, and janitors and matron were Sioux. BIA administrators were white, and clerks were Sioux. Off the reservation, Sioux graduates faced the prejudices of segregated societies and having to abandon their family support systems.

As time passed, American support for multiculturalism had the effect of supporting a greater degree of control of education by reservation communities and tribal governments. Currently, there are four types of school systems that operate on many Sioux reservations: public schools, private-parochial schools, BIA schools, and contract schools.

Most Sioux children attend public schools on or off the reservation. State laws require public schools in all counties that are funded by the state and local taxes. The federal government provides funds to replace property taxes for Indian children as it does for military children throughout the rest of the United States. These schools have elected school boards, often Indian, except where the schools are located in non-reservation communities.

Many reservations have had religious schools almost since the establishment of the reservations. Standing Rock's Catholic boarding school began in 1878, as did Holy Rosary Mission Boarding School on Pine Ridge Reservation. Spirit Lake Reservation had a Catholic boarding school earlier. Several of these schools are still operating and, often, are the higher-achieving schools on their reservations.

Bureau of Indian Affairs schools have evolved for the most part into contract schools. Tribal governments have contracted with the BIA to administer the schools through elected school boards. Funding is provided by the BIA, and contracted schools are required to conform to BIA requirements for curriculum. However, Sioux school boards do exercise powers similar to those in the states and counties. Many have cultural requirements for the curriculum in addition to the usual "three Rs." BIA schools remain on some reservations. Although they have elected school boards, they are mainly advisory, and final decisions are made by the BIA.

Although Sioux children apparently have an abundance of educational opportunities, what is really available to them are several different systems competing with one another for students and still unable to solve the problem of community involvement that is key to a culture of education. They also cannot solve the problems of poverty combined with the legacies of education as opponent.

The greatest challenge that Sioux governments and communities face in the twenty-first century is to develop a culture of education. During the latter part of the twentieth century, some progress was made. Sioux parents were starting to supporting higher standards, and governments were trying to reduce absenteeism and offer rewards for school achievement. Tribal colleges are now in place on most of the Sioux reservations. Jobs that require higher education are now under the control of the tribe for the most part, and external agencies are emphasizing hiring Sioux for their jobs too. Tribal college graduates and those who have added to their credentials after a tribal college degree are common in tribal government and as teachers in the schools. Governing boards have developed the sophistication to carry out their policy making roles. Although great strides have been made toward establishing higher standards, replacing anti-Sioux teaching with support for traditional values, and providing funding, the legacy of underachievement remains.

Despite the vicissitudes experienced by Sioux societies in the twenty-first century, there are many reasons to be optimistic. Tribal governments have only had the resources to govern the reservations since the 1960s and 1970s so the leaning curve was high. Most reservations have pursued a trend of creating a professional bureaucracy that has the education and training to administer government programs. Safeguards to assure compliance with expenditure requirements and program regulations have been added to tribal codes. The result is that most Sioux reservations are better governed than at anytime since the creation of reservations. Tribal bureaucrats are more likely to be professionally prepared, health is improving, educational levels are rising, states are more willing to recognize tribal sovereign rights, and income is increasing. Sioux cultural distinctiveness based on traditional values is emphasized more widely and institutionally than at any point in time since the creation of reservations. Self-determination is not only the U.S. policy. The Sioux people and their governments are committed to self-determination.

Appendix: Facts and Figures

Table 1
Seven Sacred Ceremonies (these are the basic traditional Sioux ceremonies)

I. Sweat lodge	Basic ceremony of purification and spiritual cleansing. Conducted within a covered wood framework lodge featuring heated rocks and steam. The physical effect is similar to a sauna, but enhanced by the spiritual experience that is integral to the ceremony.
II. Vision Seeking	As a rite of passage, a ceremony to obtain spiritual guidance that helps in the transition from boy to man. A young man isolates himself under the guidance of a holy man. During his fasting, spirits can visit him to convey supernatural means to focus his life as an adult. As a source of knowledge/answers for adults, the ceremony allows a holy man to explore problematical issues and to learn what to do for the good of the people or an individual.
III. Sun Dance	A unifying community ceremony for the Tetons-Lakota. Ideally, all members of the tribe gathered in the summer (often at the solstice), and individuals who had taken a vow to dance, if approved by the Sun Dance holy man leader. Celebrants dance until they break the ties that bind them to the sun dance pole. The purpose of this ceremony is to portray unity, pray for the good of all, and redeem a promise to the supernatural for some kind of benefit.
IV. Hunka	A public adoption ceremony that can incorporate non-Teton into the community/tribe and, more importantly, a means for an adult man to bind himself to the support of a younger man or boy. The Hunka relationship is a particularly strong commitment and an honor to the adoptee and his family. Hunka ceremonies can also cement a relationship between two men and is considered stronger even than kinship bonds.

V. Buffalo Sing	A rite of passage for a young girl. A buffalo shaman conducts the ceremony. The girl is instructed by elder women in the virtues of womanhood: modesty, generosity, child bearing, and support for her male relatives and husband during the ceremony.
VI. Spirit Keeping	A ceremony that provides a means to keep the spirit of a deceased loved one from leaving. After a year has passed, a feast and prayers release the spirit.
VII. Throwing the Ball	A ceremony thought to have begun as a puberty ceremony. In "throwing the ball," the woman throws a ball to others in order to convey blessings. Today, the ceremony is a means of emphasizing that we are all relatives, thereby, healing wounds that strained the community.

Each of these ceremonies contains sacred songs, prescribed activities, and words that are derived from the teachings of White Buffalo Calf Woman or from specific dreams received by holy people.

Table 2
Sioux Reservations and Reserves and Sioux Tribes/Bands in the United States, 2010

State	Location	Tribe/Band
Minnesota	Lower Sioux	Santee (Dakota-Mdewakanton)
Minnesota	Prairie Sioux	Santee (Dakota-Mdewakanton)
Minnesota	Prior Lake	Santee (Dakota-Mdewakanton)
Minnesota	Upper Sioux	Santee (Dakota-Medewakanton, Sisseton)
Montana	Fort Peck	Santee-Dakota (Sisseton, Wahpeton, Wahpekute)
Montana	Fort Peck	Yankton
Montana	Fort Peck	Teton (mostly Hunkpapa)
Nebraska		Santee-Dakota (Mdewakanton, Wahpekute)
North Dakota	Spirit Lake (formerly Devil's Lake)	Santee-Dakota (Sisseton, Wahpeton)
North Dakota	Spirit Lake	Yanktonai
North Dakota	Standing Rock	Teton-Lakota (Blackfeet, Hunkpapa)
North Dakota	Standing Rock	Yanktonai
South Dakota	Cheyenne River	Teton-Lakota (Blackfeet, Minneconjou, Sans Arc, Two Kettle)
South Dakota	Lower Brule	Teton-Lakota (Sicangu, also called Brule)
South Dakota	Flandreau	Santee (Mdewakanton, Wahpeton)
South Dakota	Crow Creek	Yanktonai
South Dakota	Pine Ridge	Teton-Lakota (Ogala)
South Dakota	Rosebud	Teton-Lakota (Sicangu)
South Dakota	Sisseton	Santee-Dakota (Sisseton, Wahpeton)
South Dakota	Yankton	Yankton

Table 3
Sioux Reservations and Reserves and Sioux Tribes/Bands in Canada

Province	Location	Tribe/Band
Manitoba	Birdtail Sioux (Reserve no. 57)	Santee-Dakota (Wahpeton, Mdewakanton)
Manitoba	Birdtail Sioux (Reserve no. 57)	Yanktonai
Manitoba	Canupaqakpa Dakota First Nation	Santee-Dakota (Wahpekute, Wahpeton)
Manitoba	Canupaqakpa Dakota First Nation	Yanktonai
Manitoba	Dakota Tipi	Santee-Dakota
Manitoba	Sioux Valley Dakota Nation (Oak River)	Santee-Dakota (Sisseton, Wahpeton, Wahpekute, Mdewakanton)
Manitoba	Sioux Village-Long Plain (Portage La Prairie)	Santee-Dakota (Wahpeton)
Saskatchewan	Carry the Kettle	Dakota-Santee
Saskatchewan	Mosquito-Grizzly Bear's Head	Dakota-Santee
Saskatchewan	Moose Woods (White Cap)	Santee-Dakota (Sisseton)
Saskatchewan	Moose Woods (White Cap)	Yanktonai
Saskatchewan	Standing Buffalo	Santee-Dakota (Sisseton, Wahpeton)
Saskatchewan	Sioux Wahpeton (Round Plain)	Santee-Dakota (Sisseton, Wahpeton, Wakpekute, Mdewakanton)
Saskatchewan	Wahpeton Dakota Nation	Santee-Dakota (Wahpeton)
Saskatchewan	Wood Mountain (Reserve No. 160)	Teton (Hunkpapa)

Table 4
Sioux Population Estimates in the United States

Year	Population Estimate
1880	39,342
1980	25,920
1910	27,558
1930	31,192
1962	32,913
1990	103,255
2010	155,000

Racial Statistics Branch, Population Division, Bureau of the Census; Kingsley Brady, "Teton Sioux: Population History, 1665–1881," *Nebraska History* 75 (1994), 165–188; and Guy Gibbon, *The Sioux*. Malden, MA: Blackwell Publishers, 2003.

Table 5
Sioux Population Estimates in Canada

Year	Population Estimate
1970	2,398
1999	5,420

Information supplied by Indian and Northern Affairs Canada.

Table 6
The Traditional Sioux Tribal Subdivisions

Tribe	Number of Council Fires	Location	Bands
Dakota-Santee	Four	Minnesota until after 1862 war	Sisseton, Wahpeton, Mdewakanton, Wakpekute
Yankton	One	Based along Missouri and James Rivers, near Iowa, Minnesota, and South Dakota	
Yanktonai	One	North of the Yankton and intermingled with Lakota throughout North and South Dakota and Montana.	
Teton-Lakota	One	North and South Dakota, western Montana, western Wyoming, and along Platte River in western Nebraska.	Hunkpapa, Sicangu/Brule, Sans Arc, Two Kettles, Blackfeet, Oglala, Miniconjou

Glossary

Akicita: Warrior society. All of the Sioux tribes had military societies that at various times also acted as police. Generally, they followed the direction of their itancan or of the head of their society. Membership was by invitation and was offered after some achievement in war. The Kit Foxes were one of the most prestigious societies. Akicita also functioned to unite bands because members were drawn from several bands. Today, akicita is the Sioux word for police. There has been some continuation of akicita today, but they do not have the same role.

Band or Tiyospaye: The basic political unit of the Sioux tribe. Bands were several extended families and others attracted by the success of the band leaders. Bands were politically autonomous. They could be as large as several hundred to a thousand or as small as around a hundred people. Each had an itancan, a blotahunka, and a council. The Teton-Lakota used the term *tiyospaye* (living group) to describe bands. They were often identified by the name of the most dominant leader, such as "Red Cloud's band," or by a nickname, such as Pesla (bald-headed) because of some incident, often humorous, that occurred within the group. The Dakota-Santee equivalent is the village/town. Villages and towns were also named after leaders, for example, Wabasha, or a descriptive term such as Kapozha (Little Crow's Village). Americans tended to use the terms *band, tiyospaye,* and *village* interchangeably when writing about Sioux communities.

Blotahunka: War leader. These men directed war expeditions because they were successful at war and could attract others to follow them. Often, Americans called them "chiefs" or "war chiefs," with the implication that they were political rulers with authority somewhat like kings. Their power extended only to military expeditions, and followers could cease to give them allegiance at any time. As time progressed, and war on the plains became more concentrated, some war leaders like Crazy Horse combined the roles of peace leader (itancan) and war leader.

Chief: The term favored by Americans and Europeans for Indian leaders. The term was borrowed from European history where it described the leaders of Germanic and Celtic tribes that predated formal kingship. In America, the term *chief,* when applied to Indian leaders, served create confusion about Indian leadership. There were peace leaders, war leaders, and ceremonial leaders for each band, but never for a whole tribe. Each of these leaders usually was a different person. *Itancan* is the preferred term in this book for the leaders of Sioux bands chosen by consensus. It is more accurate than the term *chief.*

Consensus: Group decision making. The preferred method of making all decisions in Sioux communities. Each band or tiyospaye had a council that was composed of the eldest males, and these men deliberated decisions that needed to be made, but all male adults and senior women were able to express their views. Discussion would continue until all were willing to accept whatever decision could be made. Itancan would then coordinate the implementation of the decision. There was little or no coercion involved because all had agreed and peer pressure provided enough impetus. In those cases in which decision by consensus did not function, families that disagreed were free to leave the band and join another band or even form their own.

Culture: All of the socially transmitted values, behaviors, and organization of a people. In Indian Studies, the term is synonymous with tribe. Members of cultures generally speak the same language, have common origin traditions and religion, inhabit a recognized territory, and are considered a culture by other cultures. Political unity is not required. The Sioux are a tribe.

Dakota: The language dialect spoken by a subdivision of the Siouan speaking people that became known as the Sioux after the 1600s. Dakota speakers make up the subdivision of the Sioux called the Santee. Dakota society spun off from the other sub-divisions of the Sioux: the Yankton, Yanktonai, and Teton-Lakota, as well as the non-Sioux tribe identified as the Assiniboine. Until well into the twentieth century, *Dakota* was the term used interchangeably with the term *Sioux.* Dakota can be translated as "friend" or "ally" or even "relative." The Dakota-Santee include four of the Seven Council Fires of the Sioux tribe.

Inyan: Rock. Inyan was the rock that gave its blood to create the world as well as the Sioux people. Catlanite, the preferred mineral for making pipe bowls, is red because it is the blood of Inyan. Before Inyan created the world, all was darkness.

Itancan: Leader. Often this position was hereditary, but leaders who did not follow tradition or were ineffective could be removed by consensus, or people simply left to join other bands. Americans sometimes called itancan "chiefs" or sometimes thought the war leaders were the itancan. Only the itancan could speak for the band, sign treaties, or conduct negotiations. Itancan did not have coercive powers, but they could send akicita to enforce decisions made by consensus, threaten those who challenged decisions of the council, or enforce traditional practices. There was no single itancan for the Sioux nation or even for all of the Teton, Dakota, Lakota, or Yankton. The United States understood that each itancan was independent of the others and tried to secure as many as signatures as possible to make sure that their bands were committed to the terms of each treaty. The United States also tried to get the Lakota to recognize a single leader who would be responsible for all of the Teton as early as 1851, but no Lakota considered himself bound by decisions made by a single person. Generally, itancan were not war leaders but probably had been so when they were younger.

Iyeska: Literally, "talks White." The term is interchangeable with mixed blood. Iyeska fulfilled multiple roles in pre-reservation Sioux cultures and, today, are part of reservation culture and society. Most are citizens of their reservation and practice the Sioux reservation culture.

Lakota: A dialect of the original Dakota language and the designation of the plains Sioux also named Teton. The Teton Lakota were divided into seven historic multi-band groups by the 1800s that were so large that they were sometimes called tribes. The seven bands of the Teton Lakota are: Oglala, Sans Arc, Two Kettles, Blackfeet, Brule, Minniconjou, and Hunkpapa. They are the largest of the Sioux subdivisions but are only one council fire. They established a separate identity later than the other fires did. The Lakota became the epitome of Sioux in the eyes of most Americans because they fought the United States with such spectacular success that they captured the American imagination and their appearance on horseback and wearing feathered headdresses was so photogenic. Red Cloud, Gall, Sitting Bull, Crazy Horse, and Spotted Tail are often mentioned in American history texts.

Mixed Blood: A person who has ancestry from both European American and American Indian ancestors. Sioux societies had long incorporated outsiders and, if they married tribal members, they became Sioux, whatever their genetic origins were. Mixed bloods were absorbed into Sioux societies and often fulfilled the function of cultural broker for the European Americans and for the Sioux. Many became interpreters. The Dakota referred to them as Kinsmen of Another Kind. Over time, mixed bloods became a distinct subculture within Sioux societies. Present-day mixed-blood Sioux are often the descendents of intermarriages dating back to the eighteenth and nineteenth centuries.

Nakota: A dialect of the common Sioux language that is often identified with the Yankton and Yanktonai divisions of the tribe. Most linguists today have concluded that this identification is the result of a misunderstanding and that only the Assiniboine spoke the Nakota dialect. For purposes of accuracy, Yankton and Yanktonai are the terms used for these two council fires.

Oceti Sakowin: Seven Council Fires. The mythical joint council of the Sioux that acknowledges the common relationship of each of the separate divisions. All of the Sioux consider that they are part of the same culture and always have been, despite being widely dispersed geographically and having developed different economies. The Seven Council Fires are the Mdewakanton, Wahpekute, Sisseton, and Wahpeton, Yankton, Yanktonai, and Teton.

Oyate: People. This is the collective term for all of the Sioux in the Sioux language.

Reservation: The federally recognized remaining territories of Sioux country held in trust for the Sioux by the federal government. Sioux leaders were able to reserve a small portion of their lands while relinquishing the majority of their land to the United States in return for goods, services, and money as described in treaties and federal Indian law. It is customary and often part of American law to designate each reservation as a tribe. For instance, the Cheyenne River Sioux Tribe, the Standing Rock Sioux Tribe, and the Rosebud Sioux Tribe are in actuality reservations, not tribes. Tribal government refers to the government of each reservation today. When Sioux refer to "the tribe," they usually mean their own reservation's "tribal" government. Reservations were not "given" to the Sioux by the United States; the legal doctrine is that they were reserved by the Sioux.

Reserves: For all appearances, reservations, but within Canada. However, the Canadian government does not recognize the continuing, inherent sovereignty of reserve governments. Canadian reserves are tiny pieces of land, usually the size of a town, but they are called nations in Canadian law.

Santee: Synonymous with Dakota. It is the founding society of the Sioux and was concentrated in southern Minnesota by about 1845. After the Dakota Conflict of 1863, most of the Santee/Dakota were refugees or prisoners. By 1867, the United States created reservation in Dakota Territory and Nebraska in return for their surrendering any claims to their homeland. Currently the reservations are Santee Reservation in Nebraska, Flandreau and Sisseton-Wahpeton in South Dakota, and Spirit Lake in North Dakota. Four Dakota communities within Minnesota are Prior Lake, Upper Sioux, Lower Sioux, and Prairie Sioux. Some Dakota fled to Canada and are based on 11 reserves located in Manitoba and Saskatchewan.

Seven Council Fires: *See* **Oceti Sakowin**.

Shirt Wearers: The Lakota Teton tried to gather at least annually in the summers, and this required that itancan be selected to provide guidance and good examples to the gathered bands in order to mediate any conflicts. Four outstanding individual leaders were chosen by the major bands and given shirts that were symbolic of their prestige and the deference due to them. Crazy Horse was a shirt wearer for a time but had this badge of authority and honor taken from him when he violated a cultural norm.

Sioux: The term applied by Europeans and Americans to the Seven Council Fires, the Oyate. It is the legal term for many of the reservation "tribes" as well. The Chippewa called them Nadewasiou—little poisonous snakes—and the Americans and Europeans picked up the term and eventually anglicized it to Sioux. Snakes in Chippewa origin traditions were powerful and dangerous but mainly evil. The names by which many tribes are known in American history were anglicized versions of the name used by different tribes. Now they are enshrined in law and custom. Most tribes called themselves something like the people. The collective term used by the Sioux for themselves is Oyate, the people.

Teton: Dwellers of the Plains and synonymous with Lakota. These are the plains Sioux.

Tiyospaye: The basic unit of the Lakota, roughly equivalent to the band. Tiyospaye were made up of a dominant leader (itancan) who provided direction to members of his extended family and others he could attract because of his achievements in leadership. Tiyospaye were fluid in membership and could grow to over a hundred individuals. Sometimes, several tiyospaye joined together for hunting or war and these combined multiband units could grow to be quite large. Crazy Horse surrendered with his tiyospaye multiband in 1877, and it numbered about 1,000 and included not only his Bad Faces, as they were known, but also Cheyenne.

Traditional(s): Refers in the context of Sioux practice, to pre-reservation culture. In present-day Sioux society, *traditional* is used as a term to describe both the old values and customs as they are currently understood and those people who are trying to live as much of their lives as possible the way life was lived in the past. This is similar to the effort of some Mennonites or Hasidic Jews who try to maintain their earlier cultural practices and beliefs. Traditionals are more likely to know the Sioux language, participate in ceremonies, and stress the values of generosity and kinship. In a way, traditionals are the fundamentalists of Sioux societies.

Tribe: Imprecisely used term. *See* **Culture**.

Wakan: In the Sioux belief system, a spiritual, supernatural, power permeating the universe.

White Buffalo Calf Woman: The supernatural Being who appeared to the Sioux and brought them their culture. She taught the Sioux what they needed to know, their culture. She also brought the Sioux the buffalo and the sacred pipe ceremony.

Yankton: One of the seven council fires. They were once thought to have developed the Nakota dialect, but they mostly used Dakota or Lakota. Yankton became distinct from the Dakota-Santee about 1500 AD and created their country in the area where the current states of South Dakota, Iowa, and Minnesota join (also where the Missouri, James, and Big Sioux rivers meet). They adopted the lifestyle of the other river tribes yet retained their sense of being part of the Oyate, the Sioux. Yankton Reservation is centered in Wagner, SD today.

Yanktonai: One of the council fires that developed as a distinct fire about 1500. They moved to central South Dakota and northward to about the Sheyenne River in North Dakota by the end of the eighteenth century. They became more like the Lakota in their way of life and are now located on both Spirit Lake and Standing Rock Reservations with smaller bands on other Sioux reservations.

Annotated Bibliography

Note: Many other studies of the Sioux and ethnographies are available but the works cited below provide a good introduction to more of the subject. Those new to the study of American Indian societies should also look at works that describe American policy like those written by Paul Prucha, of contemporary Indian law like those of William Canby, and some studies of modern tribal societies like those of Kathleen Pickering. There are, literally thousands of additional sources.

Albers, Patricia C. and Beatrice Medicine (eds.). 1983. *The Hidden Half: Studies of Plains Indian Women.* Lanham, MD: University Press of America.

Anderson, Gary C. 1984. *Kinsmen of Another Kind: Dakota-White Relations in the Upper Mississippi Valley 1650–1862.* Lincoln: University of Nebraska Press. Anderson explains the interrelationships between the Dakota and each of the several types of whites who arrived in Dakota country. French fur traders accepted Dakota insistence that they become kinsmen through intermarriage with benefits for both. English traders and government officials followed the pattern of intermarriage and conforming to Sioux protocols pioneered by the French before 1860. Americans would insist that Dakota conform to their market economy models for trade and made little effort to act as kinsmen. This study also provides a sound history of the pattern of American imperialism that culminated in the Dakota Conflict of 1862.

Biolsi, Thomas. 1992. *Organizing the Lakota: The Political Economy of the New Deal on the Pine Ridge Reservation.* Tucson: University of Arizona Press. Biolsi provides an ethnohistory of the conversion of Pine Ridge and Rosebud to Indian

Reorganization Act reservations. The explanation of reservation dynamics reveals that the Lakota directed their own political lives within the context of local issues more than within the agenda set by the Bureau of Indian Affairs.

Deloria, Ella Cara. 1988. *Waterlily.* Lincoln: University of Nebraska Press. A fictionalized ethnography of the life of a Lakota woman in the pre-reservation past. Deloria was an anthropologist who was also Yankton and her work provides a way to understand what was known about women's pre-reservation lives and Sioux culture generally. The book is often used as a text in college courses.

DeMallie, Raymond, ed. 2001. *Plains. Volume 13 of Handbook of North American Indians.* Washington: Smithsonian Institution. This volume contains a synthesis of Sioux scholarly studies for each of the three subdivisions from the Misty Past to the present as focused upon by anthropologists and historians. The Sioux portions of this two-part (two-volume) treatment of the tribes/cultures of the plains are written by Raymond DeMallie, Patricia Albers, and Dennis Christofferson. Additional articles about the Sun Dance, art until 1900, art since 1900, celebrations and giveaways, music, kinship and social organizations, intertribal religious movements, and tribal traditions and records prepared by recognized experts complement the chapters specifically about the Sioux within the context of plains Indian history and cultures.

Gibbon, Guy. 2003. *The Sioux: The Dakota and Lakota Nations.* Malden, MA: Blackwell Publishing. Professor Gibbon provides a synthesis of Dakota and Lakota research from his perspective as a senior anthropologist. He presumes a background in history and of cultural studies, so students should use his work as reference plus avail themselves of the excellent bibliography for additional material. Unlike most other studies, Gibbon's offers prehistory as well as post-contact histories. Each chapter has addenda that explore topics such as historical linguistics, women's roles, engendered objects and spaces, men's associations, and contemporary identity issues. One addendum, colonizing time, provides the author's rendition of the way Americans forced Dakota acceptance of American control. All students of the Sioux should read this book.

Goble, Paul. c. 1985. *The Great Race.* Aladdin Books, New York. This is a well-researched, magnificently illustrated sacred story of the Lakota.

Goble, Paul. 1988. *Iktomi and The Boulder.* New York: Orchard Books. This is one of several Iktomi stories adapted for children and beautifully illustrated for children. All of Paul Goble's many books are quite popular with Indian and non-Indian children and parents.

Hassrick, Royal. 1964. *The Sioux: Life and Customs of a Warrior Society.* Norman: University of Oklahoma Press. Hassrick's study represents an effort to inject psychology into the analysis of the Teton Lakota with emphasis on the perceived stress caused by the individualism of self-aggrandizing warriors within the construct of the demand for communal generosity. It is one of the few efforts to draw upon extensive testimony about what actually happened by creating an anthropological present crystallization of the 1750s. It is one of the few comprehensive efforts to describe pre-reservation Teton society in book length and despite some flaws caused by the psychological theory, is useful.

Meyer, Roy. 1967. *History of the Santee Sioux: United States Indian Policy on Trial.* Lincoln: The University of Nebraska Press. Meyer's book is considered the standard history of the Santee Sioux. For the most part, it is a political history with some attention to culture. Meyer concludes his narrative with the development of Santee reservations after the Dakota Conflict of 1862 with brief summaries of the twentieth century. Significant post-publication research has been done by many scholars, but this book remains the foundation study.

One Road, Amos and Alanson Skinner. 2003. *Being Dakota.* St. Paul: The Minnesota Historical Society. This ethnography of the Sisseton and Wahpeton of Lake Traverse Reservation (within South Dakota) provides a picture of late nineteenth and early twentieth century Dakota, along with renditions of traditional culture. Iktomi and other types of stories are a valuable feature. One Road was both a Dakota and an anthropologist.

Ostler, Jeffrey. 2004. *The Plains Sioux and U.S. Colonialism from Lewis and Clark to Wounded Knee.* Cambridge University Press. This study combines the most recent scholarship of the history of the Teton Sioux in the nineteenth century with significant and substantiated interpretations that explain both American and Sioux policies and actions. It is a masterpiece of history.

Price, Catherine. 1996. *The Oglala People, 1841–1879.* Lincoln: University of Nebraska Press. This book focuses on the internal evolution of Oglala government from band to multiband during the apogee of their power, through the conflict with the United States to the establishment of Pine Ridge Reservation. Price distills an idealized description of the governmental structure from primary sources and explains historical developments in the context of the multiband structure.

Index

Note: "i" indicates an illustration; "n" indicates a note; "t" indicates a table

About the Author

GREGORY O. GAGNON is an associate professor of Indian Studies at the University of North Dakota, Grand Forks, ND. Dr. Gagnon is a citizen of Bad River Reservation and was vice president of Instructional Programs at Oglala Lakota College (Pine Ridge Reservation) for nearly 17 years. He consults regularly with several tribal colleges. He has authored *Fiduciary for Seven Generations: The Tribal College Trustee* and *An Indian Chapbook*. He has co-authored *Native Peoples of the Northern Plains* and *Pine Ridge Reservation: Yesterday and Today* and is a regular contributor to journals in the United States and Canada. Dr. Gagnon teaches Sioux History, Chippewa History, the History of Federal Indian Law and Policy, and North American Indians.